PRAISE FOR A

THE ENFORCER: THE TRUE SAGA OF A MAFIA BOSS

"*The Enforcer* uncovers a century-old web of organized crime across Canada, the United States and abroad."
—*National Post*

"Humphreys tells his story quickly and with impact. . . . A complex world becomes marvelously clear and we even feel a perverse bit of Canadian pride that a rather tacky homebody mobster may have reached further and stayed alive longer and freer than many of his U.S. counterparts."
—*Books in Canada*

"Humphreys . . . does an admirable job of cataloguing and sorting the abundant material on Papalia's criminal career. He does so with wit and insight and honesty."
—*Toronto Star*

"A highly readable, gripping account of the life and crimes of one of Canada's most colourful, infamous, and longest surviving Mafia bosses. Humphreys has done a masterful job of separating the myth from the reality in this riveting tale."
—James Dubro, author of *Mob Rule: Inside the Canadian Mafia*

"*The Enforcer* is well grounded and crisply written—prescribed reading."
—Antonio Nicaso, organized crime specialist and author of *Rocco Perri*

"Through detailed research and original reporting, Adrian Humphreys has gathered together the strands that made up the life of one of Canada's most aggressive and enduring organized crime figures. The Johnny Papalia story, from his birth into a gangster clan to his death from an assassin's bullet, is a classic one."
—Lee Lamothe, author of *Bloodlines*

THE ENFORCER

THE TRUE SAGA OF A MAFIA BOSS

ADRIAN HUMPHREYS

HARPERCOLLINS

The Enforcer
Copyright © 1999, 2004 by Adrian Humphreys.

Published by HarperCollins Publishers Ltd.

First published in a hardcover edition by HarperCollins Publishers Ltd: 1999
First mass market paperback edition: 2000
First trade paperback edition: 2004
This trade paperback edition: 2015

HarperCollins books may be purchased for educational, business, or sales pro-
motional use through our Special Markets Department.

HarperCollins Publishers Ltd
2 Bloor Street East, 20th Floor
Toronto, Ontario, Canada
M4W 1A8

www.harpercollins.ca

Library and Archives Canada Cataloguing in Publication information is available upon request

ISBN 978-1-44343-835-3

LSC 9 8 7 6 5 4
Printed and bound in the United States of America

To Ethan, the world's biggest distraction
and greatest inspiration

AUTHOR'S NOTE

One's standing within the underworld—that nebulous segment of society encompassing the criminal milieu—is often inversely proportional to how much one talks.

Certainly within the Mafia, the code of *omertà* dictates silence towards those not of their world; and journalists are not, generally speaking, of their world. Johnny Papalia himself gave only one interview of any substance. That makes producing a definitive biography of a man such as Johnny a difficult and daunting task, one that requires drawing information from a wide variety of sources other than direct cooperation from the principal players. From that perspective, this is an unauthorized biography. The information herein comes from underworld sources, police officers, journalists, organized crime observers, the author's own experiences and observations, and from others who found themselves touched by the mob—doctors, lawyers, bankers, municipal employees, restauranteurs, bartenders, gamblers, and many others.

It does not mean this book embodies—in any way—fiction. Conversations quoted in the text are from the author's interviews, wiretap recordings, court transcripts, interviews previously quoted in the media, or the memories of credible sources who heard the conversation directly. Not one word has been invented for dramatic effect.

PROLOGUE

Stock brokers call it market manipulation.

In the underworld, however, no such distinction between an investment and a swindle exists; fiddling with the value of a company's stock is just another scam, another racket, not unlike running a crooked poker game or paying a boxer to take a dive. This was the middle of the 1990s, after all, and white-collar crime was now every bit as much a part of organized crime as crude extortions and dope rings.

For the powerful, grey-haired, 71-year-old Mafia chieftain of Ontario, this particular scam rapidly became an enormous headache. The Boss had recently invested a good chunk of change with a notorious, fast-talking, money-maker in Toronto, a man with a terrific record for turning a profit where none should really be made. The Boss was so sure of a quick return, he also piggybacked an investment onto his own on behalf of a well-known and ill-tempered crime family from Montreal.

The problem was, his money-making man didn't come through and the investment was lost. It was not just poor performance; the entire capital had evaporated. Anyone would be upset, but this old man who had muscled his way to power and prominence in a cutthroat world of swindlers, killers, and journeyman crooks was not even prepared to acknowledge the loss. He wanted the money returned in full.

It seems a preposterous demand, but this *mafioso* was always prepared to take extraordinary measures to make people see things his way.

He sent a 260-pound emissary by the name of Enio Mora, a trusted henchman and a high-ranking mobster in Toronto, to bring the financial consultant in for a little *faccia-a-faccia* with The Boss. Mora was known in the underworld alternately as "The Guy with the Wooden Leg" and "Pegleg." Mobsters are not always a particularly imaginative bunch, and the names stemmed from Mora having had part of one leg torn off by a shotgun blast some years earlier. The odd limp from his prosthetic only added to his ominous presence. Dutiful as always, Pegleg threw the nervous investment planner into the trunk of his brand-new, gold-coloured Cadillac and headed down the highway for the hour-long drive from Toronto to Hamilton to see The Boss.

The Boss wasted no time getting down to business; the market manipulator was going to experience a little manipulation himself. As if the sheer presence and reputation of the old *mafioso*—whose slightly hunched shoulders and hooked nose gave him a profile resembling a hawk—were not enough of an intimidation, the victim was promptly doused from head to foot with gasoline. The Boss casually sat beside him, flicking his metal Zippo lighter with an exaggerated clatter and chain-smoking cigarettes in a not-so-subtle threat to make this roped-down developer resemble meat loaf more than a man, if his money—and a little extra because of all this trouble—did not soon reappear.

The market man quickly avoided all the pain money could buy.

Once again, The Boss had his way.

1

The last day of May 1997 was shaping up to be a warm but somewhat cloudy Saturday. The weather, however, made very little difference to the weekend routine of Johnny Papalia. This 73-year-old man—called "Johnny Pops" by those who spoke kindly of him and "The Enforcer" by those who did not—was a creature of habit.

In his younger days, before his thick, black hair thinned and turned the colour of slush, his habits included feasts on thick steaks and mounds of Chinese food washed down by J&B scotch on the rocks by the quart, discreet meetings with high-ranking men of Buffalo's La Cosa Nostra family, late-night club hopping with notorious New York City *mafiosi*, and tours of gambling joints where he controlled a substantial piece of the action. In recent years, however, his routine had become simpler and more sedate—a routine more befitting a man who three months earlier had surgery to aid his failing heart.

On what would be his last day alive, Johnny Papalia pulled on a pair of white boxer shorts, added a white short-sleeved shirt and dark blue pants—which clashed slightly with his black socks—and a pair of black shoes. Putting on a black windbreaker and placing a soft, brown hat on his head, he left his messy penthouse apartment in downtown Hamilton, Ontario, late in the morning, and drove his dark blue Delta 88 Oldsmobile the five short blocks to his office on Railway Street, a cluttered, dead-end road in the centre of an old, working-class neighbourhood. The area around Railway Street was once dubbed the "Italian ghetto," after waves of immigrants left Italy at the turn of the century and poured into a city in need of workers for the glowing steel mills that marked the waterfront, and construction crews to build modest homes for a growing industrial city. The ghetto has since been turned over to more recent immigrants, and the former Calabrese groceries now sport signs in Vietnamese promoting acupuncture and herbal remedies. Through all the decades of demographic change, however, the Papalia family kept Railway Street for itself.

It was inside a plain, single-storey, yellow brick office building halfway down the street, at number 20, that Johnny Pops settled into his routine that day—taking care of business. It was from this utterly artless street that Johnny, who for more than four decades was one of the most powerful gangsters in Canada, kept watch over his criminal empire.

"Up until he was shot," one of the lead police investigators into Johnny's slaying wryly noted, "his day was relatively uneventful."

Railway Street is where Johnny felt the safest. This is the street where he was born and spent his childhood; where close friends and family have lived for three generations. It is a street where 13 of the 19 addresses are owned by a firm listing two of Johnny's brothers as sole directors, and tenants mail rent cheques to his sister's home. It is a street where a designated enforcer—a man who Johnny once quipped "knows nothing but my phone number"—watches traffic with a degree of suspicion. The office building at 20 Railway is the most recent addition to an old street filled with one- and two-storey red brick tenements. In April 1961, the Papalias had their old family home torn down, and, in its place, erected this small warehouse and office complex. The building stands out not only because of its more modern architecture, but because of the two or three dark-coloured, late-model Cadillacs that typically cluster in the front parking lot. The office is home to at least eight companies, officially dealing in coffee services, coin-operated vending machines, video games, pool tables, bar-control devices, and real estate.

It is here that Johnny regularly greeted people to talk business;

where he had his hair cut—in the grand mob tradition—by a visiting barber; where the Godfather fed pigeons and squirrels, and dispensed advice to friends, family, and criminal associates. Although the aging don had no children of his own, he enjoyed the sound of youngsters playing, and just days before he died had treated the neighbourhood children to some of the first Popsicles of the season.

Johnny felt more than just safe on Railway Street; he felt impenetrable. That is why he never left his Hamilton roots to live closer to Toronto, from where most of his profits came and where many of his underworld associates owned posh homes with double garages and high fences. Those who knew Johnny knew that Toronto was the best place for business and for fun—but for Johnny Pops, Hamilton was always home. Railway Street became even more comfortable for him in 1980 when the city expropriated most of the neighbouring properties—but not Papalia's addresses—to build a large park. That new green space made Railway Street a dead end, ruining much fun for city residents who had enjoyed cruising down the street to gawk at the mobsters in their snappy suits and expensive cars. With the street now abruptly ending in a tight cul-de-sac, the "gangster tour" suddenly became far too stressful.

Police intelligence officers called his locked and alarmed Railway Street office "Fort Knox." It was inside this fortress, shortly after lunch, that Johnny had an unexpected visitor.

Ken Murdock had never met John Papalia before, although he had seen pictures of the brown-eyed man with a sharply hooked nose and a scarred right cheek, the result of a car accident in 1957 after which Johnny refused to go to the hospital. Even as a bespectacled senior citizen, Johnny seemed imposing, despite his modest 5-foot-8, 177-pound frame. He was a man whose size somehow seemed to exceed his physical dimensions.

Johnny might never have realized it, of course, but Murdock carried with him for this first and final meeting with the Godfather a loaded .38-calibre revolver and a fierce determination to kill. Neither could

Johnny have known the startling fact that in the past month this 35-year-old man had already twice botched attempts to kill him.

Just one month before, Murdock, who was still on parole for an armed robbery, had visited a Hamilton home, where the gun he now had tucked in his pants and a bag of bullets were pulled from a secret hole beneath a bathroom counter and handed to him with instructions to kill the Mafia boss, Murdock claims.

According to Murdock's testimony in court at a preliminary hearing, the request came from Pasquale (Pat) Musitano. Pat is the son of an old Mafia don in Hamilton and a well-known gangster in his own right. Through his lawyer, Pat denies the allegation that he was involved in Johnny's slaying. Murdock's evidence was never evaluated by a judge or jury.

"He explained to me that there's money owed to John and . . . he was obligated to pay and there was some pressure," Murdock said. "He didn't feel too comfortable owing John money is what it boiled down to." When Murdock was told that he had been chosen to kill Johnny, he was asked how he felt about that prospect, he said. "I didn't argue. He wanted it done, I did it. He wanted John dead as soon as possible . . . It was more or less an assignment given from him to me. I went and did it."

Later, in a Hamilton restaurant, he said, he was given a white envelope stuffed with $2,000 in cash, and a promise that he would be "taken care of" if he did this considerable deed. Murdock did not quite know what that meant—more money, he assumed, and maybe something less tangible. Drugs? Favours? Murdock was then told details of Johnny's routine: the location of his office, what times he was likely to be there, the kind of car he drove and where he parked it while taking care of business. He was also told of Papalia's penthouse suite at 155 Market Street and where he habitually parked his car in the basement of that building.

Tackling a Mafia boss who is almost universally feared within the underworld—no matter what his age—is no easy task, and Murdock understandably put this low down on his To Do list. But pressure soon mounted from those who wanted Johnny dead, he said.

The first time Murdock tried to kill Johnny, he started with an evening drive to Mercanti Auto Body, an auto repair garage on John Street North. He had been given the keys to a green Ford pick-up truck by a friend who had parked it there, not because his friend was part of the plot to kill Johnny, but because he wanted Murdock to torch the truck as part of an insurance swindle. Murdock decided to put a little mileage on the truck before he sent it into oblivion. He drove it to a parking lot behind Harvest Burger, a low-rent fast-food joint popular for serving beer with its burgers and souvlaki. For Murdock, on this occasion at least, Harvest Burger's attraction was not the food and drink, but the fact that its gaudy signs mark a building with a discreet parking lot just a short walk from Johnny's apartment. The 14-storey high-rise is neither swank nor particularly run-down. The worn brown floor tiles and decorative swirls of yellowing plaster in the lobby suggest the building's former glory.

Murdock wore a heavy, knit, grey, black and white cardigan that night, which he used to conceal the revolver he had near his armpit, squeezed between his left arm and the side of his chest. From the lobby of Johnny's building he randomly buzzed an apartment on the intercom and told a man who answered that he had left his key inside the building. Murdock was buzzed through the locked lobby door and he quickly stepped into the elevator. On the top floor he faced the two opposing penthouse doors at either end of the apartment hallway. He had been told his target's apartment overlooked Bay Street, so Murdock oriented himself and knocked at the appropriate door. The man who answered was Italian, but it certainly was not Johnny; he was less than half the mobster's age. Keeping his cool, Murdock simply asked for John, and the man nodded toward the other penthouse apartment; Murdock had chosen the wrong door. He had just turned around and paused to contemplate his options, when all at once a tall, casually dressed man lumbered out of the stairwell and headed straight for Johnny's door.

"John had to have been standing on the other side of the door ever since I knocked on that guy's door across the hall," Murdock said, "because as soon as he seen the guy . . . in front of his door—the guy didn't knock—he just let him in and when he was letting the guy in he was looking back at me . . . He had a glance on me and I looked back at him." Enough was enough. Murdock jabbed at the elevator button and fled the building by the back door.

About five days later, he tried again—this time while Johnny was at work. Murdock drove his Chrysler Intrepid to a parking lot in downtown Hamilton, tucked the gun into his waistband, and walked around the corner to Railway Street. His target's Oldsmobile was parked where it should be; Murdock took a breath and stepped forward. As he drew closer, however, he was shaken at the sight of the number of people milling about—potential witnesses, potential protectors, potential retaliators. Murdock chickened out. He turned on his heel and walked back to his car, where, Murdock said, Pat's younger brother, Angelo (Ang) Musitano, was waiting to hear the news. Ang's lawyer, however, said the young man was in no way involved in Johnny's slaying. Murdock's testimony has never been tested in court.

Those who wanted Johnny dead were getting impatient, Murdock said. Over the next few days, whenever he met with the men, he was questioned about his tardiness in killing Johnny.

"What's taking so long? Why ain't you doing it? It has to be done," he was told a week later as he chatted with associates. Murdock does not take criticism well.

"I was pissed off and I said, 'Well, I'll go and kill the fucking guy,' and I left," he said. Steaming mad, he drove straight to his Knox Avenue home near Hamilton's industrial waterfront. He changed into a hooded, grey top that zipped up tight at the front, blue jeans with pockets at the side, and running shoes. They were tight-fitting clothes chosen to make him appear thinner, should there be witnesses. He covered his head with a black Nike baseball cap and his eyes with blue-tinted sunglasses. Murdock then reached for the gun he had hidden in the back of a metal dining room chair.

"I had a feeling when I was going back to the halfway house at nights that cops would go in my house and probably fish around, and if they were using a metal detector looking for guns and they were in a hurry, I felt putting it into the dining room chair with metal is going to set their alarm off but they're going to think it's just the tube framing," he explained.

Again Murdock drove to Mercanti Auto Body. After finding the same green truck, he bent the rear licence plate up to obscure its numbers and drove to Railway Street. Murdock parked in a vacant lot adjacent to the mobster's office. He made sure the truck was parked so the bent licence plate would be the one people might see when he made his escape. He tucked the gun in his belt and pulled his zipped up top over it.

It was shortly after 1 o'clock in the afternoon, and Johnny's car was again in its usual spot. As Murdock walked the 30 metres towards 20 Railway, he spotted his target just inside the front door, talking to someone whom Murdock did not know. As Murdock boldly approached the glass entrance, he reached out to tug on the door handle, but Johnny interrupted his conversation, reached forward, and pushed the door open for his killer.

"Are you John Papalia?" Murdock asked, sticking his head inside.

Johnny asked who was asking.

"My name's Ken Murdock." He asked again if this man was John Papalia.

Johnny stuck out his hand to greet his visitor, introduced himself by name, and asked what brought Murdock to Railway Street.

"May I have a minute of your time?" Murdock asked while shaking the legendary mobster's hand.

"Sure," was Johnny's reply.

Johnny walked out at ease and alone—after all, he was The Enforcer and this was Railway Street. The two walked north in silence, around the corner of the office building and into the large parking lot.

Outside, Johnny again asked his visitor why he had come to Railway Street and, while Murdock worked up his nerve, the gunman chatted with Johnny about a made-up sum of money—$10,000—that Murdock said was owed to him by Pat Musitano.

"I want my money. How do I go about getting it?" Murdock asked.

Johnny wanted to know why the gunman was bothering him with this problem.

"Well," said Murdock, "apparently you're the Godfather to him."

Johnny quietly mulled this over and the hit man filled the silence with chit chat. The two paced about the parking lot, with the mobster offering his would-be killer a menthol cigarette and lighting up one after the other for himself. The conversation lasted some 20 minutes, with Murdock doing almost all of the talking.

"What are your intentions towards Pat?" Johnny finally asked Murdock.

"Well, I don't know. That's why I'm talking to you about it," Murdock replied. "The guy owes me money, what do you think my intentions are? He's going to get hurt; it's not going to be good."

Johnny turned away and seemed deep in thought over that prospect, Murdock said. He mulled it over for more than a minute before turning back towards Murdock to answer.

"Do whatever you want. I'm not going to get involved," he said.

Those were, perhaps, Johnny's last words. His willingness to allow Pat to face substantial harm sealed his fate, Murdock said recently.

"That was not the answer I was looking for. That was the deciding factor," he said. "If he had said, 'Keep away from him, I'll go and talk to him,' stuff like that, he would not have been shot that day."

It was clearly the end of the conversation for Johnny, and few people overstayed their welcome with the don, whose demeanour could change faster than seaside weather. (One of Johnny's occasional underworld associates said he quickly learned to scrutinize The Boss's face for a sign of boredom or anger and to move out of harm's way if or when it came. "Before John could finish saying 'Get lost,' I was already gone," the associate said.)

Children played and adults strolled in the city park, a stone's throw from where Murdock and Johnny were walking. Witnesses recalled seeing Johnny and a younger man talking in the parking lot. It was a common sight on Railway Street. As an ongoing target of police surveillance, The Boss didn't talk "business" with walls nearby. Fueled in equal measure by due diligence and fierce paranoia, Johnny knew the walls—quite literally—had ears. Police who tailed him for decades called his regular outdoor sessions "walk-and-talks." They were as much a part of Johnny's routine as eating and sleeping.

As his conversation with Murdock waned, Johnny's bland day took a sudden and decidedly violent twist. He turned to walk back to his fortress, and Murdock hesitated no more. Pulling out the pistol, Murdock moved in tight behind him, briefly touched the gun to the back of the mobster's head—looked away—and pulled the trigger.

The single .38-calibre bullet entered John Papalia's head near his left ear and pushed through his brain, leaving a trail of small metal fragments. It then smashed through the skull at his right temple but, finally losing its terrible momentum, came to a rest, flattened and deformed, still beneath his skin.

Johnny fell backwards, still clutching his eyeglasses in one hand as he hit the ground. It was as if the Godfather suddenly realized something was amiss and tore them off in disbelief, preparing once again to stare down another assailant. But as Johnny lay on the pavement dying, his final attacker was fleeing, almost crashing into a car as his green truck careened out of the parking lot.

A woman who heard the shot ran to help Johnny, a man she knew as a pleasant old neighbour who was always courteous. Johnny lay unmoving, unconscious, and bleeding. All she could do was hold his hand, feel for a pulse, and wait for help. He didn't make a sound.

"There, job's done," Murdock later said.

At 1:27 p.m., Hamilton police received the first of several phone calls regarding an injury, and sent squad cars and ambulances racing to Railway Street. Paramedics fought hard to save Johnny. A tube was stuffed down his throat to pump oxygen into his sagging lungs, his shirt was cut away to allow electric shocks to zap his chest in an attempt to restart his faltering heart, and several intravenous lines were stuck into his arms and wrists. It was, however, far too late for Johnny. He was taken to Hamilton General Hospital and officially pronounced dead one hour later. He became the Hamilton region's seventh homicide victim of the year. The first call went out over the police radio as an "uncontrolled bleed," and would have been ignored by the media if not for the address given to patrol cars. Railway Street is known by most in Hamilton for one reason and one reason alone: Johnny Pops Papalia. The street came with a reputation prompting police to arrive quickly, with shotguns drawn, and the media, gingerly, with cameras ready.

On the parking lot's dark grey asphalt, an almost luminous pool of blood slowly drained with the gentle slope of the pavement. A police dog was brought to the scene but could not follow Murdock's hasty retreat. Shocked and teary-eyed neighbours were interviewed, family members were questioned, and the police began their search for a killer.

Murdock was well away from the chaotic crime scene by then, having driven directly back to the auto garage. He backed the truck into the parking space to hide the bent licence plate, retrieved his own car and headed home, tossing his sunglasses out the window as he drove.

Once inside his home, Murdock jumped into the shower, shaving off his moustache while the water washed over him. Soon on the move again, he pointed his car towards Niagara Falls, driving fast and looking for somewhere to stash his gun. He pulled into a truck stop parking lot about halfway between Hamilton and the Honeymoon Capital.

"There's trucks, there's all kinds of shit there, there's a place to hide a gun," Murdock said. "There's a restaurant to go into, there's camouflage for me. That's where I went."

He placed the gun inside an old Tim Horton's doughnut bag that he found inside his car and stuffed it in a pile of trash sitting in the open back of a truck parked outside the truck stop's restaurant. Using the stopover to watch the road for signs he had been followed, he used the restaurant's washroom—and then left, satisfied this deed was done.

It was, in fact, a singularly shoddy, undignified way for a mobster of The Enforcer's status to die. It lacked panache, dignity, and respect. It was a remarkably unremarkable murder, and stands out on the list of hits against Johnny Papalia's mob associates only for being so strikingly unimaginative.

When the boss of Montreal's Mafia, Paolo Violi, had overstayed his welcome in organized crime, he was killed in a traditional, almost respectful way. Invited to a card game at his old café in the north end of Montreal in 1978, the 46-year-old Violi is said to have been given a traditional *bacio della morte*, the kiss of death, by one of the men at the table, just before someone gently pushed a shotgun behind Violi's ear and squeezed the trigger. When Toronto Mafia chieftain Paul Volpe was executed in 1983, it was done in private, and when his body was stuffed into the trunk of his wife's leased BMW and left at Pearson International Airport to be found, it was seen by some as a message that Volpe's execution stemmed from problems he had abroad.

The sloppy way Johnny Papalia was dispatched from this world was not the last indignity to be heaped upon him. Scandal followed Johnny to the grave.

The day after his murder, as people across Canada, the United States, and Italy were reading headlines of his slaying, Bishop Anthony Tonnos, head of the Roman Catholic Diocese of Hamilton, contacted the Papalia family's parish priest—before the family did—to say that a funeral mass for Johnny in a Catholic church was out of the question. The diocese felt he was just too notorious a man to be accepted into a cathedral for a celebration of his time in this world and prayers for his passage to the next. In a choice between mercy and moral judgment, the bishop came down hard and fast on the side of judgment.

It was a surprising decision. Just two years earlier, another of Hamilton's Mafia dons, Dominic Musitano, father of Pat and Ang, was sent off in a glorious funeral spectacle inside Hamilton's largest and most ornate cathedral. Many were puzzled, if not outraged, by the decision to snub Johnny and his family in their grief. A long-time friend and relative of the Papalias by two marriages said the family was gravely insulted.

"Jesus was crucified with two thieves on the cross," said Domenic Pugliese. "Is the bishop above Jesus?"

Father Gerard Bergie of the Hamilton diocese said Pope John Paul II clearly wanted the Church to take a stand against "notorious members of the underworld." "Our sympathies are with the family, but we can't close our eyes to the fact he was involved in some pretty serious criminal activity. We have no indication he repented the criminal activities he was involved in," said Bergie.

The Church did not shift from its decision, and the result was a simple service with some 300 mourners crammed inside a private funeral chapel for a final homage to Johnny Pops.

Outside Friscolanti Funeral Chapel on Barton Street East on June 5, 1997, a raucous swell of cameramen, curious onlookers, and police surveillance officers gave the occasion a carnival-like atmosphere. Inside, however, darkly clad family and friends wept for Johnny, while Father Michael Myroniuk read a short passage from Scripture and prayed.

There was a touching eulogy by his niece, Rosanna.

"Let's remember the good things about my uncle," she urged. "Forget about the television, forget about the radio, forget about everything—he was not a tyrant." It was a poignant reminder that while police, the media, and the public often treat the violent death of a gangster with a sense of giddy excitement, for the family—the real family—the loss is one of unspeakable sorrow, one no less painful because of the deceased's notoriety.

Johnny lay in an open, solid cherry wood casket amid a sea of flowers reaching from floor to ceiling and stretching from wall to wall. At the end of the brief service, mourners lined up and, one by one, approached Johnny for the last time. With his eyeglasses back in place, a crucifix pinned to the lining of the casket's lid, a moving note to "Uncle Johnny" tucked beside his head, and a string of rosary beads in his hands, it was a striking vision of Johnny Papalia at peace.

Looking down at this old man who was clearly loved by many, who was born, raised, and finally died on the same modest street in Hamilton, it was difficult to see a man too notorious for the Roman Catholic Church.

Who was John Papalia—Johnny Pops, The Enforcer—who elicited such a harsh response? And how did this often generous and sometimes violent man from Hamilton gain the unfortunate distinction of being one of the very few Catholics outside Italy, and the first in Canada, to be denied in his death a eucharistic celebration by the Church?

2

It was grey, cold, and miserable outside—with a light dusting of snow—but the mood inside the brick house on Railway Street was crackling with warmth and joy. An adorable *bambino*, with a wet mop of dark hair and slate-blue eyes that would soon turn dark brown, was welcomed into the home.

The birth certificate would formally read "John Joseph," but his proud father, Antonio Papalia, and smitten mother, Maria Rosa Italiano, immediately took to calling him Johnny.

It was March 18, 1924, and Railway Street needed a boost. In the few years before Johnny's birth, four nearby houses were dynamited in the night; a close neighbour was pulled from Beverley Swamp with a bullet in the base of his skull—just one of eight recent slayings touching the Papalias; and a number of friends and relatives had been investigated by police and arrested. As if an ominous harbinger, the year of Johnny's birth was a deadly time in gangland. It seems a strange environment for such a fragile baby, but for the Papalia clan, this reckless milieu of crime and violence was all business as usual. As Johnny learned to walk and talk, he also learned the values of his family and the accepted and expected household behaviour.

The story of the Papalia family is, by very little extension, also the story of organized crime in Canada. The winding branches of Johnny's family tree—on both his father's and mother's sides—are inextricably tangled with the roots of organized crime. Through his family, friends, and close neighbours, young Johnny was immersed in outlaw culture from the very day he was born. He would not shy away from his daunting family legacy. Johnny himself admitted, much later in life, that he was a product of his times.

One might say Johnny Papalia came by his criminal tendencies honestly.

Johnny's father, Antonio—usually called Tony or by his nickname, "Tony Popa"—was born to Giuseppe on December 14, 1894, in Delianova, a rural village in Reggio Calabria, one of five provinces of Calabria that form the toe of Italy.

Sitting inauspiciously on the western slope of the Aspromonte, a sprawling mountain that dominates and defines the area, Delianova is not far from the thin strait that separates mainland Italy from the island of Sicily and, across a rugged spit of rock, from the Calabrian village of Platì, where Tony Papalia had many relatives and where Tony's future mob boss, Rocco Perri, was born. Delianova is a typical village of southern Italy—small, rural, and largely isolated, with a very few rich landowners and many poor peasants and shepherds who work in the rocky, difficult-to-navigate terrain of the Aspromonte.

In the summer of 1912, Tony Papalia was just five feet tall and three months short of his 18th birthday. He was a single man with little formal education, unable to read or write, but blessed with strong arms. He was earning a meager living as a farm labourer when, apparently feeling restless, he bagged his belongings and left Delianova, heading north. From the office of the Lloyd Itàliano Line in Naples he bought himself a one-way ticket to America.

On August 22, 1912, with just $30 left in his pocket, he boarded the S.S. *Taormina*, a four-year-old transatlantic steamer. Traveling in the spartan steerage section, Tony passed the fourteen days of the journey with several of his fellow townsfolk—but no direct kin—who were among the 1,646 third-class passengers. The S.S. *Taormina* landed in New York City on September 4. Tony, along with 120 other passengers destined for Canada, was then separated at the Ellis Island land-

ing from those wishing to remain in America and shepherded onto a
train for the ride north.

Two days after landing in America, Tony arrived in Montreal and
headed to the home of his cousin, Francesco Papalia, who lived on St.
James Street.[1]

The only known first-hand account of Tony's early years as a young
immigrant in Canada was given—under duress—to investigators with
the Royal Canadian Mounted Police. Inside the Mounties' old, dusty
archives is an intriguing and previously secret document recounting a
police interrogation of Tony in 1941. The truthfulness of the story
must be judged carefully—simply because he was telling it to police.
Tony was not one to talk candidly with the law and, indeed, his
account craftily weaves absolute fact with gentle fiction, and is pep-
pered with the occasional outright lie.

Tony Papalia was poor, young and single in Montreal and for three
years he used his muscles to make ends meet, working a series of irregular
jobs as a labourer in the city. He then left Montreal in 1915, heading to
New Brunswick, where he found steady but hard work in the coal mines,
he said. After two years of taxing, dirty work on the east coast, he found
cleaner employment—and a permanent home—in southern Ontario.
Tony arrived in Hamilton in 1917 and settled on Railway Street.

Once in Hamilton, Tony told police, he earned an honest wage at
the venerable Steel Company of Canada. He worked not in a blazing
steel mill, but outdoors on the outskirts of the city as a labourer in the
bush, until 1920 when he quit to again work on his own, doing odd
jobs in Hamilton. Tony claimed he did that until he found his true
calling in 1929 as a "self-employed bootlegger."

It was on the intimate subject of his family that he heaped lie upon
lie to the police. Likely out of a gentlemanly sense of honour, he told
the officers his dear wife arrived in Montreal just one year after he did

1 There has long been confusion over the early life of Johnny's father. It was previously
believed that Tony emigrated to Canada in 1900 from Platì and headed straight to Hamilton. However, the U.S. immigration records and Italian travel documents for him and his
wife were finally uncovered by this author in October, 2004, clarifying his origins and ending the debate.

and—despite her being four years his senior—the two fell in love, were married, and, a few years later, started bearing children together.

Tony was gracious but dishonest in claiming all of the Papalia children as his own.

Johnny's mother, Maria Rosa Italiano, was born in Delianova on March 9, 1890, the daughter of Domenico Italiano. In her village, she found an able husband in Giuseppe Papalia, Jr. The two remained in Calabria and had two sons: Arcangelo, usually called Angelo, on January 7, 1917, and Giuseppe, whose name would later be anglicized to Joseph, on February 20, 1920. Not long after their second child's birth, tragedy struck and Maria Rosa's husband died. With few options in her village, it was quickly agreed she would leave Delianova to marry her husband's younger brother, Antonio, who was starting to make steady money as a rumrunner in Perri's Hamilton-based bootlegging gang.

On May 25, 1923, Maria Rosa bought passage for three to America. With Arcangelo, then six, and Joseph, just three, she had her hands full but pockets quite bare as she boarded the S.S. *Colombo* in Naples. Describing herself as a housewife and saying she was on her way to meet her husband—yet retaining her maiden name, which was highly unusual for the time—she arrived in New York on June 7 and headed north by rail. Curiously, she told U.S. immigration authorities that Tony Papalia's address in Canada was 166 Bay Street, Hamilton—which was the home of Rocco Perri.

Tony and Rosie, as he called her, hit it off immediately; a little more than nine months after her arrival, Johnny was born, with Tony remembering his dead brother when choosing Joseph as Johnny's middle name.

After having Johnny, Tony and Rosie were officially married and Johnny's only sister, Antoniette, was born in 1925, followed by Dominic, in 1929; Frank, in 1930; and Rocco, in 1935. Rosie would spend most of her 80 years producing, rearing, caring for, and loving her children. Her dedication was rewarded by devoted love from each of them.

The dates Tony chose for his life story all strangely coincide with milestone events in the development of organized crime in Canada.

If the Papalias really arrived in the Hamilton area in 1917, as Tony told the police, it was just months after the *Ontario Temperance Act* became law, making possession of liquor or beer outside one's home illegal in the province. A year later, all of Canada went dry, and individual states south of the border were likewise banning booze, giving criminals of all nationalities million-dollar reasons to form organized gangs.

Prohibition changed the underworld the way civil wars and revolutions alter nations. The leap into the underworld—necessary just to have a glass of beer—became an easy one, both physically and morally. Much of the motivation behind prohibition was xenophobia. The White Anglo-Saxon Protestants in power were watching the changing world around them—one now crowded with an ethnically diverse working class—and could see their grip on power and their neatly organized view of law and order loosening. Prohibition was Protestants against Catholics and Jews; WASPs against Italians, Chinese, and Eastern Europeans; middle class against working class. The social experiment backfired—like no one in the Anti-Saloon League could ever have imagined. The act created overnight an entire industry of rumrunners, bootleggers, and black market saloonkeepers.

The new opportunities were not lost on Hamilton's Rocco Perri, originally from Platì, and his wife, Bessie, who started bootlegging out of their kitchen almost immediately.[2] In a few short years, the Perri gang served booze to thirsty Canadians and to bootlegging gangs in the United States, even ferrying liquor for the most famous mobster of them all, Al Capone, and other gangsters in cities across the northeastern United States. Selling an estimated 1,000 cases of alcohol a day in the wide swath of territory that he controlled enabled Perri to publicly declare: "Yes, they call me the King of the Bootleggers." Tony Papalia was one of Perri's trusted Calabrian associates in the bootlegging trade.

Although Tony openly admitted to police officers during his interrogation that he was a bootlegger, he was far too modest about the scope of his activities. He was active in the underworld long before his declared start date of 1929, and his "self-employed" tag masked his links to the larger network of bootleggers and drug traffickers spanning Ontario and parts of the United States. By at least 1922 he was a driver

2 For a comprehensive account of Rocco Perri, read *King of the Mob* by James Dubro and Robin F. Rowland and the more recent *Rocco Perri* by Antonio Nicaso.

in Perri's bootlegging fleet. In November 1931, Tony was arrested for breaching the *Liquor Control Act* by possessing alcohol. In short order he was convicted and sentenced to three months in jail. He beat a second charge for the same offence on July 30, 1932, and was then fined $100 on October 11, 1932, for a third bootlegging charge.

Tony was well-known as a bootlegger in his neighbourhood. Taking over two or three of the houses along Railway Street, the Papalias ran illegal bars, called blind pigs or speakeasies. Whiskey (or "ski" as it was often called) could be found there for a mere 10 cents a shot, and neighbours were happy to have a strong nip after a hard day's work.

"People would stop by all the time," said one former neighbour. "Big shots. Little shots. Cops and politicians. During the Depression they helped anyone on the street who needed help. No questions asked. They were damn good at that. I can't say anything bad about them." Although Johnny's family had a more lucrative source of revenue than most neighbours, his father's income was sporadic, rising and falling dramatically according to the vagaries of law enforcement and underworld rivalries.

The year in which Tony told police he found his calling as a bootlegger, 1929, was the height of a bloody bootlegging feud between Calabrians under Perri on the Canadian side of the border and a Sicilian gang in Buffalo known as the Good Killers. The leader of the Good Killers would go on to become a powerful and well-known boss in the American Mafia and a man wielding tremendous power and influence over Johnny: Don Stefano (The Undertaker) Magaddino. Interestingly, the year Tony claims he first started bootlegging— while his gang's war with the Buffalo mob raged—is also the year Tony and Rosie Papalia were given the deed to their Railway Street property by a Buffalo woman. On August 30, 1929, Catharine Grace of Buffalo conveyed to the Papalias as joint tenants the ownership of the lands at 16 Railway Street—the year before he made his first appearance in the Hamilton city directory, where he is listed as a peddler. Subsequent years have him listed as the owner of both 16 and 19 Railway. The family's domination of the street was under way.

•••

The period during which Tony said he was doing "odd jobs" around Hamilton coincides with a series of frightening bombings that rocked the city's Italian community.

The first came at a little past 1 o'clock in the morning on May 25, 1921, when residents in central Hamilton were jolted awake by a noise many mistook for a clap of thunder. Unsettled weather would have been a blessing. The explosion, caused by a stick of dynamite wedged into the brickwork of a house on Sheaffe Street, just a stone's throw from Railway Street, came two months after an ominous letter arrived. The letter told the head of the household to bring $1,000 to a spot beneath a railway bridge, where he would be relieved of the cash. If the recipient did not comply, the letter said, his family would be killed. In lieu of a signature, the letter ended with a drawing: a black handprint. More than 20 years of whispered stories meant the handprint was something no Italian would misunderstand, and few would not fear. It was the mark of the dreaded Black Hand, *La Mano Nera* in Italian.

The Black Hand was the name given to a particular brand of extortion that emerged at the turn of the century, perpetrated by small bands of criminals who had come to North America hidden among the thousands of peaceful citizens of Italy. The Black Hand was not a single, organized entity. It was just a convenient banner under which freelance thugs could gather in their own neighbourhood for dark purposes. The name came complete with an aura of malevolence perfectly suiting the extortionists who targeted wealthier Italians through threats and violence. In Italian ghettos across America, *La Mano Nera* extortion was rampant. Even the father of Al Capone fell victim to two Sicilians, whom Capone later shot dead. By the early 1900s, it was a coast-to-coast problem in Canada. In 1904, a labour recruiter in Montreal was targeted; in 1905, two owners of a fruit stand in Hamilton were threatened; in 1908, a Black Hand society unraveled in Fort Frances, Ontario; and in 1909, a man from the coal mining district around Fernie, British Columbia, was sentenced to 14 years for sending a threatening letter. The Black Hand was a framework for replicating old-world *mafioso* traditions, which would in turn grow to become a crime syndicate dominating the underworld.

To say the Black Hand spawned the Mafia would be incorrect, as Mafia-type organizations had existed in various forms since the 1850s. The people of southern Italy, particularly those from the island of Sicily and the provinces of Calabria, came to North America with firsthand knowledge of *mafiosi* within their communities. During centuries of repeated occupation and neglect by a series of conquerors, Sicilians responded by entrenching a deep disrespect for the legal government *du jour*. Similarly, the peasants of Calabria, long ignored by the prosperous cities of the north and the local aristocracy, developed a resentment for the state. The people did not turn to the government to solve disputes but handled them from within; men of honour emerged displaying strength, courage, and decisiveness. At first earning the respect and support of the population, it was not long before these self-appointed protectors themselves became the plunderers, positioning themselves as both cops and robbers.

The Black Hand and bootlegging gangs of North America had a profound influence over Tony Papalia's criminal development, but he was also steeped in the lore of his rocky homeland. He is said to have been a member of the *Picciotteria*, a forerunner of the *'Ndrangheta*. According to Italian court archives, each member "swears to be faithful to everyone connected to the Society of the *Picciotteria*, to help them unto his last drop of blood, to assist the other members in robberies, to present exactly all stolen goods to be divided equally with all other members cent for cent; to slash or to murder, when it is necessary, or because the boss tells him to." The *Picciotteria* made being an outlaw a way of life. They were *uomini di rispetto*, men of respect.

The *Picciotteria* was brought to Canada by Joe Musolino, who settled in Toronto with an infamous family name. Joe was the cousin of Giuseppe Musolino, a legendary figure considered the founding father of Calabrian organized crime. Giuseppe Musolino was convicted in 1898 to more than 21 years in prison for attempted murder. It was a crime, he maintained, that he did not commit, and after escaping from jail he set out on a bloody vendetta, killing all who testified against him. After his spree, he was caught and convicted to a life term. To many Calabrian townsfolk, who regularly witnessed their own injustice, Giuseppe was a hero. A folk song describes the celebrations by Giuseppe's enemies when he was convicted, and then ends with the following verse: "If I come back to the village, the eyes that were happy will cry." Italian police issued warrants for the arrest of members of Giuseppe's gang. Most were captured but some fled to the United States and Canada; Giuseppe's cousin, Joe, was among them.[3]

For Tony Papalia and Rocco Perri, to find a cousin of such a legendary figure operating in Toronto must have been an exciting and humbling experience. The gangsters looked to Joe Musolino as a superior authority and to his cousin Giuseppe as an example of how always to act: To remain true to *omertà* (the code of silence), to never cooperate with police, and to remain men of honour and respect. It is a code Tony would pass to his sons, and on one important occasion, Tony treated his family to a very public lesson in the proper *Picciotteria* conduct.

On the evening of August 13, 1930, Rocco and Bessie Perri drove through the alley that led to their Bay Street South mansion and pulled into their unlit garage. Bessie was heading for the door to the house while Rocco was turning to close the garage doors; three shotgun blasts reverberated through the garage. Rocco fled, crying out: "Somebody shot my girl."

Bessie died on the floor of the garage but her killers were never caught. One of the few clues was a stolen licence plate used on the getaway car and discarded by the killers as they fled the scene. Police hauled in two men for intensive questioning in the high-profile slaying: Tony Papalia, and his Railway Street neighbour Domenic Pugliese.[4] Just three days before Bessie's slaying, the two men had visited a garage which backed on to the Papalias' Railway Street property. From that garage, the licence plate used on the killers' car was

3 Giuseppe Musolino's end was not as glorious as his life. He died quietly in a mental hospital in 1956.
4 At the time close friends and neighbours, Tony Papalia and Domenic Pugliese would one day become family after Tony's daughter, Antoniette, proudly married Domenic's son, Anthony.

taken. Police said whoever took the plate was familiar with the garage, and concluded Tony was involved in the planning of Bessie's murder.

When Tony returned to Railway Street after his police interrogation, he was swarmed by his children. Presumably there to greet his father was six-year-old Johnny. A reporter asked Tony about his involvement in Bessie's slaying.

"I know nothing of the Perri murder," Tony said. "I am one of Rocco's friends. Call him up and ask about me. Even if I knew who did it, I would tell him first . . . not the police." Tony was not exactly telling the whole truth. It is very likely he knew more than he claimed, but neither charges nor gangland retribution came his way.

Throughout his time in Canada, Tony never learned to read or write—in English or Italian. It was the reason he never applied for Canadian naturalization or citizenship during his years in Canada—something that would lead to trouble a decade after Bessie was killed.

It was an unseasonably wet day throughout most of Ontario on June 10, 1940, and the sour sky mirrored the mood of the nation. Canadians glumly listened to Italy's fascist leader, Benito Mussolini, declare war on Britain and France. As part of the British Commonwealth, Canada was at war, too. In response, some 12,000 Italian residents across Canada were rounded up and interrogated. Hundreds were held in cells and later interned to 16 prisoner-of-war camps across the country. Newspapers carried detailed accounts of the raids, with breathless stories of guns, fascist propaganda, and even Black Shirt uniforms being seized.

The wartime internment was not one of Canada's proudest achievements. A dubious collection of prisoners was shipped off to the camps. One elderly Italian even had to ask a fellow prisoner whether Italy had declared war on Germany or on France. Among the fascists, possible saboteurs, and innocent tailors and labourers were several *mafiosi*. After years of attacking the Italian gangs with little success, the RCMP turned to the relaxed rules of civil liberty forged during wartime hysteria. Among those arrested was Johnny's father, Tony, despite his clear lack of political interest.

Tony, then dividing his time between bootlegging and working as a baker for the Hamilton Baking Company, was rounded up in the early days of the Italian conflict, but not immediately interned. He was paroled as an enemy alien on July 5, 1940, with stiff requirements to report regularly to police. He complied for a bit, but on September 6, 1940, two days after his regular monthly visit to police, he packed a bag and left Hamilton. He headed north and lived for a year with friends in North Bay. In late summer of 1941, Tony returned to see his family and take care of business. At 11 a.m. on August 25, he was arrested and taken to RCMP headquarters in Toronto, where he was fingerprinted, photographed, and interrogated. Tony again clung to the *Picciotteria* code.

"He refused to disclose the names of the people that shielded him from police," the RCMP officers wrote in their notes. "He claims that he left Hamilton and went to North Bay where he resided with friends, but under no circumstances would he divulge their names." It was a decision that angered his captors and was a contributing factor in their decision to imprison him at the camp in Petawawa, Ontario, despite the fact that he had a house full of Canadian-born children to support, including 17-year-old Johnny. The Custodian of Enemy Property probed Tony's financial affairs and concluded that he had no bank account and no insurance, and that the house and property at 16 Railway Street was his only asset. The house was valued at $1,130 and the land at $540. On September 12, 1941, Tony signed a letter on Prisoner of War Mail letterhead with a smudgy "X" in lieu of a signature. Addressed to the Custodian of Enemy Property and mailed from Petawawa it reads: "I have read over your letter of recent [sic] requesting a statement of my assets and liabilities. My assets consist of premises No. 16 Railway Street, Hamilton, Ont. My liabilities consist of approximately $600 in groceries, furniture and two years' taxes."

Tony's stay at camp Petawawa was curiously short. While Perri and others spent years in the camp, Tony was released on October 23, 1941—just two months after his arrest.

Correspondence over several years regarding Tony's file flew between government officials. It had nothing to do with Tony's notoriety; rather, it concerned a squabble over an outstanding bill of $6.90, a sum the government expended to seize Tony's property. The government tried to pass the bill on to Tony.

In an amusing letter sent in May 1944 to "Antonio Papalia, Esq." from the office of the assistant deputy custodian, Tony is advised: "The custodian's charges in connection with the investigation into and the administration of your affairs during your internment amount to $6.90. I would, accordingly, appreciate receiving a money order for this amount in favour of the custodian."

Months later, an internal memo to the custodian noted with some alarm that Antonio Papalia, Esq., seemed quite unwilling to pay. "I have written to him," writes a bureaucrat in the custodian's office to his boss, "but so far have been unable to collect this amount." There is no record of Tony ever having paid the bill.

Maria Rosa Italiano brought more than a devoted mother's love into Johnny's life. Her side of the family, the Italiano clan, provided Johnny with additional outlaw role models; several members of Rosie's family played an even more active and integral part in Rocco Perri's gang than did Tony Papalia. From the 1920s until well into the 1980s, some of the Italiano clan were participating in Papalia criminal affairs, including representing the family at a meeting in November 1986 with Frank Commisso, a resident of Italy who visited Canada allegedly to discuss drug distribution. In 1924, Alex Italiano was convicted for breaching the *Ontario Temperance Act*, and in 1931, Dominic Italiano, who lived next door to the Papalias, faced a far more serious charge.

It might have been dismissed as a street brawl if a gun had not been drawn when Dominic Italiano and Luigi Gasbarrini laid into each other. After a private detective heard a gunshot and rushed to the scene, he found Gasbarrini on top of Dominic in the street, beating him and screaming that Italiano had just shot him. Police arrived and arrested Italiano, but at his trial a year later Gasbarrini's memory evaporated. Gasbarrini said he could not remember how he had been shot. Police testimony was a little more revealing. An officer said he found a revolver in Dominic's coat, with one bullet having recently been discharged. His bullets had a peculiar scratch mark across the percussion cap. A detective then testified that several months ago he had searched Dominic's home and found six cartridges with the same markings. Dominic was found guilty.

Rosie's cousin, Nazzareno (Ned) Italiano, had his Toronto home raided by police in 1929. Officers uncovered a large cache of drugs and marked money used by an undercover agent in recent heroin buys. To the surprise of everyone involved, while police were still turning his home upside down, in through the front door strolled none other than Bessie Perri, carrying a large roll of bills, although none of it marked by police. At his trial for drug possession, Ned obeyed the code of *omertà* and remained silent on the involvement of his bosses, Rocco and Bessie Perri. Ned took the fall for the Perris, and was jailed six months and fined $300.

Like many immigrants, the Papalia family acted as a single economic unit, working together, pooling resources, each helping all. The economic alliance extended, to a certain degree, to encompass the Italianos, in an experience blurring the lines between colleague and kin. And as such, the incarceration of Ned Italiano had deep ramifications. While Ned wasted away in jail in place of his boss, his family was left uncared for by Rocco and Bessie. Police reports from the time note how this breach of gangland etiquette—a boss should provide for the family of underlings who hold their tongues—caused a rift with some of Perri's gang. Chief among those slighted would be Ned Italiano's family, including Tony Papalia.

This goes a long way in tracing the Papalia clan's alienation from Rocco and Bessie Perri, and is a milestone in their journey from loyal friends to likely assassins. It was just a year after Ned Italiano was sentenced and then slighted by Bessie and Rocco Perri that Bessie was slain with the apparent complicity of Tony Papalia. Fourteen years later, when Tony had returned to Hamilton from his wartime internment a full two and a half years before Rocco Perri was released, a secret agreement had been struck among Tony, other Hamilton-area *mafiosi*, and Stefano Magaddino in Buffalo. It was an accommodation that did not include Perri.

It was almost one month after Johnny's 20th birthday when, on April 20, 1944, Perri returned to Hamilton to try to recapture his place as king of the mob. Perri moved into the Murray Street East home of his cousin, Joe Serge. Three days later, at about 10:30 in the morning, Perri told Serge he had a headache and was going for a walk to clear it. He was never seen or heard from again. With Perri gone forever— lying dead, mob lore had it, encased in concrete, at the bottom of Hamilton Harbour—Tony and his sons took a sizable share of the booze and drug trade that Perri had forged. Perri's disappearance, like the murder of his wife, was never solved. And as with Bessie's slaying, rumours persist that a Papalia—this time perhaps even young Johnny—played a hand in the mysterious affair. The Hamilton police file on the case remains, technically, open and contains unmailed Easter cards that Perri left behind.[5]

A systematic elimination of loyal Perri lieutenants followed, but the Papalias and Italianos were left unscathed; their place in the under-world swelled substantially. The Papalia and Italiano clans were not the only beneficiaries of Perri's disappearance.

Perri's absence hardly ended bootlegging and drug-running in Ontario. Emerging as a notorious force of underworld power were three *mafiosi*, all former senior members of Perri's gang, each laying claim to a portion of his territory in such a peaceful co-existence that it is impossible to fathom it not being an arranged coup d'état. The cross-border feuding ended with the Calabrian-Canadians serving up their boss—and their allegiance—to a new Sicilian master south of the border. Money and power meant more than quaint notions of nationalism; the new dons of Ontario drew power from Buffalo and paid tribute to Stefano Magaddino.

From Guelph emerged Tony Sylvestro, a Perri ally who was well known for bootlegging and loan sharking, and after Perri's demise he

5 New research by organized-crime writer Antonio Nicaso suggests that Perri was not abducted and killed. A recently uncovered letter implies that Perri was alive in 1949, and an Italian cousin of the mobster told Nicaso that Perri died in 1953 in Massena, New York.

became the biggest heroin importer in the country, flooding Toronto and Vancouver with his powder. Sylvestro maintained his position as an old-style Mafia don with direct access to the Buffalo chieftain until his death in 1963.

From Hamilton emerged Calogero (Charlie) Bordonaro, one of three members of Perri's gang arrested for the 1923 Black Hand bombing of a Hamilton home. Before the case could get before the courts, however, the main witness disappeared, leaving authorities no option but to free them. Bordonaro blossomed from a Black Hand thug into an old-world Mafia don, investing his profits from his rackets wisely into real estate, all in the names of family members and in-laws. Bordonaro went on to a long and distinguished career in organized crime, maintaining great influence and power throughout the 1950s and 1960s, and bringing some members of his family into the inner circle of the Mafia.

The third don moved from Buffalo to Hamilton, but the relocation was prompted by more than an affinity for Canada. Santo Scibetta faced criminal charges in Buffalo and was deported from the United States. Rather than return to Italy, he came to Hamilton, where his older brother, Joseph, spent considerable time. Joseph Scibetta was an old Black Hander and was charged along with Bordonaro in the notorious bombing case. Younger than the other dons, Santo Scibetta relied upon his close contact with Buffalo for his power, and to his mortal end he commanded great respect from even the most powerful young *mafiosi*. As an old man, after seven decades of Mafia activity, Scibetta became a sort of universal *consigliere* for Ontario's Mafia groups, and would slowly wander from his modest Hamilton home on Dundurn Street South near Aberdeen Avenue to all manner of offices, restaurants, and parking lots, listening to proposals by young mobsters, giving his nod of approval for the plans and reaping a cut of the profits. When he died in May 1985, his funeral was attended by most major underworld leaders, including Johnny, in a rare display of solidarity.

Tony Papalia was subordinate to these three dons as he made his way in the underworld. Tony taught Johnny how to show proper respect for authority, and Johnny followed his father's lead, always respecting and frequently consulting these old-world, senior Mafia dons. As Johnny matured, the dons thought well of the young son of their faithful soldier and were always ready to lend their support when advice or references were needed.

Johnny grew in an environment not only of crime but of tradition. He was given a valuable calling card to enter the doors of the criminal cartel, for he was shaped by the world of his family as surely as his ancestral home of Delianova was shaped by the sprawling Aspromonte.

3

Johnny Papalia's childhood was not an easy or always happy one.

His early years were marked not only by the mayhem of his family's life in crime, but also the mundane experiences of childhood; his performance at St. Augustine's Roman Catholic school on Mulberry Street in Hamilton was unremarkable, and he had his tonsils out at the age of 10. While Johnny's father spent much of the war era imprisoned or on the lam, Johnny, in his early and mid-teens, fended off anti-Italian taunts on Hamilton's streets with his fists. Street-fighting became a forte, even though he was neither big nor always well.

Hamilton doctors, as it turned out, did things to Johnny that police and his gangland opponents were always struggling to accomplish: they stripped him naked, punched holes in his body and locked him up for months on end. For all of Johnny's eventual tough bluster and magnificent power, a peek back into his youth finds The Enforcer a sickly child.

Johnny had contracted tuberculosis, or TB as it is commonly known, a life-threatening infectious lung disease. Although uncommon in developed countries today, TB was once a serious and deadly affliction. Called the White Plague during the Industrial Revolution, it was the leading cause of death among children. Once contracted, the bacterial infection can slowly form a cavity in the lungs with effects often lasting a lifetime.

Johnny's left lung was hit hard. Several times he was admitted to the

Hamilton sanatorium for treatment. It was a way for the Health Department to deal with a patient while keeping him out of school so as not to infect other children. Johnny's enforced absence from the classroom was too much for the already-fragile student's academic progress. In a move he would rue later in life, he did not return to school after the eighth grade. Leaving school was Johnny's biggest regret. With a better education, he said, looking back at the age of 62, his life might have taken a different turn.

His injured lung continued to nag him, and around 1943, late in his teen years, his doctor ordered six months of bed rest after the onset of pulmonary flu with dry pleurisy. The doctor's order was largely ignored; after just five or six weeks of dawdling around the house Johnny cracked. Insisting he was strong enough to get up, he returned to his favoured hangouts in Hamilton and Toronto.

After all, he later admitted to his doctor, "I was a wild kid."

Wild, indeed. Johnny was already developing a taste for fast women, and at the age of 19 contracted syphilis, which required him, for several weeks, to make regular visits to Hamilton General Hospital for penicillin injections.

It is unfortunate that Johnny contracted both TB—a lingering ailment often inflamed by damp, confined spaces—and a desire to commit crime. Johnny did not just have the normal, expected aversion to jail cells; they literally made him sick. His first stint behind bars in 1945 set his coughing off anew. Complaining of significant weight loss and a severe, continuous cough, he headed to the doctor's office and was promptly sent for chest X-rays. Doctors checked him every few months, and in 1947 found a shadow at the top of his left lung, a sign his TB was digging in. At the age of 23, Johnny was again admitted to the dreaded sanatorium for a four-month stay.

His treatment there was brutal. He suffered through a physically taxing procedure called a pneumothorax. A hole was punched through his chest wall and into his sick lung, purposely collapsing it. Since TB is a bug that requires air to survive, collapsing the lung is designed to kill it, hopefully before it kills the patient. In Johnny's case, both seemed to survive, and he was put on an intensive three-month regimen of daily medication. It was all a little too much for the impatient gang leader and he left the sanatorium against all medical advice.

A year later he was coughing up enough blood to cause him to exclaim to his doctor that he was "hemorrhaging." He was again sent to the sanatorium for months of medical intervention. The sanatorium was fast becoming his home away from home, albeit one where all sorts of uncomfortable and unpleasant things happened to him. While there he had an appendectomy, regular chest X-rays, and plenty of poking and prodding. The last set of X-rays showed his lung lesion was starting to mend, and that news was enough for him to again hop out of bed and leave against doctor's orders.

Johnny's early health problems were far from over. He faced more invasive treatment for his tuberculosis while visiting Detroit for several months near the end of 1948. There, he was given a plural drain, an uncomfortable and undignified procedure in which a rubber hose was stuffed between his ribs and into his chest cavity, where it stayed for several days draining fluid.

It is said his close call with TB made Johnny fatalistic and unusually daring. This perhaps accounts, in some part, for his love of the fast-paced, do-or-die world of the criminal underworld into which he was born, and to which he would devote the rest of his life.

4

Using an old, brick icehouse at the corner of Railway and Mulberry streets as a base of operations, a gaggle of teenaged hoodlums ran a small gang, dividing its time between adolescent high jinks and chronic petty crime.

It was late in a troubling decade, the 1930s, and setting an example for this loose-knit confederacy of street toughs was Johnny Papalia, the skinny Italian boy just in his mid-teens. He was years younger than the oldest member of the gang, but still managed to be a little more daring and to have a little more presence—enough to prompt other boys to look to him for leadership. He could talk proudly of his part-time duties helping his father in the bootleg trade and could whisper to the gang about the syndicate, Rocco Perri, and big-time crime.

Some said he was fearless, perhaps even stupidly so.

As a teenager, Johnny was rough and often unruly but always managed to remain respectful to adults, while bullying their kids about behind their backs. Once, after cuffing a much younger boy, sending him sprawling across the room, the child's mother chastised Johnny. Johnny hung his head low, and—peppering his speech with "Yes, ma'am. Yes, Ma'am"—he apologized profusely, promising it would never happen again. The mother quickly relented, but the moment she was out of hearing distance, Johnny turned to the aggrieved boy and snarled: "I'll do it again when she's not around, you little bastard." Johnny was a born intimidator. It was a talent he realized early in life.

With members of this ragtag neighbourhood gang, Johnny found himself breaking into houses just a stone's throw from his own. From there, the ambitious street punk's scope of criminal endeavours grew.

In 1942, just four days shy of his 18th birthday, Johnny was charged by Hamilton police with vagrancy, which was a bit of a catch-all charge often laid when cops knew the guy they nabbed was up to no good but evidence of a more serious offence was scant. It was the same year Johnny tried his hand at a labourer's job. His older half-brother, Angelo, found Johnny a job at the company for which he worked, Gartshore-Thomson Pipe and Foundry Company, a factory just a few blocks north of their home. Johnny worked off and on at Gartshore-Thomson for the next few years, squeezing casual labouring in between criminal activities.

On January 27, 1944, Hamilton police again collared Johnny, this time for failing to register for the draft. Who could blame him? Not only was he too unruly and likely too unhealthy for the military's tastes, but this country he was supposed to protect had locked up his own father and many of his friends under some dubious circumstances.

"You had to know what it was like to grow up in Hamilton during the Depression," Johnny later said. "I grew up in the thirties and you'd see a guy who couldn't read or write but who had a car and was putting food on the table. He was a bootlegger and you looked up to him."

By 1943, Johnny had left most of his old Hamilton crew behind and turned to Toronto, a city just an hour's drive from his home. He ran with a tough crew of Toronto hoods including Roy Pasquale, Alberto (Bertie) Mignaccio, Pasquale (Pat) Giordano, and Paul Volpe. The group became close over the years, committing crimes together, dreaming big dreams together, and planning larger and more profitable scams together. Most remained friends or associates for decades, although criminal competition fractured some friendships—especially Johnny's relationship with Volpe.

Roy Pasquale was a couple of years older than Johnny and went on to be a successful independent loan shark in Toronto. He was at least Johnny's underworld equal until Johnny got all mobbed-up. Pasquale maintained close ties with Johnny until he died in a frightful domestic dispute in 1983; he killed his wife and then turned the gun on himself.

Pat Giordano was a boxer, a tough hombre who fought under the name Patsy Gordon. He was later involved in many intricate schemes, including loan sharking, body rub parlours, dodgy home repairs, and fraudulent aluminum siding installation. Bertie Mignaccio, four years Johnny's senior, would soon distance himself from the others as they embarked on more violent escapades. He did not travel far. He became the owner of the Lansdowne Athletic Club, a notorious Toronto boxing gymnasium once described by sports writer Dick Beddoes as "an exotic little museum of mayhem," filled with "more guys who have stood before a judge than have kneeled before a priest." Signs in the gym warned patrons the phones there might be monitored by the police. Bertie was the victim of an unsuccessful hit in 1974 when he took two bullets in his leg and a third in his chest.

Paul Volpe, on the other hand, was three years younger than Johnny and would rise with him as a Mafia boss of great power and distinction in Toronto. Volpe took a page out of Giordano's book, reveling in home-repair swindles in the early 1950s, then moving into gambling, major loan sharking, labour racketeering, and casinos abroad. Volpe's rise in the Mafia was aided by Johnny's all-too-frequent sabbaticals from the street when he found himself behind bars. The two would go on to have an often uneasy co-existence at the top levels of the Mafia in Ontario, until Volpe's unsolved murder in 1983.

"They were a very tough bunch," said someone who knew the members of the gang and spent time with them in Toronto. "They had a lot of balls. John himself talked tough, although he wasn't as tough himself. He was smart enough, though, to make sure he was with people who were. John was the type of guy—even back then—that if he sensed fear in you he tried to prey on it."

In this early stage of their criminal careers, the gang members fed on each other's sense of daring, leading to at least one successful armed bank heist. In the early 1940s, with a colleague remaining behind the wheel of the getaway car, Johnny, Pasquale, and Giordano burst into the Toronto-Dominion bank at Dundas Street West and Ossington Avenue in Toronto, making tellers reach for the sky. It was a big score for Johnny—who was not more than 20—even after it was split four ways. This was not loot to be squandered. This was venture capital. These ambitious young people talked excitedly about how this was the score that would set them up in a less dangerous, more reliable line of work for men of their abilities and demeanour. This was to be their loan-sharking money; cash to be lent out to desperate souls at crippling rates of interest. All they had to do, they told each other, was lend it to people who would be too frightened to go to the police. Businessmen were off-limits; but if they put it out to the right people, "one way or another the people will pay it back," they said to those close to them. Much later in life, whenever they found themselves in the area of Dundas and Ossington, they would jokingly say: "Hey, there's my bank."

In 1945, at the age of 21, Johnny got his first taste of jail. He was caught during a house break-in and sentenced to four months' incarceration. If Johnny's lot in life had not been cast by his family tree, or the day he dropped out of school, then doing time settled things then and there. Bars, rough bunks, and cellmates were to become surroundings Johnny would see much of in his life. From this first incarceration until his slaying in 1997, Johnny would spend nearly one-quarter of his life behind bars.

Not long after his release from jail, Johnny's interest in gambling started to show itself. On February 10, 1947, he was charged by Hamilton police after being found in an illegal gaming house.

Johnny then turned to drugs.

The recognized drug czar of Toronto was Harvey Chernick, according to an internal RCMP report from the late 1940s. Chernick built a sweet pension fund by retailing heroin to Toronto's 800 or so addicts. Most addicts were chasing their habit to the tune of $10,000 to $50,000 a year. Chernick employed young hoodlums to sell his capsules of dope, removing himself from much of the risk. Police knew what he was up to, however. A police report from 1947 noted with some surprise that Chernick was believed to be traveling to—of all places—Hamilton to get his dope in bulk from the Sylvestros in

Guelph. Through Johnny's increasing criminal activities in Hamilton and Toronto, he hooked up with Chernick and went on his payroll, peddling dope on the streets of Toronto. On June 27, 1949, Johnny, then 25, was arrested by Toronto police near Union Station, the city's central railway station. He was carrying 50 pharmaceutical-size capsules filled with heroin, ready for street sale. Each capsule contained a pre-weighed portion of white powder, equivalent to one hit for an average junkie.

In court, with tears running down his cheeks, Johnny pleaded his case down from conspiracy to distribute narcotics to simple possession. Leaning on his litany of medical problems as convincing evidence, he told the judge he would not survive a lengthy prison term. The judge bought it and handed him a sentence of two years less a day in the Guelph Reformatory. Perhaps Johnny's narrow escape from serving major time for such little reward forced him to re-evaluate his role in the underworld. Perhaps he received some sound advice from his father, or the Sylvestros, during his enforced stay in Guelph. Perhaps he met a fellow con who passed along news of big things happening elsewhere in the country.

Whatever happened in the reformatory, or shortly after his release in 1951, his first move dramatically—and permanently—changed his life. After dabbling in all manner of petty crime and racking up a troublesome criminal record, Johnny was ready to take his chosen career to a whole new level.

It started with a simple act. He packed his bags and headed for Montreal.

5

"**V**ice spread itself across the city with an ugliness and insolence that seemed assured of impunity."

It was a tough condemnation of the sparkling city of Montreal, intoned with judgment of biblical proportions. It was 1924 when a judge wrote those words after probing the penetration of the upper-world by the underworld; his harsh words hardly stemmed the flood of high crimes and misdemeanours. Montreal has always been plagued by colourful crooks with a flair for organization and exploitation. It is a city where many of the country's most important criminal leaders made their fortune—and met their messy end. Part of the blame must be placed on civic leaders who early on decided the key to a successful city lay in its being vibrant and lively. With that semi-official seal of approval, the city's centre spilled over with some 200 nightclubs and bursting-at-the-seams brothels. If that did not attract hoodlums and racketeers, nothing would. Appropriately, Montreal gangsters became early leaders in organized gambling, prostitution, robberies, and drugs.

This hyperactive underworld within Montreal—which Johnny Papalia was about to walk into—had produced strong men with ambition to match. Vincenzo (Vic, The Egg) Cotroni had emigrated from Mammola, Calabria, to Montreal at the age of 14 in the same year Johnny was born. While Johnny was more or less attending school in Hamilton, Cotroni assembled an impressive criminal record including theft, assault, bootlegging, and rape, the latter a conviction he dodged by marrying his victim. Vic Cotroni, along with his younger brothers—Giuseppe, often called "Pep," and Francesco, known as Frank, "Santos" and sometimes "The Big Guy"—ran nightclubs, engaged in electoral fraud, and worked with Antoine d'Agostino, a Corsican drug baron, in making Montreal an important heroin smuggling centre.[1] Luigi Greco, once an enforcer for the city's crime lord of the 1920s, was a practical and unpretentious man who realized his city's vast potential: major international shipping along the St. Lawrence Seaway; a paved, 620-kilometre highway to New York City; and politicians and police already on the underworld's payroll. Greco and another career criminal, Frank Petrula, traveled to Italy in 1951, and are believed to have met with Charles (Lucky) Luciano, the top American Mafia leader who was exiled to Italy, to whom they offered up Montreal. It was the start of a radical realignment of the city's underworld, already well under way when Johnny was drawn to Montreal after his release from an Ontario jail. Extraordinary attention from America's underworld turned towards the north for another reason as well.

Estes Kefauver, a United States senator from Tennessee, launched extensive public hearings on organized crime after taking a keen interest in the syndicate. From May 1950, through a cross-country tour, to his grand, televised finale in New York City the following year, Kefauver spoke with some 600 witnesses who spat out more than 11,500 pages of testimony. The New York hearing was broadcast nationally and showcased the galvanizing effect of both television and the mob, sparking the world's first television spectacular. An estimated 30 million people watched Mafia boss Frank Costello—the "Prime Minister of the Underworld"—and a parade of other mobsters, most of whom refused to answer questions on the grounds they might incriminate themselves. Kefauver's committee ordered the U.S. Immigration and

1 For a wonderful account of the Montreal Mafia, read *Blood Brothers: How Canada's Most Powerful Mafia Family Runs Its Business*, by Peter Edwards.

Naturalization Service to review the status of 559 immigrants, shone a spotlight on some previously shadowy faces, and prompted a federal gambling tax. The tax was seen as a particularly devious trick by bookies in those states where gambling was illegal, particularly New York. If they paid the federal tax, they would be arrested by state police for illegal gambling; if they ignored the tax, they risked arrest by the feds for tax evasion. The answer for 100 or so American bookies was to head north.

It is a truism that where the money goes, the mob follows.

This underworld migration to Montreal prompted Joseph (Joe Bananas) Bonanno, head of the powerful New York crime family that bore his name, to send his best man to Montreal to organize the city and ensure an appropriate kickback traveled south. In stomped Carmine Galante, opening a fresh chapter in the already bloody history of both the city of Montreal and Johnny Papalia.

Carmine (Mister Lillo) Galante came to Canada clenching a cigar between his teeth and with the confidence that came with being willing and able to kill anyone who crossed his path. Galante was Bonanno's underboss, the second most powerful position within an American Mafia family, and was a man of distinction. If someone not to be trifled with ever walked St. Catharine Street, it most certainly was the uncontrollably greedy Mister Lillo.

Galante's antisocial tendencies showed themselves just 10 years after his birth in East Harlem in 1910, the son of *émigrés* from the picturesque Sicilian fishing village of Castellammare del Golfo. Galante was unpredictable, contrarian, and psychopathic. To police officers, Galante was an enigma; they would both link him to some 80 gangland murders and follow him while on a quaint family visit to Disney World with some of his five children. A New York City police lieutenant said of Galante: "The rest of them are copper. He is pure steel." There was much power and little compunction packed into his wiry, 5-foot-4 frame. When he arrived in Montreal at the age of 43, he was already slightly paunchy and his hair was starting to thin. He could have passed for a deli owner or, with his Don Diego stogies, a businessman who was slumming it. Galante's ice-cold eyes were just starting to fail him, but he had no trouble seeing a city ready to fall at his feet.

He was a very motivated and motivating man, and his organizing drive in Montreal was alarmingly thorough. With a gang of strong-arm enforcers, led by Petrula, the city wept and bled as he worked protection rackets on nightclubs, brothels, booze cans, and even back-street abortionists. Galante's sadistic streak resonated with Petrula. It is said the pair once smashed a table full of beer glasses onto the floor of a nightclub and forced a busboy to dance barefoot on the shards.

Within a year, the city was as much Galante's as it was the mayor's. But despite the fun from bullying busboys and profiteering from illegal abortions, Galante's primary concern was making Montreal the major North American beachhead for massive heroin importation. Although he never touched the stuff himself, drugs were Galante's enduring passion.

He brought Greco in close to him, and when Petrula started screwing up, installed Greco as his *de facto* underboss.[2] In turn, Greco contracted out the heavy lifting to younger hoodlums who quickly gathered by his side.

One of his admiring new hires was Johnny Papalia.

A young man of 29, fresh from jail, with a family name that meant something in Ontario, and impressive references from the three dons of Hamilton and Guelph, Johnny signed on with Greco's goon squad. It was his duty to help Galante convince business owners and gambling operators to fork over regular protection dues to the new mob, and to ensure any dissenters were left whimpering.

It was a fortuitous coupling. Johnny was being exposed to an ever-widening circle of made Mafia men, gaining their trust and approval,

2 One slip Petrula made was keeping a list of politicians and journalists paid by the mob during Montreal's 1954 municipal election, which fell into police hands. Gangsters had dropped more than $100,000 trying to defeat reformist mayoral candidate Jean Drapeau.

and using his connection to Galante as his *entrée* into New York City's underworld. Most important for Johnny, with his quick wit and eagerness to please, he was rapidly earning respect. He became known as a tough guy who remained cool under pressure. His father had taught him well.

For Galante, when it became necessary for him to extend his reach a little into Toronto, Johnny was the perfect employee to take care of the hands-on details. Galante was not content to extort just merchants and bookies; he moved in on dodgy stock salesmen. Financially savvy white-collar workers were burning up the telephone lines making high-pressure sales pitches for dubious stock offerings to suckers across Canada and the United States. Galante saw rich men already skirting the line between fraud and legality with their stock schemes, and that meant men who did not want police snooping around their affairs—the perfect targets for extortion. In Montreal, Galante had Johnny and the other members of Greco's strong-arm squad work their baseball-bat diplomacy on the stock marketeers. These boiler rooms often worked simultaneously in Montreal and Toronto, however, and in order to catch it all, Galante sent Johnny back east.

It was a heady time for Johnny, the ambitious hood, shuttling back and forth between Toronto and Montreal in the name of Galante. But it wasn't all fun and games. In June 1955, while on a collection run in Montreal with former Toronto boxer Norman (Baby Yack) Yakubovitch as his designated muscle, Johnny's overture to one victim was met with a blast of bullets. Spry Johnny ducked in time, but poor Baby Yack took a painful slug in the buttock.[3]

By 1956, an estimated 60 percent of North America's heroin touched down in Montreal. Galante, however, was not there to personally enjoy this pinnacle. In the spring of 1955, his thunderous presence there suddenly ended; a probe of his immigration status forced Mister Lillo back

---

3 Yakubovitch did not fare well with guns. He was again shot and wounded during the mob's goon play in the 1958 federal election.

to New York. After two subsequent Bonanno representatives were likewise tossed out of the country, Galante realized he had two dependable homegrown hoods who could keep things going just fine on their own. Appointing Sicilian-born Luigi Greco and Calabrian-born Vic Cotroni as joint heads of the Montreal branch of the Bonanno family was also an astute political move, launching a Calabrian–Sicilian alliance that would keep relative peace between the factions for years.

Johnny learned a great deal from Galante and had formed a relationship with the older and more seasoned mobster, Vic Cotroni. Having watched one of North America's most efficient, ruthless, and bloody-minded mobsters at such close quarters, having made enough contacts to circulate among New York's men of La Cosa Nostra, and having dodged bullets and swung bats, Johnny was now ready to carve out a criminal empire of his own.

Back in Ontario, the postwar years were shaping up to be an intoxicating time. Great rolls of cash changed hands quickly in a world populated by greedy grifters, high-rolling gamblers, journeyman crooks, dirty cops, and corrupt politicians. The top racketeers hosted flashy parties and gleefully mingled with society's upper crust—from politicians and businessmen to sparkling socialites and police brass. By the mid-1950s, there was a smorgasbord of enticing illicit activity to attract the attention of young, ambitious men wanting a piece of this kind of action.

Johnny, turning 30, was eager to make his mark on the underworld, but forging a central role for himself in this golden era of criminality must have seemed a daunting task. Everywhere he turned he saw older, more experienced men who were often connected to larger interests. Johnny, however, was now a graduate of the Galante school of underworld domination. He had truly completed his apprenticeship in crime. With his attention shifting back full-time to Ontario, Johnny was returning home a new man. Gone was the skinny young street urchin; here was a bold man with a keen sense of power. Gone was the sickly child. Here was a man of respect.

In a firm fit of confidence he picked up where his work with Galante's organization left off. Establishing his own gang of trusted criminal underlings in Hamilton and Toronto, and using temerity, fearlessness, brains, and brawn, Johnny would concentrate on three areas of classic underworld activity: extortion, loan sharking, and gambling.

6

"Johnny Papalia—does that mean anything to you?"

The young, intense, well-dressed man asking the question had just burst through the inner office doors of a Toronto stock broker after talking his way past the receptionist. The startled Bay Street broker looked up from his desk at Johnny, the unexpected visitor asking the rhetorical question. Johnny repeated himself.

"Johnny Papalia—does that mean anything to you?"

The broker, confused, astonished, annoyed, said it did not.

"Well, it's going to. I'm your new partner."

The stock broker, who later recounted the Papalia sales pitch, had just met the man who had picked up more than a few pointers from the American Mafia's man of steel, Carmine Galante, while in Montreal. Johnny was now making something of himself in Toronto. This startled stock broker was not the first—or the last—person to hear that his sudden, unexpected new partner was Johnny Papalia. And like the rest of them, this broker was not anxious to share his wealth. He promptly told the intruder that he was, in fact, "crazy."

"Don't you know who I represent? I represent people from the other side," replied Johnny. The broker became angry.

"Now look," Johnny said, "I don't want any trouble with you." Johnny was asked what he *did* want.

"A thousand dollars a week—for protection." The broker asked what kind of protection Johnny offered.

"Protection," Johnny said, smiling, "against everything."

When the broker ordered him out of his office, threatening to call the police, Johnny became indignant.

"Call the police, eh? We'll have to learn you the ABCs. We'll have to give you a few lessons." And with that, Johnny promptly left, as casually as he had come in.

Before the broker really had time to ponder what had happened, two of Johnny's men came crashing into his office, one swinging a blackjack. Ignoring the waiting customers, they pushed past four secretaries and beat the broker unconscious on the floor of his office. The reception from the broker would be very different the next time Johnny came calling.

The young gangster started making good money on Bay Street— without buying any stock.

The move against Bay Street brokers was just one leg of Johnny's comprehensive plan to become a bona fide crime lord. Following Galante's lead, Johnny pressed hard to personally influence many facets of underworld and upperworld life in Ontario. His techniques were a little crisper and more modern, but really not all that different from those of the Black Hand gangs of his father's era. As the Black Handers had done a generation before, the new breed of gangsters targeted victims to be harassed, beaten, or otherwise coerced into paying "protection" money to make it all stop. Of course, the money was being paid to the very thugs manufacturing the imminent danger. Miss a payment or go to the cops, and it could become nasty for the victim or his family. It might mean a disturbing visit from a soft-spoken enforcer, a sound thrashing with a lead pipe, a broken leg or kneecap, a missing thumb, or even a bomb or bullet.

One stock broker quickly coughed up $12,000 after his family was threatened, and others were making regular $1,000 payments. A delinquent broker had just walked out of his Toronto office when a stranger silently stepped up to him and smashed his arm with a crowbar before slipping away into the closing-time crowd. A Toronto pimp who was lax in forking over money was confronted by two of Johnny's collectors in a tavern on Bay Street. He was forced to sign over the ownership of his flashy convertible, which was then sold to one of Johnny's associates for a fraction of its value. The cash was then applied to ease the pimp's debt.

One stock salesman did complain to police after moves were put on him by Johnny and his boys. Police arrested Johnny—but the salesman backed out of testifying before the case got to court. Johnny Pops walked away a free man. Police were incensed, but this was only the beginning.

Hamilton's chief of police at the time, Leonard Lawrence, said Johnny was a suspect in several attacks that left victims bloody but uncooperative. "We have heard rumours that gangland beatings have taken place here recently," Chief Lawrence told the press, "but when we question the people who are said to be involved, nobody—including the victims—shows much interest in talking to us. It is typical of what happens when a syndicate tries to take over and organize crime."

Not all phony stock sellers were Johnny's enemy. When Johnny saw a good thing, he was always willing to listen, learn, and bring new talent into his fold. Such was the reception given Barney Altwerger (also known as Barney Auld, Barney Alt, and Barney Alvey). Altwerger was Johnny's size exactly, and when the two born swindlers met in Montreal, he earned recognition from Johnny—who partnered with the operator on a number of schemes—as well as from police. Altwerger's past included crimes of violence, and he worked his way onto Canada's Most Wanted list, where he stayed for five years. He would go on, over the decades, to spread his manipulating ways to Calgary, Edmonton, Vancouver, America's deep south, and to brokerage houses in Amsterdam and London. From a Vancouver boiler room in which Altwerger was sales manager, sincere-sounding salesmen pitched so much stock that they amassed a $64,786 phone bill in just 40 days in the autumn of 1957. By the time police raided the facility the scheme had folded, and officers found 19 empty phone lines and Altwerger, who innocently asked the cops: "What do you fellows want?"

To this day, extortion and loan sharking go neatly hand-in-hand: extort money and then put it to work on the streets through high-interest loans. Loan sharks employ similar incentives as extortionists for those on the wrong end of the payment plan; limbs are shattered over unpaid debts of just $200. The term "shark" is a bastardization of "Shylock," the name of Shakespeare's famous moneylender in *The Merchant of Venice*, and indeed, "shylocking" is the preferred underworld name for the moneylending business. It was what Johnny called it.

"I did shylocking and bookmaking, but that was back in the '50s," Johnny admitted decades later. Extortion and loan sharking became the lifeblood of the mob, and few did it better than Johnny. Johnny lent out his money on the streets of Toronto and Hamilton, where it soon tripled. He started small, lending to cabbies, waiters, and dock workers. He soon had men making loans on his behalf in most of the large factories around Hamilton—including Stelco, Dofasco, and International Harvester.

Johnny then developed a specialty clientele, roughly described as those involved in the night life. Gamblers were among his best customers. The need to pay a gambling debt, or a really good feeling your luck at dice is about to dramatically change—neither looks good on a bank loan application.

Johnny also made loans to bartenders and regular bar clients. His approach was clever but haphazard. Johnny liked to buy the bar tabs of heavy drinkers at hotels and taverns. He is said to have cleared the entire arrears of the regulars at popular downtown hotels. The bar owners were happy to get immediate cash for what could be difficult accounts to collect. Johnny would then let the barflies know that five percent a week was the Bank of Papalia's current rate of interest. It seems petty and strange, but it was obviously a ploy that earned Johnny money—enough to even hire help.

Heavyweight boxer and renowned street fighter Howard (Baldy) Chard was eight years younger than Johnny when they met in the early 1950s. Baldy was a brute of a man who, although possessing more than enough power in each of his hands to quickly convince people to see things his way, had such an awesome physical presence that he rarely needed to lift a finger. He was the perfect picture of frightfulness: 5-foot-10, more than 300 pounds, and a putty-like face bearing scars from a thousand street fights. He was the former heavyweight champ of Kingston Penitentiary—a title that really meant something on the street.

Baldy first went to work for Johnny as an enforcer and a prop. Baldy would collect money from the punters who owed Johnny interest on their bar tab and others. He was also trotted out to stand quietly at Johnny's side during important meetings. Most of the guys Johnny met with knew of Baldy's fighting prowess both inside and outside the ring, but even those who did not needed only to catch a glimpse of him to learn all they needed to know.

Baldy had a career dotted with triumphs and embarrassments. In the summer of 1948, he dropped before an unworthy opponent when the gamblers' odds were firmly in his favour. Those placing the right bet made a killing, but the paying customers in Syracuse, New York, were not so thrilled; nobody, not even his opponent, saw Baldy take a single punch. Baldy suffered a knockout of a different sort a few years later. Up on charges for selling booze to minors, Baldy was conducting his own defence. He called to the stand the teenage girl whom police found lightly toasted inside the boxer's house. He had arranged for the girl to tell the court she had had nothing to drink. After she was sworn in, Baldy asked if she ever drank booze in his home. The muscle man almost choked when she replied: "Yes. And I'm glad of a chance to tell the truth." She then turned to the judge and said Baldy had told her that if she testified against him he would find her and "fix" her. The surprise evidence doomed Baldy, the fledgling legal eagle. This conviction was followed by charges of robbery with violence, assault, operating a bawdy house, and living off the avails of prostitution, all while under Johnny's tutelage.

Baldy did have his share of glory. In 1965, Baldy bested former Canadian and British Empire heavyweight champion James J. Parker in a bareknuckles brawl before Johnny Papalia and 100 other invited guests in an infamous Toronto match-up. The fight became legend. Parker was a hard man himself and had knocked out 70 of 81 opponents. The non-stop, winner-takes-the-door bloodfest was the last known bareknuckles boxing match in the country.

"Our gangs started it," Parker said of the match years later. "His gang said he'd beat the crap out of me and my gang said I'd lick Chard easy. We almost killed each other. Some said we fought 59 straight minutes. Somebody else said he timed us at 44 minutes. I had no respect for Baldy. He was a pimp and a stoolie and a bully. But he might have been the toughest guy in the world."

Johnny and Baldy remained close friends and business associates until their relationship was shattered in the mid-1970s. For years, Johnny had let Baldy and his family live rent-free on an untended farm the Papalias quietly owned in Waterdown, a rural community on the outskirts of Hamilton. In about 1975, in the early spring, Johnny decided to sell the land, and had prospective buyers ready to see it. He could not reach Baldy to tell him to prepare the property for viewing, however. The next day Johnny—typically dressed in a fine suit with razor-sharp creases in his trousers, and a long, expensive topcoat—drove out to the farm with four associates.

"Where the hell were you?" Johnny raged at Baldy. "I phoned you yesterday. You were supposed to be here. I had someone coming out to have a look at the farm. You are supposed to be here." Baldy thought Johnny's notion preposterous and pointed out that he still had to earn money to buy food for his family. He could not stay housebound day and night. The two argued fiercely in the muddy lane beside the farmhouse.

That's when Baldy slugged him.

Johnny went down like everyone did when Baldy lashed out, and those with him gasped, unsure of what to do. Johnny got up quietly, scraped some of the mud from the back of his topcoat, looked up at Baldy and said: "We'll talk about this another time." He then turned and left. Word soon filtered down to Baldy that he would be left alone despite his impertinence—as long as Baldy never spoke of the embarrassing incident. He also was to move off the farm. Johnny had one last message for his former henchman: "Our relationship is over." Baldy Chard later died from complications stemming from diabetes.

Johnny's loan-sharking enterprise eventually grew into a highly organized and efficient operation that for many took on the role of neighbourhood bank. He became, in effect, a full-service underworld financial company. It was a far-reaching effort—stretching across the Golden Horseshoe. Problem borrowers, however, faced stiff retribution. One man was bashed around in his Hamilton home and was bleeding profusely when an ambulance arrived. His place had been torn apart by street muscle giving him some incentive to pay back his loan, and police were soon at the scene.

"You know what he said to me?" a detective asked after talking to the victim about the attack. "He said he fell down the basement stairs. It looks like a tornado hit the place but he insists he fell down the stairs."

Such was the fear of the Papalia name and sanctioned muscle.

7

If extortion was a bit blue-collar, gambling was the underworld's white-collar alternative. It certainly was held in higher esteem by mainstream society, for many of the men in blue uniforms, men in black robes, and even those wearing white collars liked to put a few bucks on the line when the Toronto Maple Leafs faced the Montreal Canadiens, or to back boxer Sonny Liston in a title match. While few would see threatening a man's livelihood—or his children—as a legitimate way of earning an income, gambling was given a discreet nod of approval by a substantial segment of society.

Like Prohibition before it, outlawing betting was a losing proposition. The Second World War had been a time of low unemployment and high household income, which frustratingly clashed with profound rationing. It all fueled a tremendous interest in an easy, enjoyable outlet for all of that disposable income: gambling. As the 1940s waned, gambling—cards, dice, and betting on anything that moved—became a national pastime. Long before the government was tempted to wade into the gambling business, those wanting to lay a bet were forced to come face-to-face with a mob-approved bookie. From dockworkers betting 50 cents to doctors laying down thousands of dollars, gambling had gripped the nation. An estimate in 1961 suggested Canadians would place bets worth $1.8 billion that year. In the United States, business was more than 10 times that. It became an incalculable and essential source of untaxed profit in the cash-intensive world of organized crime.

It was a racket Johnny intended to dominate. First loosely and then systematically, he forced his way into the games that people played. It was a passion he maintained until the day he died.

For his foray into gambling, Johnny Papalia followed his usual pattern. He made big plans but started small; gathered around him a core of skilled operators; established a base of operations; learned the ropes—and then burst out in a splendid eruption, flowing in all directions.

In the early 1950s, Johnny enlisted waiters and bartenders around Hamilton to call in bets from regular customers. Even an elevator operator at St. Joseph's Hospital took bets from staff and patients on Johnny's behalf. Johnny cut these freelance staffers in on the action, giving them a return on every dollar they collected in his name. Once the waiters and bartenders entered into this arrangement, however, they soon found they were equally responsible for recouping all losses, and if they had trouble collecting from their customers they were personally on the hook to Johnny Pops to make up the difference. And they always did. It was an effective way to keep overhead low, reach out to a cross-section of gamblers, and insulate Johnny from prosecution.

Johnny gathered to his side four key lieutenants: Red LeBarre, Freddie Gabourie, Frank Marchildon, and Jackie Weaver.

Donald (Red) LeBarre was a faithful Papalia underling who amassed three decades of loyal service before his death. He earned his nickname Red from the colour his face turned whenever he drank, which meant he spent considerable portions of his life quite red-faced. Later in life, he would at times be Johnny's driver, bodyguard, roommate, and almost constant companion. He would regularly visit Johnny in prison. But when Johnny was building his empire, Red was his popular front man for sports betting. A large, affable man, Red contacted his regular roster of compulsive gamblers three times a day by phone. His round of calls grew so heavy, he needed an answering service to ease the burden. Red was also something of a "mechanic"—a man who could rig a crooked game of craps or cards—and later ran high-stakes canasta games out of a beauty parlour on Hamilton Mountain, the part of the city that sits on top of the Niagara Escarpment.[1]

Where Red was gregarious, Frederick (Freddie Gabe) Gabourie was a looker.

"He dressed like a duke and had the manners of royalty. He could have been a movie star," said a friend. Handsome, suave, and a terrific dresser, Gabourie really did flirt with an acting career in Hollywood, working as an extra in several films before being kicked off the Metro-Goldwyn-Mayer movie lot for taking bets. He moved back to Ontario and settled into a job as a strong-armed goon and gambling impresario on the Papalia payroll. Gabourie drove other gangsters nuts by impressing their women with his smooth manners and grace. Each time he reverently stood up when a mobster's girlfriend or wife entered or left the room, the women always demanded to know why their men could not be more like Freddie Gabe. Gabourie offered a strange mix of attributes—impeccable clothing and Victorian manners blended with a swindler's eye and a mean right hook. It made him an enviable catch for a fledgling crime lord. Gabourie's loyalty to Johnny was never in question. He ate several gambling-related charges and one for fraud without ever turning on his boss.

Jackie Weaver tried to play the government like the suckers he coaxed to his Toronto crap tables. It was not one of his more successful scams; he was caught and convicted of failing to file an income tax return. Weaver was a broad-shouldered gambler who kept his hair in a military-style buzz cut. He followed Johnny's lead of always dressing as if he were on his way to a formal dinner. Only a few inches taller than Johnny, Weaver was not a big man, which once or twice got him into trouble when he traveled far from his usual stamping ground and was caught fiddling with the dice at crap games. He was the youngest of the gang and also the quietest; he rarely started a conversation but was a comfortable conversationalist to those who approached him. Weaver

---

1 Red, near the end of his life, was suffering badly after repeated hospital scares from heart trouble and diabetes. Fed up, in the summer of 2000 he decided to end the strain he felt he was putting on his family.

and Gabourie were a good team and were always looking for a new score. One year they rode the Grey Cup football train from Winnipeg to Toronto, cleaning out the Bluebombers' fans at makeshift dice tables along the way.

In a room above a Toronto restaurant, Johnny, Gabourie, and Weaver ran late-night, high-stakes crap games. A couple of heavies—including Baldy Chard—remained downstairs to make sure only the right kind of people ventured up, and Gabourie and Weaver made sure everyone left with a light wallet. Johnny financed the games, throwing up the $2,000 to $3,000 float needed to start each night's gambling from a giant wad of cash rolled up in his pocket.

Frank Marchildon was two years older than Johnny, but a loyal underling nonetheless. Less dexterous and glamorous than Gabourie and Weaver, and less affable and boisterous than LeBarre, Marchildon's strength lay in his loyalty, toughness, and genuine affinity for Johnny. The son of a French father and East Indian mother from the shores of Georgian Bay, Marchildon had known Johnny for more than a decade and had become an intimate member of his inner circle. Of all his lieutenants, Johnny perhaps trusted Marchildon the most.

"Marchildon was a tough little bastard," said an old friend. "He wasn't a big guy but he got things done."

Marchildon owned a dress shop and a heating oil business in Hamilton, but gave them up when Johnny asked him to move to Toronto. Once there, Marchildon set up a hairdressing salon as a front for his activities. Loyal and long-suffering, Marchildon stayed with the Papalia clan for more than three decades, and was still working for them in 1979 when members of Johnny's family were investigated for an elaborate fraud. Marchildon and Johnny were close personally, as well. Johnny was named godfather to the Marchildons' youngest child.

When Johnny's boys all got together—as they did constantly—they fed each other's bravado through a rollicking sense of dark humour.

"They were so inventive and creative and were always coming up with different scams to pull on naive people, scams that you and I would never think of in a million years," said a friend of the men who often accompanied them on social outings. "It was always such a waste of brain power. I kept thinking in those days, if they had just sourced it out better, what good could they have created?"

Schemes, scams, cons and outright heists became a way of life, creating deep social, as well as professional, bonds.

"We ate together a lot. We partied together. If anybody opened up a new place, we all went to it together. There were a couple of bars that we hung out at. It was always lots of laughs—lots to drink, the best of food, everywhere we went the best waitresses waited on us just to get the big tips," said the friend. "They drank, smoked a little pot, reminisced and laughed at themselves. They had a morbid sense of humour and to hear them, you'd think they were the Gang That Couldn't Shoot Straight."

They loved to rib each other over the scams that went awry. There was the time some of the gang were pulling a heist and just could not get the safe open. Refusing to admit defeat, and with morning coming, they lugged the safe outside and dumped it in the back of their car so they could continue to work on it in private. It was so heavy, however, that the car's shocks could not support it; as they peeled away, the back end of the car scraped along the road, sending out a noisy shower of sparks.

"They always had crazy stories. They poked fun at one another, but no one else could poke fun at them. They could do it amongst themselves, but they wouldn't take it from someone else."

Organized gambling was a surprisingly intricate but efficient operation, requiring constant communication and interaction with other gambling enterprises in a loosely affiliated, continent-wide network. The lifeblood of the bookmaker is information.

For horse racing, the source of that information is the racewires. While one legitimate company teletyped racing results to news organizations to fill their sports pages, a shadow wire fed the bookies. Sometimes it came directly from a sports publisher discreetly redirecting the legitimate flow of information. Other times it came from an army of men with binoculars, cooped up in rooms overlooking racetracks, who read the results directly from the track's board and called it in to a central office. Using daily racing forms listing horses, post times, track conditions, and odds, the gamblers would daily assess their options, make their picks, and usually lose their money.

For sporting events, a bookie's best friend was "the line," the calculated odds for each race or competition. Professional handicappers across the continent assessed the relative merits of each match-up and decided who was favoured and by how much. Bookies used codes to call secret services to get the line by telephone. So long as a bookie's bets from his clients were fairly evenly spread between the horses in any given race or between the two combatants in a sporting event, his profit was assured. But when gamblers heavily favoured one team, one horse, or one boxer, he stood to take a bath in sudden losses. To ensure profits, a bookie would "lay off" bets, hedging against a loss by making bets of his own with an allied bookmaking joint. This was called "spreading the action," "balancing the books," or sometimes "come-back money."

The odds were always kept in favour of the house.

Johnny's next move was into established gambling clubs.

In 1954, he made arrangements to pay to the government all the arrears of the Porcupine Miners' Club, a long-defunct social club from Timmins, Ontario, incorporated in 1929 as a bona fide place for miners to socialize. The mandate of the Porcupine was to improve social conditions in the Town of Timmins, but Johnny's interest was less noble. Gaining a social club charter was the first step in opening any large gambling den. Professional gamblers—Johnny included—were transferring incorporated social club charters, originally issued to veteran groups, ethnic organizations, and social clubs, and using them as fronts for cards, dice, and betting operations. Charters did not make gambling legal, but having one threw up a reasonable screen behind which to hide; it provided an excuse for men to gather night after night, and by the time police got through the bolted doors, evidence that the card games were part of a set-up involving a house bank for gambling would have been cleared away.

Johnny had a hand in getting his first club charter from Tony Sylvestro of Guelph. Sylvestro had shady contacts in Timmins from past gold scams (stolen gold was bought directly from corrupt miners and resold on the black market). Johnny's business partner in this new gambling venture was to be Dante (Danny) Gasbarrini—Sylvestro's son-in-law—assuring Sylvestro's assistance in the enterprise. Danny Gasbarrini grew up in Johnny's neighbourhood and was the son of Luigi Gasbarrini, the man shot in the leg by Johnny's relative, Dominic Italiano, decades before. In just a few months, Gasbarrini was due for release after a lengthy prison term and would need to get back on his feet.[2]

On April 7, 1955, the club advised the provincial secretary that the Porcupine was being revived, but no enquiry was made as to why a miners' club from Timmins was suddenly of interest to the people of Hamilton. Johnny and Gasbarrini set up their club at 15½ John Street North, just a few blocks away from Hamilton's police headquarters. It ran without interference for several years.

"It was a strictly honest game and we took our profit on the house percentage," Gasbarrini later said of his days with the Porcupine. "For two years the police never bothered us although they knew it was going on. But we never paid anyone off. It was just that we ran an honest game and had some of the best people in town coming. Then one night no one came into the club and we found the police at the door sending people away."

Despite Gasbarrini's protestations, when it came to cards and dice, gangsters were running notoriously crooked games. Unwary and unconnected gamblers walking into a club were like lambs jumping the queue to be fleeced. Dice were loaded with weights, forcing particular combinations to show when they were tossed. Edges were rounded or the cubes cut at irregular angles to favour certain numbers. The dots on the faces were even altered, eliminating the standard

---

2 Danny Gasbarrini was arrested in Vancouver on October 27, 1949, while distributing heroin for his father-in-law. He was convicted of conspiracy to distribute narcotics and sent to prison for seven years, the maximum sentence for the crime.

spotting on the die's face; suddenly—after an unseen switch to bogus dice—it became impossible to shoot a winning roll.

Cards were often marked using white ink or bleach. The backs were altered by scraping off small bits of the artwork with a sharp knife. Slight and almost unnoticeable dents in the surface of the card would tip those in the know to the card's value. The edges of high cards were trimmed ever so slightly and could be discerned in the deck by a dexterous dealer; he would then assign them to the people at the table who were in on their racket. A clip was often attached to the bottom of card tables, and key high cards were secretly removed from the deck and placed in it until being returned to the game—into the winning hand of the house. Skilled dealers could even take an ordinary deck and turn it into a money-fleecing machine as cards were quickly dealt over tables on which cars, homes, and businesses were lost. And if all else failed, there was the professional pickpocket, working outside the club as a last line of defence in separating fools from their money.

The cheating, of course, could only run one way. When a gambler was caught cheating at the Cooksville gambling club, club owner James McDermott himself swung the baseball bat that shattered the man's arm.

Johnny's gambling enterprises spread. When police picked off one, another was ready to take its place. In February 1958, police finally moved against the Porcupine, and three men, including Michael Genovese (alias Genessee), were convicted of keeping a common gaming house. Genovese was a man named in secret RCMP reports from 1947 as a key lieutenant for the Sylvestros' drug-smuggling operation and the front man for dope sales to Harvey Chernick in Toronto. The Porcupine's charter was scrapped on January 8, 1959, but Genovese was already running another set-up, this one out of the Alexander Motel on Highway 20, just outside Hamilton. When the motel was also raided, police found Norman (Nemo) Joseph of Lewiston, New York, at the helm. Nemo was a big player in Buffalo's syndicate. Inside the motel, officers seized betting sheets showing an average daily volume of $22,900 in bets. Nemo is estimated to have taken $8 million in lay-off bets from across the United States. Interestingly, despite Genovese's tight relationship with Tony Sylvestro, he insisted on taking the fall for Nemo and was jailed for two months. This shows how Buffalo's *mafiosi* outranked even senior members of Ontario's mob.[3]

In September 1957, the outstanding arrears of another social club were paid, and on October 10, 1957, the renovated premises at 1284 Queen Street West in Toronto welcomed gamblers to the West End Bridge and Social Club's opening night—where bridge was a game few played. The Queen Street location was the home of a previous club shut down by Toronto police not a year earlier, when two of Johnny's lieutenants—Freddie Gabourie and Jackie Weaver—were charged with keeping a common gaming house and bookmaking. A "branch" of the West End Bridge and Social Club—boldly using just a photocopy of the original charter—was found to be hopping in Hamilton when police raided a club at 25½ MacNab Street North in July 1958. Inside they found a large-scale, full-service sports betting operation complete with a ticker-tape machine relaying play-by-play information on most sporting events. Papalia lieutenant Red LeBarre was running it with assistance from Johnny's brother-in-law, Anthony (Tony) Pugliese; Johnny's younger brother, Dominic, was the club's vice-president and his older half-brother, Joseph, the club steward. The branch at 25½ MacNab Street closed down and the equipment was moved—to just down the road. At 9-A MacNab Street, the same operation was immediately re-established under the name the Divion Club, listing Weaver as the president and employing two more of Johnny's brothers, Rocco and Angelo.

On April 13, 1960, the West End club on Queen Street was raided. Weaver and two others were convicted of engaging in betting. On May 27, 1960, the West End's charter was finally canceled. Less than a

3 Less than a year later, Nemo was arrested in Toronto for another offence, and promptly sprinted from the courtroom. He was captured and let loose on $10,000 bail, which he happily skipped, heading back across the border.

month later, Toronto police again raided 1284 Queen Street West and were alarmed to find it now occupied by the Divion Club. When the Divion was shut down, up popped the Checkers Club, again run by Red LeBarre and Rocco Papalia.

When Checkers was raided by police on July 31, 1961, Dominic Papalia did his very best to warn his brother and associates inside. Arriving on the scene to find police cars pulling up outside the Merrick Street gambling den, the shocked gangster drove his truck in front of the cruisers, leaned on the horn, and started shouting out warnings. He was charged with obstructing police. Despite Dominic's efforts, police arrested Rocco Papalia and LeBarre inside, charging them with keeping a common betting house, engaging in bookmaking, and recording bets.

Johnny's chief frontmen were getting to be well known to police officers in cities and towns across Southern Ontario. Some members of Toronto's anti-gambling squad first met Johnny face to face during a surprise raid on the notorious Bellevue club, another popular gambling den that answered to The Enforcer.

"We were executing a routine search warrant one afternoon when Freddie Gabourie and another man came out of a backroom," said a retired Toronto police officer who conducted the surprise raid. The mystery man was dressed in a black suit with a white-on-white tie and shirt combination, and from his demeanour the officers could tell he was the man in charge. "When we asked him for his name, he gave us some lip. Perhaps it was the first time a Mafia chief was grabbed by his tie and banged up against a wall. From then on, he was always polite when we ran into him," the officer said.

The names of the clubs changed, the addresses switched, but in each case the man in charge was Johnny Papalia. Still, he saw that there was much more money out there to be had.

Johnny would not have dared to go after the province's big gambling kings—or likely even thought of it—before his graduation into the uppercrust of the underworld through his tutelage in Montreal under

Carmine Galante. As a growing man of respect, however, with as much strong-arm experience and as many well-connected associates as he had, it really became the only move to make. "Go big or go home" might well have been Johnny's motto, and with that idea entrenched in his ambition-soaked brain, Johnny went after the single most profitable piece of gambling action around—the lucrative Cooksville club. Standing between him and all that money were James McDermott and Vincent (Pete) Feeley, two major players, who along with a partner were known as the Three Thieves.

McDermott and Feeley rose, literally, from rags to riches through gambling, crime, and corruption. McDermott exercised horses for a living in his early years, and in 1939 faced his first conviction, a breaking and entering charge.[4] By 1959, however, he owned an airline operating out of Toronto Island Airport and would soon buy a personal helicopter for $44,000, drawing the money from a suitcase full of cash. Feeley, a grade nine drop-out, waited on tables after forging his own army discharge papers in 1942. But by 1960, he had a swank Toronto apartment in which police once seized $20,500—$10,000 of it hidden in a shoe. McDermott and Feeley were involved in high-rolling clubs around Toronto, including the lucrative one on Centre Road near Cooksville that attracted Johnny's interest. They also ran the Riverdale Club, first set up on Eglinton Avenue and later in Downsview; the Finnish Club, a large, refurbished building on Sixth Street, which they ran with James Ryan; the Roseland Club near Windsor, which they ran with partner Vito (Billy Jack) Giacalone, who supervised the gambling interests of the Detroit Mafia and would later be one of the mobsters working with Jimmy Hoffa, the doomed head of the Teamsters union; the profitable Tisdale Club in Peterborough;

4 McDermott joined the army to gain sympathy from the judge by appearing in uniform; the move assured him a suspended sentence.

and the Frontier Club in Bertie township in Niagara, which they ran with partner Benny Nicoletti, who supervised the Buffalo mob's gambling operations.[5]

McDermott was perpetually crafty and surprisingly well read. Feeley fancied himself a ladies' man and used his considerable charm on women in positions to help his enterprises. He dated the wife of a corporal with the Ontario Provincial Police's anti-gambling squad, hoping to pull from her valuable information. The woman greatly enjoyed Feeley's company. She was not alone. Feeley rode the buses that passed OPP headquarters, flirting with police secretaries when they took their seats.

In typical Papalia fashion, Johnny marched up to the Thieves and introduced himself as their new partner. McDermott and Feeley did not fall down right away. After all, they were rich and powerful people and had contacts with heavies of their own; a partner in one club was a Magaddino man, and the Detroit Mafia had a piece of another. What McDermott and Feeley failed to grasp, however, was how interconnected and monolithic an organization the Mafia could be when it wanted to be. Although Johnny was not likely yet a made Mafia member, he had close ties and tight associations with a growing circle of *mafiosi*. When astute people looked at Johnny, they saw the shadow of the three dons standing behind him. People like Johnny did not act in a vacuum. McDermott and Feeley went to Detroit and hired some muscle to rough up Johnny, whom they saw as little more than an impertinent young punk. But when the hired heavies came to size up their target and realized Johnny's deep criminal ties, they wished him well and went straight home. McDermott and Feeley soon welcomed Johnny as their protector, enforcer, and partner.

5 Proving that sometimes the fruit doesn't fall far from the tree, Benny's son, Benjamin "Sonny" Nicoletti, Jr., took over the family's interests in illicit gambling and continued to run cross-border games. In September 2002, the FBI accused Sonny, then 62, of Lewiston, New York, and Adam Thomas, then 32, of St. Catharines, Ontario, of running a gambling empire that boasted both sophisticated off-shore casinos and low-brow extortion against Southern Ontario illicit gambling dens. Authorities claimed Nicoletti and Thomas were taking in more than $25,000 in bets each day, much of it in Canadian currency.

The Cooksville cash made Johnny's pockets bulge.

Like his relationship with Galante, Johnny's pairing with the Thieves brought benefits to both sides. It was actually a pretty decent fit. Now, along with Feeley's soft touch with the ladies, the operation had Johnny for the hard sell. It brought Johnny into regular contact with the top players and racketeers on both sides of the border, this time as something of a success story.

His role in the clubs was an important but nebulous one. He smoothed problems, he was a fixer: part public relations, part strike force. Johnny was once called upon to quiet an angry partner of McDermott's and Feeley's who had paid the pair $500 a month for their influence in keeping police attention away from his club. Dominic Simone ran one of the biggest crap joints in the province. It was a profitable venture, with crooked dice being used at the tables and a series of doors—each with a watchman armed with a warning buzzer—erected between the front entrance and the gaming room. But when Simone's dice set-up was busted by police in December 1953, he did not feel that the more than $50,000 in payoffs had been such a good investment. When Simone got out of jail he demanded a refund. Feeley paid Simone a grand or more to shut him up, but he continued to squawk. The gamblers unleashed The Enforcer. Johnny reminded Simone that this gambling business was strictly *caveat emptor*. Johnny handled the enforcement with extreme panache; rather than belting away at Simone, he merely suggested McDermott and Feeley be left alone, and then, after tucking $200 into Simone's breast pocket, told him the issue was now "personal."

Gambling was exciting to Johnny, blending his interest in sport, love of competition, sneaky underhandedness, and dumb luck. Johnny loved running the gambling show, and late into his life maintained it as his goal to control gambling in the province. Ironically, although eventually serving prison time for drugs, extortion, and assault, it was his gambling rackets that really occupied much of his time and enthusiasm. In fact, Johnny would have been content just to run a well-oiled bookmaking operation all his life. He once took aside an RCMP officer who regularly investigated his many activities and—over a bottle of anisette—told him that if the force would just look the other way and let him have two lines coming in to his headquarters so he could run a quality bookmaking joint, he would drop everything else—and police would never have to worry about The Enforcer again.

The offer was, of course, refused, but one can only imagine how different things might have been had the government taken Johnny at his word.

8

The Bonanno and Magaddino families were not the only powerful American Mafia clans eyeing the action in Canada and watching Johnny Papalia's activities. While Joseph Bonanno had Carmine Galante beating the underworld of Montreal into submission, and Stefano Magaddino was strengthening his ties with *mafiosi* in Ontario, the Genovese family of New York City, under its violent and troll-like boss, Vito Genovese, also had expansionist dreams.

Genovese sent a young, beefy *mafioso* north of the border to look after his family's interests in this newfound land. Their interests ran heavily towards drugs. Vincent (Vinnie) Mauro, also known as Vinnie Bruno, was a favourite of Genovese, although his rank within the crime family was still low. Mauro would have a big impact on Johnny's life, and Johnny on Mauro's.

Mauro, born in 1917, was the product of the street gangs of Greenwich Village, an area of Manhattan encompassing a wildly popular nightclub district. A street fighter, robber, and dope peddler, Mauro was eventually recruited into the New York Mafia by none other than Joseph (Joe Cago) Valachi, who would later become the first Mafia turncoat. When Mauro was exposed to the larger criminal concern, he was fascinated. He stood by, reverently absorbing the comings and goings.

"He used to come around to this poolroom where we hung out on 108th Street and First Avenue," Valachi said of the young Mauro. "He looked like a nice kid, quiet and all that, so I got close to him and I used to take him downtown to the Village Inn and the Hollywood, and Tony Bender took a liking to him."

Mauro's deep-set, brooding eyes contrasted with his quick, mischievous smile, often creating an unnerving effect. Once invited into the inner circle of New York's crime cartel, Mauro's quiet, nice-guy schtick gave way to his Greenwich Village streetpunk nature. At his core, Mauro was pure New York: loud, brash, and easily lapsing into crudeness. He was a huge leap from the image of the quintessential *mafioso*, one able to quietly command respect and give orders with a gentle nod.

Mauro, however, was also a lot like Johnny: bright, ambitious, and possessing a gleeful love of life that made him instantly attractive to those around him. After all, even mobsters like to have fun, and Vinnie Mauro and Johnny Papalia made fun happen. Mauro blossomed into an impressive career criminal with admirable business interests. He partnered with Valachi and their boss within the Genovese family, Anthony (Tony Bender) Strollo, in a profitable juke box operation. By being cut into a business with the likes of the notoriously greedy Strollo, Mauro showed his ability to ingratiate himself with his bosses. Strollo was a very senior *capo* in the Genovese family and in charge of the rackets across Greenwich Village. Mauro, said Valachi, was Strollo's "pet."

When Johnny met Mauro in New York City around 1955, the pair of thirty-something bachelors immediately hit it off. They found they shared many passions: show girls, race tracks, gambling, and an egoist's interest in their own advancement. Both unencumbered by a wife or children, Johnny and Mauro spent long nights together in New York, both dressed in sharp suits, rolling off $100 bills and arguing over who would pick up the tab for a table full of associates and newly made lady-friends in posh nightclubs. The fact that these two men were operating in cities worlds apart helped erase the natural rivalry that might normally have welled up between two such men. They also soon realized they could help each other out.

Mauro jealously eyed what Carmine Galante had created in Montreal and felt he could do the same in Toronto. Such a move, of course, would be easier with a man of Johnny's position, contacts, and considerable abilities. And so the two men started talking business. For Mauro, more often than not, that meant talking drugs. His plans for Ontario never materialized, partly because of a reluctance to relocate and partly because his obsession with becoming a drug baron consumed most of his energy. It was an obsession that would send him into treacherous waters, dragging Johnny along with him.

Vinnie Mauro was not Johnny's only American friend. Frederico (Freddie Lupo) Randaccio of Buffalo was a pal far closer to home. Like Johnny, he was always a careful dresser and had a penchant for wearing dark glasses in public; if not for Randaccio's greying temples, he could easily have been mistaken for Johnny from across a crowded room. The two met in the early 1950s, when Randaccio was rising fast in the Magaddino mob in Buffalo and Johnny was a young protégé. A full 17 years older than Johnny, Randaccio was more mentor than friend, but it is said the American mobster was rather fond of Johnny, despite his being Canadian—and Calabrian as well.

Randaccio arrived in the U.S. on July 6, 1910, at the age of three aboard the S.S. *Mendosa* from Palermo, Sicily. Then named Frederico Fassi, he traveled with his mother, who was joining her husband in New York City. Freddie attended school in New York until the end of grade four, when, in 1918, his family moved to Buffalo. At the age of 15, he was arrested for the first time and subsequently dropped out of school. He moved deeper into the underworld and hooked up with Magaddino. Randaccio later became Magaddino's underboss when Salvatore John Pieri was sent to prison on a drug charge on December 11, 1954, in Cleveland, Ohio. Some Buffalo mob members could not resist the lure of narco-dollars, but never close to their homes. Police noted four other members of the organization were drug traffickers, but each confined their sales to the east-side black neighbourhoods or away from the city altogether.

On the outside, Randaccio was a calm, unobtrusive, polite man. Inside, however, he had problems. Labeled as psychopathic by the psychiatric department at Auburn State Prison in New York, he became well known in the underworld for making people see things his way. Randaccio showed his smiling, smooth-mannered side to the ladies, and his fearsome side to men who crossed him. His sadistic tendencies made him a feared man in a tough town, but police who tailed Randaccio also noted he had a number of young, very pretty, and extremely devoted mistresses around Niagara Falls and Buffalo.

When it came to taking care of business, Randaccio made frequent visits to Magaddino's funeral chapel for meetings with the grand boss, or would meet the don at a Buffalo laundry service company that Magaddino owned. They also met over early-morning breakfasts in the restaurant of the Peace Bridge Motel. As Randaccio's stature in the mob grew, he cut off his nightly visits to the rowdy nightclubs where common hoodlums gathered, although he silently invested in many of them. Like Johnny, Randaccio owned a vending machine company, although Buffalo police pressured him and his partner, Fred Mogavero, to sell Delaware Cigarette Vending Machines Co. to other—that is, legitimate—business owners. While Randaccio followed Magaddino in every detail, he also had influence over the old don, especially in matters involving personnel. Randaccio was a formidable friend for Johnny to have.

Johnny made friends in the American mob not only because he helped them take care of business, but because they liked him. In such a cut-throat world, where mobsters kill their own brothers for perceived slights and breaches of honour, to be considered not only an associate but also a friend of the likes of Mauro and Randaccio suggests the force of Johnny's personality when he was not on display for the media. Johnny was a great conversationalist who cracked jokes to his peers and listened well to his superiors. He could be forceful, but always knew how to show proper respect.

From the early tutelage of his father and the counsel of the three Ontario dons, to advanced studies in crime under Carmine Galante, Vinnie Mauro, and Freddie Randaccio, Johnny had wisely chosen his mentors in crime. He was now approaching graduation day.

9

"**Q**uesto è il santo della nostra famiglia. "

In English, it means "This is the holy image of our family." Within the underworld élite, these words become excruciatingly important because they form part of the secret blood oath of initiation into La Cosa Nostra. While the words are spoken, a picture of a saint, often an image of the Virgin Mary herself, is ignited in a candle's flame and bounced from hand to hand by the initiate as it smoulders in his palms.

"As burns this saint," the pledge continues in Italian, "so will burn my soul if I betray this organization."

As with almost all Mafia initiation ceremonies, there is no record of Johnny Papalia's official induction into the most important club in crime. Membership, said Joseph Pistone, the Federal Bureau of Investigation's special agent who spent six years undercover as "Donnie Brasco" to infiltrate the powerful Bonanno crime family, "is the most secret and protected bastion of all Mafia activities."

Although there are no records, what likely went on between Johnny and his prospective new family members can be pieced together from the few initiation ceremonies that police have managed to capture on tape. One took place in 1985 in London, Ontario, and featured an undercover RCMP officer actually being inducted into a Calabrian Mafia cell while police secretly videotaped the ceremony. The operation was code-named Project Oaf. Another, in the United States four years later, was more formal but no more important. What is astounding is the remarkable similarity of practices and words between the two ceremonies—words that would have been spoken at Johnny's initiation.

"In this sombre ceremony men actually become *mafiosi*—they are 'made' or 'baptized' or they 'get their badges,'" said Pistone. "They become 'wiseguys' or 'friends' or 'good fellows' or 'one of us' or 'straightened out.' To become 'made' is the hallowed goal—the highlight of a lifetime to every mob associate, or hanger-on, or every Italian street-corner punk who prefers being a thief to having a job."

While the word "Mafia" is now used as a general term for organized crime, technically, the true Mafia is only the Sicilian crime groups, also known as Cosa Nostra, meaning "Our Thing." Other groups have their own proper names, including the 'Ndrangheta or "Honoured Society," from Calabria, and the Camorra from Naples. The transplanted American version of the Mafia has a slightly blended membership of Italians from various backgrounds, although it is generally ruled by Sicilians. It was dubbed La Cosa Nostra by the Federal Bureau of Investigation. Each organization has its own structure and rules, but to the casual observer today, La Cosa Nostra, Cosa Nostra, 'Ndrangheta, or Camorra, are all seen as different aspects of "the Mafia."[1]

Johnny Papalia was eligible for membership in either a Calabrian 'Ndrangheta cell, because of his father's roots and close contacts with the Calabrian criminals in the Hamilton area, or in America's much larger La Cosa Nostra, because of both his Italian heritage and contacts and friends south of the border.

One does not apply for membership in the Mafia; one must be "proposed" by a member who is willing to go on record with a current boss that vouches for this newcomer and claims responsibility for his conduct.

"That privilege doesn't come easily," said Pistone. "You have to be a good earner, and you have to be trustworthy—and to ensure that

---

1 *Global Mafia: The New World Order of Organized Crime* by Antonio Nicaso and Lee Lamothe is an excellent source of information on the origins and operations of the many disparate crime groups operating today and thoroughly updates our knowledge on these syndicates' globalization and cooperation.

you possess these qualities, the mob watches you for years prior to nominating you. A sponsor is risking his life to propose an associate for membership. If a member goes bad, those who vouched for him are totally, unquestionably, immediately held responsible; they are subject to the death penalty."

The Calabrian initiation ceremony in London was a more casual affair than its La Cosa Nostra counterpart, perhaps because the group itself was very small and most members inexperienced. But despite the wine and laughter, the words were solemn and the threats against betrayal believable.

Giovanni (John) Zangari, a leader of the cell, led the ceremony in an apartment on Proudfoot Lane. He gathered six fellow mob members and a man he thought was a promising young recruit—but who was instead a clever undercover cop—into a circle and spoke of entering into "the Honoured Society of Calabria" and "the family." Each member present voted three times to accept the initiate into the organization. The ceremony and rules explained to the officer sounded remarkably similar to the oath of the *Picciotteria* probably taken by Johnny Papalia's father six decades before.

"I swear on the tip of this knife to forget father, mother, all the family, at whatever call, to answer to 'Corp of the Society,'" the inductee was prompted to say in a rather disconcerting blend of English and Italian. (Interestingly enough, when the knife was first pulled out for the ceremony, the police officer said in English: "Don't use it, please." It is not known if he was joking around or genuinely frightened, but it must have provided a few tense moments for his police colleagues who were secretly listening in.)

"There is a dark tomb wide and deep under the depth of the sea. Whoever uncovers it shall die with four knifings to the breast," the vow continued.

Zangari explained some of the rules, the "codes of the court," as he called them. Cooperation, communication, dividing of profits, and punishment are crucial elements.

"If we make a penny, a penny . . . is what is divided amongst us. If [one of us] is in trouble, we are all in trouble. These are not things that are discussed with anyone," Zangari said. "You are older than my brother, but because he entered [The Society] before you . . . you have to respect him. I'll tell you something. When one does a swearing in, they have to do a swearing in that will last. It is not a swearing in that you can say you want to leave . . . If he does [a profitable activity] and I don't know, I don't know but if I find out, if he does something light, small, there are other methods in which he can pay. And you don't pay with words . . . You know how it is paid? With death, that's how it is paid."

And finally, catch-all words of wisdom: "If you are respectful, you are respected by all. When one has respect the other things will come."

Zangari did not speak of punishment without pointing out benefits, including the connections that came with being a made member. He spoke of his "friends" in other cities, in groups far bigger and more powerful than his. He spoke of friends in Toronto, Montreal, Winnipeg, Sarnia, and Windsor.

In October 1989, the FBI planted two bugs in the basement ceiling of a house near Boston, Massachusetts, to record a Mafia induction ceremony. At the ceremony, Carmen Tortora, a young associate of Boston's Patriarca family, took a blood oath to join the family.

"Do you have any brothers, Carmen?" Joseph (J.R.) Russo, the 59-year-old *consigliere* of the family asked him.

"One," he answered.

"If I told you your brother was wrong, he's a rat, he gonna do one [of] us harm, you'd have to kill him. Would you do that for me, Carmen?"

"Yes."

"So you know the severity of this Thing of Ours?"

"Yes."

"Do you want it badly and desperately? Your mother's dying in bed and you have to leave her because we called you, it's an emergency. You have to leave. Would you do that, Carmen?"

"Yes."

"All right. This is what you want. We're the best people. I'm gonna make you part of this Thing."

Russo then turned to Biagio DiGiacomo, an alleged family *capo*.

"Carmen, oh Carmen, we're going to baptize you again," DiGiacomo said. "You were baptized when you were a baby, your parents did it. But now, this time, we gonna baptize you. And you repeat after me."

"Io, Carmen, voglio entrare in questa organizzazione," he pledged in Italian, meaning, "I, Carmen, want to enter into this organization."

"Per proteggere la mia famiglia e per proteggere tutti i miei amici." (To protect my family and to protect all my friends.)

DiGiacomo explained what that meant: "We protect you and your family, and you're going to protect us and our Family."

"I swear," Carmen's oath then continued, "not to divulge this secret and to obey with love and *omertà*."

Carmen was asked to produce his "trigger finger." He held up his index finger and it was pricked with a knife to draw blood. That was when the saint's image was ignited.

"I want to enter alive into this organization and I will have to get out dead."

Johnny got out dead. But how did he get in?

He had plenty of friends and colleagues who were made *mafiosi* in Montreal, New York, Buffalo, and Hamilton. Some were Calabrians, some Sicilians; some were born in Italy, others in North America. Although he had been steeped in a culture of crime since the day he was born, he did not come to the attention of La Cosa Nostra until he moved to Montreal and worked under Carmine Galante, the Bonanno family underboss from New York City. It is unlikely that Galante or his right-hand man, Luigi Greco, formally inducted Johnny into La Cosa Nostra, however, for that would have made him a soldier in the Bonanno family, the family to which Montreal's Cotroni family answered. Johnny was clearly not Bonanno's. Later, in 1968, when discussing Mafia business with Giacomo Luppino, an old Mafia don in Hamilton, Johnny complained Cotroni was not answering to Magaddino in Buffalo as he thought he should be. Luppino sagely counseled the young *mafioso* that it was not a matter for Johnny to concern himself with, but for La Cosa Nostra's ruling commission to decide: "We are all under the Commission," Luppino said.

Johnny was also close friends with Vinnie Mauro, but Mauro, too, was a member of a rival family, the Genovese clan of New York City. That would have been an even harder alliance to make work in Ontario. If Johnny had chosen the Bonannos, he would at least have had strong allies in Montreal. But as a Genovese soldier he would have been alone facing substantial pressure from Buffalo and Quebec. Galante and Mauro had a profound influence on Johnny's criminal and personal development—and gave him influence and power by association—but they are unlikely to have initiated him formally as a member of La Cosa Nostra.

The many strands of Johnny's life all knotted in Buffalo. From his father's accommodation with Magaddino in the postwar years to the influence of Buffalo's Scibetta family in southern Ontario; from his friendship with Freddie Randaccio to Hamilton's close proximity to the strong La Cosa Nostra base there. Clearly Johnny's true ties ran to Buffalo and Stefano Magaddino.

Johnny Papalia's induction into the Mafia as a soldier in Magaddino's La Cosa Nostra crime family probably occurred in 1955, after Johnny's triumphant return from Montreal.

With Galante having yanked Montreal firmly into the Bonanno family's sphere, Magaddino was anxious to maintain his Canadian base in Ontario. Some years later, after Bonanno visited Montreal, Magaddino was furious. "He's planting flags all over the world!" Magaddino bemoaned. The Buffalo boss had a number of older, respectful associates in Ontario who aligned with him over the years, including Johnny's father and the three dons. But he needed a young, firm, hands-on boss to move the organization into rich, new areas of growth. He took a keen interest in a number of rising hoods in Ontario. Two men in particular caught the old don's eye.

In 1955, Magaddino traveled across the border to meet separately with Roy Pasquale and Johnny Papalia. Pasquale, older and perhaps wiser than Johnny at the time, was elated to host such a celebrated figure at his home and discuss with him the future of crime. Pasquale was big in Toronto, a leading loan shark, a volume mover of stolen merchandise, and a bankroller of dice games on the side. Magaddino is said to have been impressed and to have told him Buffalo was formally taking the province. Magaddino then made Pasquale an impressive proposal: be his number-one lieutenant in Ontario. Pasquale must have been floored by such an opportunity, but he was also torn. He loved the idea of the money and power that would flow from being in La Cosa Nostra, but he was also an inveterate individualist and shivered at the thought of answering directly to a formal boss. With regret, he declined Magaddino's offer. Magaddino said he would then make the same offer to Johnny.

Days later, Pasquale went to see Johnny in Hamilton and told him to expect Magaddino to make him an offer.

"He already did," answered Johnny. "He did, and I'm accepting."

If Johnny was not already a made man in the Magaddino family, his acceptance of Magaddino's offer meant he would have been inducted immediately, probably proposed officially by Randaccio. His formal tie to Magaddino was a serious one. Johnny cut his Godfather in on all profits, and the Godfather gave him the connections and clout of the Magaddino name. For the rest of Johnny's life, he kept a flow of tribute money—in varying amounts—going to Buffalo. How often and how much depended to some degree on how warm his personal relationship was with each of the subsequent bosses of the Magaddino family, but Johnny maintained his allegiance to Buffalo in good times and in bad. Johnny was never lazy with his loyalty.

His territory, in alliance with other Magaddino-friendly mobsters, was more or less officially the land stretching from the Ontario–New York State border, through Niagara Falls, Welland, St. Catharines, Hamilton, Burlington, Oakville, and as much of Toronto and the rest of the province as he could grab. He never fully took Toronto—it is really too big and diverse a city for one crime boss to run—but did extend his reach north to North Bay and south to the Lake Erie waterfront. His influence and reputation went farther afield, however, to touch on matters, to some degree, from Vancouver to Montreal.

Johnny was not to supersede the older dons of Ontario who already answered to Magaddino, but rather work with them, taking on the role of hands-on boss, with the old dons remaining almost as *consigliere*, advisors, and arbitrators; spiritual leaders who were paid tribute through both respect and cash payments. Although insolent with anyone from outside his criminal fraternity, Johnny remained acutely respectful of his *mafiosi* elders, allowing these old dons to maintain influence over him. When Giacomo Luppino came to Canada from Castellace of Oppido Mamertina, Reggio Calabria province, in 1956, and settled in Hamilton, his longevity in the Mafia, his respect earned in Italy, his keen wisdom, and his close relationship with Stefano Magaddino meant he, too, would be treated by Johnny as a man of respect.[2] At Luppino's funeral in March 1987, Johnny showed his respect for the old man by leading a small crew of enforcers—including his brother Rocco—out to, quite literally, beat the bushes around the cemetery where Luppino was being buried, in an effort to flush out hidden police officers and nosy journalists. They found two reporters up in a tree.

Johnny brimmed with excitement at his new place in the underworld. It was what he had wanted most of his life and what the family he was born into had prepared him for. He immediately announced who was to be in his organization. His inner circle of Red LeBarre, Freddie Gabourie, Frank Marchildon, and Jackie Weaver were getting plum positions, of course. He relied also on some members of his family, particularly his younger brothers: Dominic, Frank, and Rocco.

Johnny juggled his organization to accommodate his planned expansion. With Marchildon sent to Toronto, he promoted a renowned Louisville slugger, Hilton Harmes, as the replacement watcher of his Hamilton rackets, and the much-feared Joe Hasler was moved into Harmes's spot as designated enforcer. For less physical work, he relied upon Louis (Keckle) Bowmile, whom Johnny greatly admired for his keen intellect. Keckle was often referred to within the local underworld as "Canada's Meyer Lansky," after the legendary

---

2 Luppino is said to have publicly hacked off the ear of a man who failed to commit a crime as ordered; he then carried the leathery ear around with him for years.

financial mastermind of the American mob. In keeping with Canada's cultural melting pot, Johnny's crime "family" was diverse, proving Johnny was to be seen as a crime lord from Hamilton rather than from Italy.

An aggressive move for control of an underworld as large as Ontario's needed to be well financed—even when backed by the considerable shadow of Stefano Magaddino. In the years following the induction of Johnny as the Buffalo point-man in the province, there was a rash of jewel heists. More than $36,000 in jewels were snatched from one diamond merchant when bandits pistol-whipped and tied him down in his room at Toronto's King Edward Hotel. Most of the gems found their way into Hamilton jewel shops. Police looked to Johnny's gang, but charges could not stick; a jeweler charged with selling stolen property skipped his bail and fled to South America rather than testify about where he had gotten the hot rocks.

Johnny's next step was to let it be known—far and wide—that he was now fixed up with Magaddino.

"He didn't let it be known he was answerable, he let it be known he had the association," an old underworld figure said of Johnny's public relations campaign. "It was always a careful line he walked."

Like Vic Cotroni's Mafia group in Montreal, Johnny Papalia's organization in Ontario was now a branch-plant operation of the American La Cosa Nostra. Cotroni's head office was in New York City. Johnny's orders came directly from Buffalo.

10

It was March 21, 1961, and Johnny Pops wanted in. At stake was control of the biggest prize in Canadian crime: the lucrative enterprises of Maxie Bluestein, Toronto's independent gambling king. This was to be a night of high drama, a night of blood; the night Johnny would announce—to those who had not already figured it out—that he was a new man. This was the night Johnny would earn the name, rather than just the job description, "The Enforcer."

The time was late evening. The place, inside the 125-seat dining room of the Town Tavern, a restaurant and bar that once stood near the corner of Queen and Yonge streets in the heart of Toronto. The dining room was filled to capacity and the doormen were telling customers they would have to wait in the bar area for a table. The Town was a popular club for underworld travelers, defence lawyers, professional athletes, minor celebrities, businessmen, and night-life gadflies. The Town had all that was needed: decent dinners, a well-stocked bar, attractive women, and a place to see, be seen, and talk business. It was a place, naturally, where both Johnny and Maxie were regulars.

Maxwell Bluestein was perhaps the biggest and brightest of all the gambling kingpins in Ontario. Bluestein was called "Max" or "Maxie" by his friends, and was also known as "Max Baker," his real name before he co-opted the last name of a wealthy Jewish family to give him an air of respectability. Maxie was a tough man with deep blue eyes and very dark hair, which only accentuated the pallid flesh of his harshly featured face. Although a man of very few words—he hardly spoke at all, in fact—he was bold, cocky, and clever, and was into gambling's biggest bucks.

Maxie ran a number of gambling dens, including the Lakeview Athletic Club and a swank dice game inside the Royal York Hotel in downtown Toronto. But most of Maxie's money came from sports betting. He had at least 200 runners in downtown Toronto, each hanging around a specific spot—perhaps a pool hall, bar, or cigar store—taking bets from regular clients. The runners memorized a half-dozen bets each before calling them in from a pay phone. Stiffer law enforcement had ended the time-honoured tradition of "bookies" writing the bets in little books. When police raided one of Maxie's clubs, they seized slips showing a daily average over the previous nine days of $37,700. All told, Maxie's gambling operations raked in an estimated $13 million a year. He was smart enough to know where his skills lay, and stuck to gambling almost exclusively, leaving the more violent activities to others. Within this fringe of society, Maxie was the gentleman gambler, despite his sometimes abrasive personality.

"The police pretty much left him alone to operate," said an old friend of Maxie's. "With Max, if you owed him money and didn't pay, he just didn't let you play again; but with the others, if you didn't pay, they'd break your legs. In the police view, Max was better than a Mafia bum from Hamilton or Buffalo."

Despite all his activity, Maxie's business only ever brought one charge of keeping a common gaming house.[1]

The meeting between Maxie and Johnny could have happened anywhere, but it could not be avoided. The moment Johnny turned his full attention to the gambling industry, he and Maxie were destined to clash.

1 Maxie Bluestein's punishment, laughable given the money rolling in from his operations, was two months in jail and a $15,000 fine. In a strange twist, he was released early due to a clerical error. An investigation by the Deputy Attorney General's office was satisfied there was no dishonesty involved in the mistake.

That night in the Town was not the first time Johnny and Maxie had met. Maxie had known Johnny when he was a mere street punk and still thought of him as the skinny, dope-peddling kid from Hamilton. To make things worse, Johnny's early dope boss, Harvey Chernick, was a distant and none-too-favoured relative of Maxie. Several times over the past few months, Johnny had made overtures to Maxie about a business arrangement. First, Johnny wanted to be a partner in his profitable dice game at the Royal York Hotel. Johnny was prepared to negotiate—he was not just muscling in. Johnny's contribution would consist of putting Freddie Gabourie, Jackie Weaver, and Frank Marchildon into the action on the house's behalf. But Maxie did not need Johnny's men or money. He was doing just fine on his own, and that was the way he liked it. As Maxie's refusals became increasingly terse, Johnny's demands likewise grew. One by one, from Windsor to Toronto, the major gambling bosses had fallen before Johnny. Only Maxie held out. Maxie had moxie.

"Maxie was a guy you couldn't intimidate," another friend of the gambler said. "You just could not intimidate him. The man had no fear, or if he did, he certainly didn't show it. They kept pushing to buy in and he kept saying no. Something had to give."

It became a decidedly one-sided offer—Johnny gets a piece of Maxie's operation and Maxie doesn't get all busted up—but one Maxie felt he had to refuse. Soon after an earlier meeting between Maxie, Johnny, and two *mafiosi* from Buffalo at the Westbury Hotel in Toronto, Maxie applied for a permit to carry a gun. Toronto police turned him down.

Johnny ran out of patience and let it be known that March 21, three days after Johnny's 37th birthday, was, almost literally as it turned out, do-or-die night for Maxie. There was a planned spectacle by Johnny, who had learned well the ancient lessons of the Mafia: Punish one to teach a thousand.

Maxie, it seems, was to be Johnny's object lesson.

This was all prologue when the pair arrived separately at the Town Tavern on the first day of spring 1961. Johnny was ensconced in a booth at the back of the club and his table became the buzzing nerve centre of the intrigue-filled bar. A rotating cast of characters approached the gangster, greeted him, chatted and laughed, whispered and listened, retreated, and watched.

At Johnny's side was Frank Marchildon, perhaps his most loyal lieutenant. Gabourie and Weaver were also with Johnny that night, although they spent much of their time at Maxie's table. Weaver knew Maxie particularly well and acted as the go-between in the Town, shuttling back and forth between Johnny's and Maxie's tables, trying to get Johnny's way without Maxie getting damaged. Nearby, two other on-again off-again Papalia hirelings, Joseph Irwin and another man, lurked. They were the B-team, backup boys and part of the cleanup crew, ready to spirit away bloody blackjacks and other weapons that might make an appearance during the night.

Maxie said later that he had known Johnny "since he was a kid," and also knew Gabourie and Weaver, but not Marchildon.

Late in the evening, Weaver joined Johnny at his booth, and Johnny called the waitress over to his table.

"Johnny Pops said to me, 'You go over to Baker's [Bluestein's] table and see what they'd like to drink,'" waitress Anita Leduc said of that infamous night. At Maxie's table, Gabourie and another man whom the waitress did not know ordered crème de menthe, but Maxie said he wasn't interested.

"So I told Johnny," Leduc said, "and then Weaver said to go over and tell him 'I'm buying the drinks,' and I did and Baker had one."

Maxie knew well the symbolism of the underworld. It was crucial for him to know who was offering the drink. If Maxie accepted a drink from Johnny, it would be seen as a sign he accepted him as a partner. So later, when Johnny himself sent over a drink, Maxie waved it off with a flourish of his hand. Another account said Maxie scrawled an obscenity on a cocktail napkin and had that sent back to Johnny's table by the waitress. Whether with a flick of the wrist or a scrawl of a pen, refusing was a fateful gesture.

It was past 1 a.m. when Maxie called it a night. He was satisfied with his performance—he had stood up to Pops in public and nothing had happened. He was confident that Johnny was all bustle and no muscle, even going so far as to send his own enforcers home early. He got up from his table and walked to the tavern's lobby, where hats and coats were checked in by the club's long-time hat-check clerk, Eva Anderson. She knew Maxie well, and that night Maxie gave her a nice tip—a crisp $5 bill which he called an early "Christmas present."

Johnny, Marchildon, Gabourie, and others were also on their feet. Johnny walked past Maxie and turned to face him, standing between the gambling king and his only exit. He pulled a menacing blackjack from his breast pocket. Gabourie and Marchildon, the latter carrying a short length of rubber hose—another favoured gangland weapon for inflicting non-lethal punishment—positioned themselves behind Maxie.

"I'd like to talk to you," Johnny said to Maxie. Maxie was as dismissive face-to-face as he had been with the drink. "I'm talking to Eva," he said, turning away from Johnny and back towards the hat-check clerk. Maxie caught a whiff of what was afoot in time to pull out a small fishing knife he was carrying in lieu of the gun he had wanted.

Iron bars—dangling at the end of rope to give better leverage and an accelerated swing—suddenly rained down on Maxie's skull, across his forehead, eyes, and crashed deep into his cheekbones. Blackjacks and brass knuckles were bashed into Maxie's face until he dropped. While he lay in a growing pool of blood, he was kicked in the face, and a broken bottle was ground into his mouth.

Before going down, Maxie lashed out at his attackers with his narrow blade and stuck Marchildon six times in the back, once puncturing his lung cavity. Both Marchildon and Maxie bled profusely. When the Town's doorman and bouncer, Wayne Russell, a 20-year-old heavyweight boxer, tried to stop the fight, Johnny grabbed him by the arm and told him to steer clear. When Russell saw a knife flash, he again tried to step in, and again Johnny warned him to mind his own business.

With the damage done, the gang fled. The weapons were quickly passed to Irwin and his colleague, who then disappeared into the crowd.

Running out of the tavern, Johnny saw the worrisome wounds to Marchildon's back, and the pair climbed into the back of a cab to get to a hospital and have the slashes stitched. Johnny told taxi driver Edward DeMarco to hurry. DeMarco was turning his cab around when he was stopped by a mob of people fleeing the Town. Some patrons were yelling at Johnny and Marchildon in the cab, and the driver knew something was not right. He pulled over. Marchildon bashed the cabbie on the back of the head and ordered him to drive on, but he refused. Anxious to be far from Maxie's crumpled body, the pair jumped out and ran towards Victoria Street. The cabbie's strange ordeal was not over, however. Just as police arrived, a man approached from behind and told him that he had better keep quiet—or an iron bar might clang down on his head. (Later, in court, DeMarco said he was very unclear about who hit him inside his cab. The judge leaned in and asked: "The thought of this man with the iron bar might deter you from talking?" The cabbie answered forthrightly: "Well, the people involved in a thing like this might make trouble for me. I have a wife and two children. I'm in a public position because my picture is in my cab and I could be found easily.")

With blood flowing from his lower back, Marchildon was forced to abandon Johnny—who raced to safety—and turn to the police to get him to a doctor. He arrived at St. Michael's Hospital in a cruiser.

Gabourie, meanwhile, made a clean escape. He changed his clothes and doused his suit in water to wash away the stains from Maxie's spilled blood. Weaver, however, got sidetracked on his way out and was drawn into a scuffle in the dining room with Toronto Argonauts football player Freddie Black. Weaver was swapping blows with Black, rather than running for cover, when police arrived.

Soon after the attack—and before Maxie had even been removed from the floor where he lay—a telephone call came in to the club for the hat-check clerk, a woman who had the best view of the whole bloody mess. Eva Anderson took the call.

"You'll be filled in if you talk," she was told by the caller. Others who saw the attack received similar calls that night and over the next few days. They were told it would be "healthier" for them to forget what they had seen.

Police were called to the Town Tavern at 1:39 a.m. and quickly realized this was far from the usual barroom brawl.

Maxie was on the floor, now propped up against a wall, floating in and out of consciousness and swimming in his own blood. The Town's manager, Leo Cournoyer, used a tissue to pick up a bloody knife he had found on the floor near Maxie's almost lifeless body, and handed it to the hat-check clerk to keep an eye on. It would soon disappear, as would witnesses. Wherever police turned for eyewitness accounts—asking people who had been right there when it happened—they were met with stony silence. Everyone said either that they could not see the fight or did not know any of the attackers. For clues, police were left with innuendo, many frightened people, and three coats still in the coat-check room. But even the coats were not much help; the labels had all been removed, and the only person who could connect those coats to the people who handed them across the counter was not in a talkative mood. Eva Anderson had worked at the Town for 11 years, but Maxie's vicious beating and the telephone threat took a serious toll on her mental health. She became extremely nervous, paranoid, and jittery.

Police did what they could. Weaver and Marchildon—the only ones they knew were involved in some way because of Marchildon's wounds and Weaver's being found at the scene—were charged with creating a disturbance.

Maxie, meanwhile, was rushed to hospital. An intern at St. Michael's used more than 20 stitches to close just one of the gaping wounds on his head. Maxie was in bad shape. But the very next day, Maxie insisted his son drive him to the busy intersection of College Street and Spadina Avenue. Drawing on all of his remaining strength and ignoring outrageous pain, he pulled himself out of the car and defiantly walked around the block for all to see. He wanted to send a clear message of his own to Johnny: Maxie was alive, still standing, and invincible. It was a bold display—and quite a charade. Maxie was more messed up than anyone, including himself, fully understood.

The conspiracy of silence—or more aptly, the conspiracy of fear—

that kept Maxie's beating from becoming known outside the under-world was shattered in April by journalist Pierre Berton in a shocking exclusive published in the *Toronto Star*. Berton said the gang administered "as terrible a beating as it is possible to give a man without killing him." His indignation at the lack of cooperation by witnesses was scarcely hidden. He called the incident "perhaps the most remarkable case of mass blindness in scientific history," one worthy of a write-up in medical journals.

"My enemies should feel as well as I do," Maxie defiantly boasted to Berton during his brief interview. "I was beaten up at the Town Tavern. Why don't you go to them to find out what happened?"

Reporters tried. Everywhere they went, people clammed up. At the Town Tavern, reporters were met with a rousing chorus of silence.

"They're scared people," the Town's owner, Sam Berger, said of his staff. "I guess anybody who knows anything and won't talk is scared. They fear for their own safety." Hat-check clerk Anderson told reporters: "I don't want to say anything at all about it, understand?"

Freddie Black, the pro football player who got in Weaver's way, said he turned towards the action when he heard a commotion, but was knocked to the ground by a punch. "I wouldn't know who hit me if I stepped on him, it all happened so quickly. I don't know what went on. I might have been on the floor for 10 seconds or 10 minutes."

Police were no better a source of information for reporters chasing Berton's scoop. Deputy Police Chief George Elliott said Maxie had told his officers he was being shaken down by the mob for money, and detectives suggested the savage beating might have been related to Maxie's gambling activities. A special squad of detectives, dubbed the Bluestein Squad, was formed to probe the attack. Police offered anonymity to anyone who would come forward with information.

The more the newspapers and politicians talked about the "failure of citizenship" and the "frightening breakdown of law and order," the more they unintentionally touted the power of The Enforcer. It was Johnny's power—and his ability to spill so much of Maxie's blood—that created the fear that smashed civility in the heart of Toronto. But the cloak of invisibility could not last forever under the public pressure sparked by the intense news coverage. The explosive stories caused an uproar; newspaper editorials responded with suitable outrage. Toronto politicians demanded the province do something to ensure U.S. crime syndicates did not gain a toehold in their fair city.

The connection to Johnny did not take long to make. Newspapers began reporting that "a Hamilton man, said to be a Mafia leader," administered the near-execution. While Toronto police were starting to understand the new status of Johnny, his home town coppers were still out to lunch.

"It's hard to believe," a Hamilton police spokesman said at the time. "Toronto is a big city and can take care of itself. If the claim was the other way around—that Toronto mobsters were sent to Hamilton— then it could be more likely."

Between the shame heaped by the press and the promises of safety by police, several witnesses finally cracked. Exactly one month after Maxie was pulverized, a clandestine court hearing was held in Toronto. A dozen witnesses whispered their testimony. Elaborate plans were made to ensure word did not leak out—telephones in the courthouse were even fiddled with so outgoing calls could not be made. Within hours, arrest warrants for assault occasioning actual bodily harm were issued against Johnny, Marchildon, Gabourie, and Weaver.

In Hamilton, police swooped into a downtown parking lot and arrested Marchildon as he tried to get into his car, which had been under surveillance for hours. In Toronto, Gabourie and Weaver walked into City Hall and gracefully surrendered.

The ringleader, however, was nowhere to be found. The homes of Johnny's relatives, several of his favourite downtown bars, and many known gambling haunts were all put under surveillance. His parents' Railway Street house and his brother Frank's Herkimer Street apartment were searched several times, and police started using civilian cars to scour the streets because the gangsters could easily spot the police cars and perhaps warn Johnny. As the manhunt dragged into its third week, stories spread of Johnny being seen in cities all over Canada and the United States. He did head south for at least part of his time as a fugitive, visiting Florida and Las Vegas, a city already into its second decade as a gangster-run hot spot. But there were also sightings of the mobster much closer to home. Stories were told of Johnny ordering drinks in downtown Hamilton bars and chatting with well-wishers at Toronto parties.

It was almost suppertime on May 11, 1961, when Johnny surfaced. Neatly dressed in a dark, expensively tailored suit, long trench coat, and dark sunglasses, he strolled into his lawyer's office and told the receptionist: "Tell him Johnny's here."

The plan was for Hamilton lawyer John Agro to arrange Johnny's peaceful surrender to Toronto police. An arranged arrest was important to Johnny; he feared he would be beaten by police if they grabbed him unexpectedly on the street. He even went to a Hamilton doctor for a thorough checkup before the surrender, to document his fine physical condition. A tight lid was not kept on his surrender plans, however. Inside the waiting room was a reporter and photographer from the *Toronto Star* and outside were a pair from the *Hamilton Spectator*. Johnny paced about the tiny waiting room, growing impatient.

"Hey, what's keeping that guy Agro in there?" he said to the receptionist. "He knows I'm waiting. Hey, what's going on, anyway? Why isn't he ready? It's all arranged. I don't like this."

Johnny was soon joined by his brother Frank, and minutes later, acting on their own tip, Hamilton Morality Squad officers arrived to make a pinch they had been itching to make before Johnny could take his trip to Toronto. On the way down in the elevator from Agro's ninth-floor office, *Star* reporter Fred Hollett squeezed in some questions to the mobster: "Where have you been?"

"Around," came the curt reply.

"Why are you giving yourself up?"

"There's nothing wrong. I just want to get the truth told. You have already got me tried and convicted. I gotta have a chance to talk. Don't I get a trial?"

"Why are you mad at the papers?"

"I'm not mad at anybody. I just want to be treated fair. There's nothing wrong with me. I don't know about gangs." Johnny was testier to photographer Andy Sharp: "Watch it with that camera, creep."

As Johnny, Agro, the arresting officers, and a growing press corps walked the block to the waiting police car, Johnny kept up his aggressive stance—despite his assurance that he was not mad at the papers. With a handkerchief partially covering his face he warned reporters to back off.

"I've got nothing to say to you at all. I don't want my picture taken.

"Look at the dirty rats. The creeps. Those crummy, rotten cameras and all you crummy, rotten guys," he was quoted as shouting before being stuffed into a police car and whisked away. (Although "crummy" and "rotten" were the words published in the newspapers the next day, it is very likely that Johnny, who could swear a vicious blue streak without a moment's notice, actually used less family-friendly terms.)

Johnny spent six hours in the Regent Street police station in Toronto before being released on $2,000 bail. The cash was put up by E.J. Orzel of Hamilton, who pulled the money from a great wad of $100 bills. Justice of the Peace Gordon Hainer, who accepted the bail money, later said in amazement: "If I'd asked for $10,000, I'm sure it would have been supplied."

After appearing in a Toronto courtroom the next day, Johnny waited to avoid photographers massing outside. When it came time for him to run the gauntlet, he did not do so graciously. Still wearing his dark glasses and a nice suit, he spat at a newspaper photographer when he burst through the doors, and stomped on the feet of another. Despite being rather photogenic, in a gangsterish way, Johnny maintained a strong dislike of photographers throughout his life. Media coverage of his court appearances usually had a twin message: Johnny Papalia appeared in court today; Johnny Papalia attacked photographers today. Although he had little fondness for reporters, it always seemed to be the presence of photographers that roiled him the most.

"They've been writing about my family for years," Johnny said in 1986, when approached by reporter Peter Moon for comment on what police were saying about him. "You just go ahead and publish your story. I don't care. It's disgraceful what they do," he said of reporters.

On June 27, 1961, the trial of Johnny and his associates for assaulting Maxie Bluestein opened amid newspaper headlines dubbing Johnny "The Enforcer" and "Canada's Capone."

The trial dealt with blood-splattered clothing and laboratory testing that, although crude by today's standards, captured the public's attention. Johnny's lawyer was Clive Bynoe, a man who would later play an important role in the Papalia family's history. Gabourie's lawyer was Malcolm Robb; Joseph Sedgwick acted for Marchildon, and Claude Thomson acted for Weaver. The defence team was irate at being denied transcripts of the depositions made against their clients in the closed-door hearing prior to the arrests. Crown Attorney Herbert Langdon argued the witnesses' safety was at risk. Judge Joseph Addison directed that the trial begin and defence counsel be supplied with copies of the depositions only as each witness was called to the stand. The court wanted to get to the witnesses before any gangsters could.

Johnny's ability to instill fear was clearly visible. One witness who did not show up at court had to be brought in by police the next day. Witnesses remained hazy, changed their stories several times, and were hesitant to point a provoking finger at Johnny, who sat in a dark suit just yards away. It seemed the witnesses were being threatened. Judge Addison even refused to grant a request by defence lawyers for a brief adjournment because he did not want the tavern's cashier to leave the witness stand before cross-examination was complete.

"I want her testimony without distraction," Judge Addison said.

Maxie was the first witness called by the Crown. He said he was unarmed and on his way out of the Town Tavern when hit from behind.

"I was gone. I was on the floor. I don't know what happened. I didn't see no one," he told the court. "Someone hit me. I was in a fog. But I can remember seeing a fellow swinging a rope with an iron bar on the end of it. I could not tell who that fellow was . . . If I had a knife, I must have taken it from one of the fellows who was hitting me."

Who had hit him? "It could have been Weaver, could have been Papalia, could have been anybody. Could have been a waitress. I don't know."

A waitress at the club, Elizabeth Tergsteegen, who moved to Peterborough after the beating, said Johnny and Maxie were talking a few minutes before she heard a noise that sounded like a body hitting the floor. When she turned to see, her view was blocked by patrons standing and watching. She ignored the commotion because "When people like Maxie Baker and Johnny Pops have a fight, it's better to walk away."

Club hostess Arthena Griffin and waitresses Elena Jogi and Anita Leduc told similar stories. Bouncer Wayne Russell, who quit his job at the Town the day after the fight, said he saw Johnny holding a billy club a few feet from where Maxie was being beaten, but never saw the mobster strike a blow.

"Bluestein was conscious, because he screamed," Russell said. "There was a man on top of Bluestein and they were fighting. I think he was sticking him [with a knife]. When I went over, he was getting smashed over the head with the billies. I saw two men twisting Bluestein's legs as if to break them." Russell, it seems, had a pristine memory for everything but faces; he could not identify any of the accused.

Hat-check clerk Eva Anderson said she remembered little about the incident and could not identify any of the attackers. She said she saw the butt of a gun—"just like you see on television or in a Western"—but didn't know who had it. Her testimony so rankled the judge that he declared her a hostile witness for the Crown.

"This witness apparently remembers nothing. I have no hesitancy in declaring her a hostile witness," Judge Addison said. Five witnesses said Anderson answered a telephone call right after the beating and was bothered by what she was told. But Anderson denied answering the phone. She denied being handed a knife that the manager had picked up. When the tavern manager said it was unusual for coats and hats to be left behind at the club during the winter months, Anderson said it happened every night. After listening to all of the witnesses, Judge Addison sent police officers to Anderson's home to bring her before the court for a dressing-down because her testimony was sharply at odds with that of every other witness.

"One of my functions is to say when a person is telling the truth," Judge Addison said. "I say to you now, you were not telling the truth. You did see who hit Bluestein and you did get a knife. In these instances it is just your word, but unless you change your testimony and search your memory and remember a telephone call you received early that morning, I will recommend to the attorney general that a perjury charge be laid. Five other witnesses testified you answered the phone." He then warned her that the penalty for perjury could be as high as 14 years in prison. He asked her again. "Did you or did you not get a telephone call?"

Anderson replied: "I'm sure that I did not get a telephone call."

Marchildon was the only accused to take the stand, and his appearance added a little unintentional levity to the proceedings. He told the court he was not carrying a club or length of hose in the Town that night, as witnesses had said, but rather a comb.

"You have a short haircut," interjected the judge. "Why is it you have to carry a comb?"

"My scalp is itchy," said Marchildon, who then produced a long comb that folded in the middle and scratched his head with it.

"But why were you walking around with a comb in your hands?" asked the judge. "You certainly didn't intend to comb Bluestein's hair, did you?" Marchildon had no answer.

The judge was not happy with anyone involved in this case.

"The diffidence of the witnesses in giving testimony in this case is far more serious than the crime itself," he said when passing judgment on the accused. Nobody—including the victim—seemed concerned by the attack. The judge was as angry at Maxie as he was with Johnny.

"As to the assault itself, I would be inclined to say . . . a plague on both your houses. Apparently [the beating] is an occupational hazard and one [Maxie] did not want to complain about to this court. Bluestein is observing the code of the underworld and saying nothing that will make him out to be a squealer. . . . But the place, the number of patrons at the tavern, and the viciousness of the attack make it advisable that the guilty parties and others who live by this law be discouraged."

Johnny was found to be the ringleader of the attack. The judge noted that Johnny had never been convicted of a violent crime, but that a deterrent was needed for others in the murky gambling world. He sentenced him to 18 months in jail. Antonio Papalia was in the courtroom to hear Johnny's sentence. It may well have been the last time Johnny saw his father.

Despite Marchildon's stab wounds—and his unique comb defence—the judge found him to be an aggressor in the fight and guilty of assault. He was sentenced to nine months. Gabourie was handed a four-month sentence. (He got off much lighter, however, as his conviction was overturned on appeal.) Weaver was acquitted. The judge said Weaver was clearly involved in this mysterious dispute and acted as some sort of liaison between the mobster and the gambler, but that there was no direct evidence he attacked Maxie. He might even have been acting as peacemaker, Judge Addison suggested, albeit a rather poor one.

Why had Maxie refused to work with Johnny? It could have been arrogance. He could also have grossly misread the street. Maybe he disbelieved that little Johnny was now a big shot. Of course, it might also have been that he firmly believed what he told police after the attack: "I won't be shaken down."

The beating and the trial were big moments for Johnny, and certainly a mixed blessing. Despite ending in a jail term, the judge's statement—a stinging condemnation by mainstream standards—reads like advertising copy for any mobster. Here was a modest-size man from Hamilton, a grade school drop-out, able to make everyone in a tough Toronto bar quake. The judge summed it up nicely: The witnesses were more afraid of Johnny than of the court's ability to punish them for perjury. After taking an oath on the Bible to tell the truth, witness after witness showed more fear of Johnny than of God.

To the underworld, the case proved what astute gangsters and rounders already knew: Johnny Pops was now in command. If there were others who—like Maxie—had failed to recognize Johnny's new power, their doubt evaporated.

Johnny knew the value of decisive, highly targeted action, but the beating of Maxie Bluestein was also terribly, terribly messy. Many in the underworld felt it was grossly déclassé. In the final analysis, the beating was a tactical blunder. The press, police, and public were now sharply eyeing what had previously been a private affair. One of Johnny's critics may have been Magaddino himself. The old don loathed publicity and is said to have been furious at Johnny's garish display at a time that might jeopardize other, more profitable ventures.

Even 15 years later, Johnny had no regrets.

"Bluestein started it," he said. "He had a stiletto and he stabbed Marchildon twice. We had to defend ourselves. Bluestein was greedy. He wanted it all for himself."

For his part, poor Maxie Bluestein was never the same. Following his merciless beating he became a disturbed, understandably paranoid man. After four sticks of dynamite strapped under his Cadillac failed to detonate, his downward spiral accelerated. He suspected his wife, his two sons, every delivery man, every waitress to be part of an elaborate plot to rub him out. Delusional, certainly, but with good reason. Johnny was still after Maxie's enterprises and was again making overtures to his people. In 1973, Maxie shot and killed his best friend, who was making his regular visit to see the old gambler. At Maxie's trial, defence attorney Edward Greenspan presented a mentally troubled man, and Maxie was found not guilty by reason of insanity. He was committed to the Clarke Institute of Psychiatry, and died following a heart attack in 1984.[2]

Although Johnny did not know it while settling into his new home in Millbrook Reformatory near Peterborough, his time behind bars—in Canada—would be unexpectedly brief. While he was getting to know

2 Journalists Peter Edwards and Antonio Nicaso chronicle Max Bluestein's sad demise in nice detail as part of their excellent examination of Canadian Mafia murders, *Deadly Silence*. Along with James Dubro's *Mob Rule* and Edwards's *Blood Brothers*, *Deadly Silence* completes a triumvirate of solid reporting on Canada's modern Mafia history.

his new cellmate, the reverberations of the beating were still ringing through Ontario and even south of the border. After the trial of Johnny and his crew, Metro Toronto Chairman Frederick Gardiner spoke to the press, giving what would later seem a rather prophetic statement.

"It looks like real gangsterism is coming to Toronto."

Indeed, it had. This "real gangsterism" now had many names—Johnny Pops, Canada's Capone, The Enforcer—but only one face. That of John Papalia. And if Canadian police did not yet fully realize it, the U.S. government did. The Papalia name had become a prominent if unexpected one in a large probe, involving *mafiosi* in New York City, which had secretly started a few years before Maxie's beating but was not made public until months afterwards.

11

Vito Scuderi, an honest automobile mechanic from Sicily, stepped off a passenger ship and onto American soil thinking he had left behind the sad trappings of crime that tainted his homeland. It was March 7, 1960, and he carried with him everything needed to start a new life in Brooklyn. He also carried a suitcase that was not his own.

Six months before leaving for the United States, Scuderi retained the services of a 'travel agent' who offered full-service emigration packages. For the thousands of illiterate farmers, mechanics, and labourers heading to North America, a trip to an agent—who prepared the documents, handled passport and customs forms, and booked passage for the trip across the Atlantic—was a crucial first step. All, of course, for a considerable fee. For citizens of Sicily's Trapani province, such an agent was Salvatore Valenti. He was a man of many occupations: a contractor who owned trucks and worked on government construction projects, a ticket agent for inter-city travel, and a "man of respect." Although Valenti had forged connections with government officials, his name appeared in police files as a local Mafia leader.

The day Scuderi left his home, Valenti appeared on the dock to meet him.

"A friend of mine left for the United States last week in an airplane and could not take with him this valise," Valenti said. "You could take it with you." Valenti opened the suitcase, showed him the heavy quilt inside, and said someone would collect it at the dock when he reached

New York. Scuderi agreed, and in New York was greeted just as Valenti had told him.

"I am a friend of Salvatore Valenti," said a man waiting at Pier 84, on the banks of the Hudson River in New York City. There to collect the suitcase was Matteo Palmeri, a Sicilian who had made New York his home some years before. Palmeri took the case, placed it in his truck, and drove to his mother-in-law's apartment. There, he removed the thick quilt and with a razor, gingerly sliced at its fabric, revealing five packages hidden in the lining. He had almost finished cutting the bags free when the razor slipped, cutting deeply into one of them. Out trickled a fine, white powder. Palmeri grabbed at the hole to stop the flow, and with his other hand reached to scoop up the small pile on the floor. Moving too quickly, he found himself in a mess; white powder floated about the room, trickled down his clothes, and tickled his nose. He started sneezing and his head spun. Nauseated, Palmeri dashed for the bathroom, reaching it just in time for the toilet to catch his thick stream of vomit. Sick, confused, and sweating profusely, Palmeri crawled into his mother-in-law's bed to sleep.

A baker by trade, he was more used to breathing in flour than nearly pure heroin.

Inadvertently sampling some of the merchandise was not the first or the last mistake Palmeri made during his two years in a heroin conspiracy cobbled together by three Mafia men: Johnny Papalia, Ontario's young, new Mafia boss; Vincent (Vinnie) Mauro, Johnny's *mafioso* friend in New York City; and Alberto Agueci, a Sicilian who emigrated to Canada. Twice before, Palmeri had met immigrants from Sicily at the pier and walked away with a suitcase sent by Valenti. Unknowingly, these immigrants were each bringing with them between 5- and 16-kilo loads of high-grade narcotics, forming a crucial link in a $150-million drug ring that spanned the globe.

Importing the heroin was Alberto Agueci's idea, and one he had long before he even left his home in Trapani, Sicily, and headed to America in 1950 at the age of 28. His plans were postponed when U.S. immigration turned him away, and he settled instead in Windsor, where he joined a road construction crew. He carried with him a letter of introduction from Rosario Mancino, an important drug trafficker from Sicily who had ties with Lucky Luciano. Mancino's was a formidable reference to carry, and after Agueci presented it to a certain Windsor travel agent, he was soon able to drop his job with the road crew and move to Toronto, where he became co-owner of Queen Bakery. His partner in this enterprise was Benedetto Zizzo, brother of Salvatore Zizzo, a Mafia leader in Agueci's home town.

"Alberto was a very warm person," said a former associate of the mobster. "He was happy to be involved with the mob because it made him feel important. He was a very incompetent individual when it came to anything else but the mob. He couldn't really earn a living any way else. He didn't have particular mental skills, and he didn't have particular physical skills. He couldn't have been an electrician or a carpenter. But he got into this thing and was very happy about it. He was a very nice guy and very hospitable. His wife was too. When I was at their house they wouldn't be able to do enough for me. Alberto was also quite scared of John."

After Johnny's triumphant return to Ontario from Montreal, he met with Agueci, who was just two years his senior, and the pair embarked on a number of illicit enterprises.

In 1957, they were taking a sizable percentage from an ingenious scam that ripped off hundreds of churches and service clubs across Canada. A small Toronto company undercut all competitors on the price of bingo cards sold to organizations running charity bingo games. The unknown catch was that the company's people were secretly appearing at the games with a tiny printing press concealed in a woman's handbag. As the bingo numbers were called, a winning card was quickly manufactured to match the official game cards in use. The crooks had a lock on winning and walked away with hundreds of thousands in prize money. The scheme was first pulled in communities all across Ontario, from Ottawa to London, North Bay to St. Catharines, and then extended nationwide. Charities in Nova Scotia, Newfoundland, New Brunswick, Alberta, Manitoba, and British Columbia all fell prey.

The following year, Johnny and Agueci became partners in Star Vending Machine Company. Business boomed as the men muscled their machines into stores where owners felt they had little choice but to acquiesce. Police were powerless to intervene because no one who had been beaten or threatened would agree to testify. The coin-operated machines were then stocked almost entirely with stolen goods. From warehouses, railway cars, and truck-trailers, cigarettes were poached on a massive scale and found their way into Star's machines.

Later, the pair went after the owners of bars and after-hours clubs, forcing them to buy their illicit booze, which was smuggled into Canada. Agueci knew that as lucrative as these schemes were, they were penny ante compared with the money to be made in heroin.

Addicts are drawn to heroin because of the explosion of euphoria it provides once the needle jabs into their vein. The euphoria settles into a numbing feeling of warmth and peace—until the high wanes and the craving builds for another fix.

Gangsters are attracted to the powder because of the exponential profits it generates. In the early 1970s, the opium gum needed to produce a kilogram (2.2 pounds) of heroin could be purchased for $220 in Turkey. By the time it was processed into heroin, that kilo would fetch a price of more than $240,000 in America.

Opium comes from a certain species of poppy, a hardy, flowering plant that grows well in the temperate climes of Southeast Asia and the Middle East. Johnny's primo powder began its journey in the Republic of Turkey, a strategically placed country straddling Europe and Asia. Poor farmers in the centre of Turkey's rolling agricultural lands have planted the tiny, yellow poppy seeds each fall for more than 10 centuries. Each spring they watched the colourful flowers bloom with great, fleshy, white and purple petals. Come July, the plant's pods would ripen and were, in a technique practised by generations of Turkish farmers, sliced open and left overnight. Onto the outside of the pods seeped a light-coloured resin. Once collected, the sticky paste turned brown and was molded into small loaf-like mounds. Often before leaving Turkey, or after it was smuggled by camel convoy to Beirut, Lebanon, the gum was changed into morphine by a simple chemical process that turned it from a bulky clay into an easy-to-smuggle, off-white powder.

The morphine base was then smuggled to the raucous French port of Marseilles. On the outskirts of the city, in a number of secluded villas tucked away among the mountainous slopes that rise from the seacoast, were a string of secret laboratories. The port attracted underground chemists who had learned the 17-step science of turning morphine into the pure white crystals of European heroin, the most valued drug on the planet. This was *L'Ecole Française,* the French School of production, which achieved legendary purity with no trace of the yellow tinge common in less-professionally generated heroin. One of the experts was Dominique Albertini, a lumpy former seaman who somewhere in his shady life learned the art of producing heroin from a depraved scientist, and soon became the consummate underworld chemist. In the 1960s, the chemists of Marseilles were cooking up an estimated 600 kilos of heroin a year, almost all of it destined for the eastern seaboard of North America.

From Marseilles, the heroin made its way into Sicily, courtesy of the Sicilian Mafia, who had perfected smuggling techniques by feeding the nation's hunger for black market cigarettes. The Mafia was looking for ingenious ways of getting the heroin off their island and into the arms of America's addicts. They found it by linking key *mafiosi* on both sides of the Atlantic, an arrangement forged in a series of important and supposedly secret meetings.

Over the better part of a week in mid-October 1957, an American delegation of La Cosa Nostra members from New York City, led by Joe Bonanno and his underboss, Carmine Galante, met with ranking members of the Sicilian Mafia in Palermo's Grand Hôtel des Palmes. Sicily's delegation was led by Genco Russo, grand master of the Sicilian Mafia, and with him were promising Sicilian mob boss Gaetano Badalamenti and the man who would later become the most prominent Mafia rat in the world, Tommaso Buscetta. Up for discussion was how each of them could become rich beyond measure by working together to bring large shipments of heroin into America.[1] Stories—perhaps legends—circulate of what went on at the meetings. One snatch of conversation apparently overheard by a waiter involved Russo's reasons why they needed to work in unison: "When there are too many dogs after a bone, happy is he who can keep well away." The arrangements they made—bringing the heroin cooked up in Marseilles to Italy and then shipping it to America for distribution by La Cosa Nostra members—were the basis for several smuggling rings known as the French Connection.

The Palermo meeting was followed one month later by a summit of La Cosa Nostra representatives from every Mafia family on the continent at the country estate of Joseph Barbera in Apalachin, a rural town in upstate New York. The idea behind the now-infamous meeting was to gather away from the prying eyes of big-city cops. It became a red-faced fiasco. A New York State trooper was suspicious of the number of dark limousines carrying silk-suited men to the home of the area's richest resident and set up a lonely roadblock. By the time reinforcements arrived, the Mafia policy-makers had abandoned hundreds of pounds of barbecuing beef in a panic and were scampering away—many on foot through the woods. Police nabbed some 60 mobsters while another 40 escaped, including, it is believed, Luigi Greco and Pep Cotroni from Montreal. Drugs were a dicey subject within La Cosa Nostra families, a theme forming much of the tension in *The Godfather* book and movie. The profits were dazzling but so were the risks. Narcotic convictions brought long prison terms, especially for repeat offenders, and that meant the loyalty of indicted soldiers was difficult to maintain. The quandary meant La Cosa Nostra had a patchwork approach to the drug trade. Many family bosses officially banned their soldiers from involvement in dope, but turned a blind eye if a cut from a profitable narcotics enterprise was handed over. Despite the massive

1 Thirteen of the 30-odd men at the meeting would later be indicted by Aldo Vigneri, an Italian judge, alleging their involvement in "a criminal conspiracy to enrich themselves, not hesitating to kill and kidnap, and organizing the drug traffic to the United States via Sicily." Galante was one of them.

narcotics enterprise that Johnny was about to embark upon, he, too, despised the use of hard drugs, his friends insist.

"John really was old school and did not approve of drugs. He did not like them, he did not want to be around them and did not want to be around people who used them," said a high-ranking underworld associate of Johnny's. "This thing in New York was really a situation; it was not really John's doing. It was something he was called upon to put together, and he couldn't turn his back on it. We don't always get to do in this life what we want to do," he said of the heroin conspiracy.

The French Connection ran with uneven success. Tons of dope had made its way to America's shores, but this had not gone entirely unnoticed.

In 1958, Carmine Galante, Johnny's early mob mentor, was among 36 men indicted for international drug trafficking. A year later, Pep Cotroni, of Montreal, was arrested in Quebec. At Cotroni's trial, precise testimony by an undercover Bureau of Narcotics agent, who had tricked Cotroni into trusting him, damned the *mafioso*. On the third day of testimony, Cotroni changed his plea to guilty and was sentenced to 10 years.

Cops often compare the battle against drugs to grabbing a balloon; when you squeeze one part, another expands. And so it was with the French Connection. For every mobster busted, there were two others greedily ready to take the place of their fallen comrade.

Alberto Agueci and Johnny Papalia were ready to take their turn.

Agueci's contacts with the Sicilian Mafia secured the heroin from Antoine Cordoliani and Joseph Césari, a pair of notorious Corsican underworld leaders. It was quality merchandise from quality hoods. Cordoliani was a former partner of François Spirito, who established the first global network for French heroin, in the 1930s, dubbed the Orient Express; Césari was the half-brother of the famed heroin chemist Dominique Albertini, and was himself capable of producing some of the best dope on the planet. Salvatore Valenti, the travel agent, with his partners, would send the heroin to New York and Toronto via unsuspecting immigrants. A portion of the heroin that came into Canada would be directed to Toronto, Windsor, and Vancouver. Most of it would go on to New York City, where half of America's 500,000 heroin addicts lived. The heroin going to New York directly would stay there, be cut with confectionery sugar and peddled on the street. Johnny had the right friends who could arrange for tons of dope to disappear into the arms of hungry addicts not only in New York but also in Southern Ontario and Vancouver. Supply and demand. Johnny could link the two ends of the dope cycle. It seemed perfect.

In October 1958, the new dope ring took shape. Johnny introduced Agueci to Vinnie Mauro, and Mauro introduced the Canadian connection to his right-hand man, Frank (Frankie the Bug) Caruso. These four men formed the nucleus of a network that would encompass more than 32 people in three countries. Johnny would be the money man—paying the bills and handling the profits. Perhaps he insisted on it, or, more likely, since he was the one who brought Mauro and Agueci together, he was the only one everyone knew and trusted.

The ringleaders next had to secure the blessings of their bosses. For Mauro that meant his *capo*, Anthony (Tony Bender) Strollo, who answered to Vito Genovese. For Johnny and Agueci, it meant a trip to Buffalo to see Stefano Magaddino. It was not a difficult sell. The fledgling ringleaders knew how to speak the language of the mob; they went bearing cash. Agueci gave Magaddino $4,000 as a tribute payment, and the boss said he was expecting to reap half of the new venture's profits. The young mobsters had no intention of coughing up that kind of dough, but they certainly would keep the tribute flowing to keep the boss happy.

By May 1959—even though Palmeri, their New York front man, still thought he was joining a diamond smuggling operation—the first shipment of Johnny's heroin was on its way. Mauro's intermediary, Luigi LoBue, visited Palmeri's bakery to give him instructions.

"I received a letter from Italy, from a partner of mine," LoBue said of a message sent by Mario Mazzaro. "You have to go to the pier and pick up this valise for me." LoBue told Palmeri the name of the passenger he was to meet. "Tell this passenger that you are Salvatore Valenti's friend and he will give you the valise."

Palmeri abandoned the bakery and went straight to the pier to meet the 11 a.m. ship from Sicily. He talked his way past the guard at the gate and quickly found the passenger.

"I am Salvatore Valenti's friend," he said. The passenger handed him a suitcase, and Palmeri drove it back to the bakery and gave it to LoBue. LoBue rubbed the suitcase's inspection stamp off with a wet rag and left. Two days later he returned carrying a shopping bag.

"I have five packages in this bag. Put it away somewhere in your bakery where nobody will see this bag for a while," Palmeri was told. He hid it behind the flour.

"Now," continued LoBue, "go call up Vinnie Mauro and tell him that you are ready to make a delivery for him." Palmeri did as he was told.

"I want to talk to you," Palmeri told Mauro on the phone.

"I know," replied Mauro. "Come over tonight and see me."

That night Palmeri took the shopping bag and drove to Manhattan. Palmeri pulled his car to the side of the road, and Mauro emerged from a doorway and leaned into the open window.

"Look down farther in the direction of your automobile," Mauro said. "There is a car there, a black car, with a man sitting behind the wheel. Do you see that man?"

Palmeri nodded.

"Drive up there and stop right behind his car . . . This man is going to come over to your car and he is going to say 'hello' to you. As soon as he says 'hello' to you, you get the shopping bag, give it to this man, give him a chance to pull away, and then come back and pick me up."

Palmeri did as he was told. After returning to pick up Mauro, the two rode several blocks in silence before Mauro spoke.

"How do you feel about this?"

"Well," answered Palmeri, "I did what you told me."

"It was not too bad, after all?"

"It wasn't too bad," agreed Palmeri.

"Well, okay. I will get in touch with you in a few days."

When they next met, Mauro handed Palmeri an envelope flush with cash. If Palmeri thought this was his payoff for his role in the scheme, he was soon deflated.

"Bring this $5,000 to Luigi LoBue, and I will call you in a few days," Mauro said. When Palmeri got back to his bakery, LoBue was there waiting. Palmeri handed him the money, which LoBue counted before leaving. Over the next few days, Palmeri brought another $10,000 to LoBue. At the end of May, Palmeri finally received some money of his own. LoBue gave him $300.

Almost two months passed before Palmeri heard from LoBue again. Around noon on a warm July day, LoBue sauntered into Palmeri's bakery with another letter from Italy.

"Do the same thing you did the first time with the other valise," LoBue said, giving him the name of another passenger. Palmeri did, bringing back another suitcase.

"Go outside your bakery and sit there," LoBue told Palmeri. "Give me a couple of hours. I am going to go to work on this valise. See that nobody comes down." An hour passed and Palmeri, bored and curious, walked back into his bakery. LoBue was at Palmeri's large worktable with a thick quilt which he was cutting open with a razor. Stacked on one side were small white packages that Palmeri thought looked like cotton tightly wrapped in plastic. Startled by Palmeri's sudden appearance, LoBue nicked one of the packages. It wasn't cotton; powder spilled out.

"Is the diamonds in between the powder?" Palmeri asked, perplexed by what he saw. LoBue flashed with anger.

"Look," he yelled, "sooner or later you are going to know what is going on. I don't deal with diamonds. This is narcotics. Now what are you going to do about this? I suppose you are going to quit. Well, suppose you quit and then later on, when the valise gets caught, who do you think they are going to think did it?"

Palmeri was silent. He was not averse to crime—in the 1930s he had been a bootlegger and had a prior conviction for conspiracy to sell whiskey.

"If you think of quitting the job now, how could you do it?" LoBue continued to screech.

"You do all the talking. I ain't saying nothing," Palmeri said quietly.

"All right, let's forget about it," LoBue said, calming down.

"You go outside now and let me finish my work."

The heroin was again tucked away behind the flour. Palmeri again contacted Mauro and passed the bag of dope to the man in the black car and returned to collect the New York mobster. The gangster was worried about Palmeri, who now knew they were not smuggling diamonds.

"Is everything all right with you?" Mauro asked.

"Yes," answered Palmeri.

"You are nervous?"

"Well, a little."

"Don't worry about it," Mauro reassured. "It's easy. Just be careful and don't do anything, like, fast. Always take it easy." Mauro laughed and got out of the car.

In July 1959, in a diner on Lexington Avenue, Mauro introduced Palmeri to a new member of their organization. Salvatore Rinaldo was at times a construction worker and at other times a bookie, drug dealer, and thief. Rinaldo's first conviction was almost 30 years earlier, for unlawful entry. Over the years he would be arrested three more times, each for taking bets on horse races. Rinaldo was hired to take the dope from Palmeri and get it into the hands of the network of distributors, replacing the mysterious man in the black car.

"From now on," Mauro told the baker, "you are going to deal with this fellow here. Forget about the other man. He is no longer with me. Give your phone number to Salvatore Rinaldo and wait for my orders."

Rinaldo and Palmeri got along well, although Rinaldo was amused at how green Palmeri was in the "junk" trade—which is what they called heroin. The first time Rinaldo collected the dope, he pulled his car up near the bakery and the baker nervously walked the shopping bag out to him. As soon as Palmeri reached Rinaldo's car he threw the bag in the window.

"The way you were walking with that package," Rinaldo said, "it looks like you got a licence to carry junk."

Rinaldo was an experienced drug merchant. After the arrival of each shipment, he removed a dash of powder from each bag, poured some nitric acid into a cup and sprinkled the powder into it. He watched it turn yellow and then green. He then put a dash more of the powder into a glass test tube, tied the tube to a thermometer, dunked them into a pan of mineral oil, and put it on the gas stove in his kitchen. He watched the temperature gauge rise to 235 degrees Centigrade when the powder started turning yellow, then to 240 degrees when it turned brown, and then to 245 degrees when it dissolved completely. That was what Rinaldo was looking for: the two signs of high-grade heroin.

By now, regular clients were clamouring to buy a percentage of Johnny's heroin shipments, generally for $8,500 (U.S.) a kilo.

There was Joseph (Joe Cago) Valachi, who at the time was just a veteran soldier in the Genovese family, but would, in just a few years, become famous for breaking *omertà* by outlining to authorities for the first time the inner workings of the Mafia cartel. Valachi's involvement in Johnny's ring started in December 1959, and he usually had others handle his share of the dope, including Ralph Wagner.

"I forget who sent him to me," Valachi said of his relationship with Wagner. "Anyway, this guy said he's a good kid, and I liked him. He was handy to have around; he helped me paint the house. Ralph was dying to get into junk, so I put him to work. He wanted to get in the mob too, but of course, he can't as he was a mix-breed, meaning he was part Italian and part German."

Wagner would put the dope into the hands of several black dealers, including William (Shorty) Holmes, 38, who was supplementing his part-time wage from the *New York Times*, where he stacked newspapers, with street sales of heroin. Holmes and Rinaldo had a little code— each quarter-kilo bag was called "a ticket."

"Bring me a ticket," Holmes would always say over the phone. Rinaldo knew the voice and where they met, and would go to the music section of Gimbel's department store in Yonkers, where Holmes would always be waiting.

There was a trio of hoods who worked together: Charles Shiffman, Charles Tandler, and Morris Taubman. Shiffman was their boss, and had a lengthy criminal record. Shiffman and Rinaldo also had a code. Shiffman would phone Rinaldo, working a dollar amount into the conversation. The numbers corresponded to the time of the meeting; if he said $530, they would meet at 5:30 p.m. that day at Yonkers Raceway.

Another team was Robert Guippone and Anthony (Porky) Porcelli, Rinaldo's partners in a Brooklyn numbers racket. They came to Rinaldo's home to collect the dope, and sat in his basement mixing 10 ounces of confectionery sugar to two kilos of heroin to make it go farther.

Mathew Palmieri (not Matteo Palmeri, the baker) was another regular. He would arrange a different street corner for each delivery, and Rinaldo would drive there and wait. Mathew would climb into Rinaldo's car, pass over a bag containing $8,500, and give a hand signal. His brother would then walk across the street and collect the dope and disappear.

Rinaldo also had "special customers" who were close associates of Mauro's and Caruso's. For them, the dope went out on consignment. Salvatore Maneri was a made Mafia soldier who was called "Sheer" by everyone except Caruso, who always referred to him as "The Little Guy." Maneri was small in stature but his bankroll was large; he bought in five-kilo loads. Caruso would phone Rinaldo when Maneri was ready to buy, and Rinaldo would go to Maneri's apartment with the dope packed in a briefcase. Maneri's wife would tell Rinaldo where to park his car, and when Rinaldo arrived at the right spot, Maneri appeared.

"Have you got the five packages?" Maneri would ask, and Rinaldo would hand over the briefcase. Maneri would walk a block down the street and toss the case on the backseat of his car through the open window, then walk away. Seconds later, Maneri's brother would come and scoop up the case.

Arnold (Wash) Barbeto and his partner, a man whom police only knew as "Andy," were introduced to Rinaldo by Mauro. Mauro said to do whatever Wash asked. That usually meant kilo bags on consignment when they met at cheap diners around the city.

The client list for Johnny's dope grew as his reputation for quality and reliability spread.

Near the end of January 1960, LoBue left the ring—but not willingly. He had been arrested by police in an unrelated matter, and was found to be an illegal alien. The ring went on without him, with the Italian connection writing Palmeri directly. It was when Palmeri tried to do LoBue's job of removing the dope from the quilts that he got dizzy and sick from breathing it in. From then on, Rinaldo agreed to do that part, and Palmeri stuck to collecting the suitcases at the pier.

A little after 1 p.m. on a crisp April day, Palmeri was summoned to a meeting at a small restaurant in New York's Little Italy with Mauro, Caruso, and Agueci. Sitting at the table was a man he did not know, a man wearing sunglasses despite the dim surroundings of the restaurant. Palmeri was introduced for the first time to Johnny Papalia, described by Mauro as one of the bosses of the operation.

Johnny had news.

"From now on there ain't going to be valises anymore. We are going to start working with trunks. What do you think of this?" Johnny said to Palmeri.

"Well," said Palmeri, "what can I say?" Trunks rather than suitcases meant twice as much dope in each shipment.

"It is not going to be easy like when you pick up a valise and you walk away from the pier," said Mauro. "It is going to be rough. You can handle some trunks by yourself, but you got to think, you got to be careful. It isn't going to be easy. Of course, this trunk has to be opened on the pier and you might get nervous."

Agueci interrupted the conversation. "Whoa, he doesn't have to get nervous because there is nothing in the trunk. It is only clothing when the inspector opens the trunk because the narcotics is on the bottom, in between two bottoms. Nothing to worry about. Write your address and give it to me. I have to give it to my brother, Vito, because he is going to go to Italy, and then he is going to write to you when he is ready with the trunk."

Then Mauro turned to a matter of far greater interest to Palmeri.

"I'm going to keep giving you $300 for a while because we are kind of tight at the present. We need a lot of money to get the rest of the trunks in, but that is not your payment. We will give you all your money all at one time, so don't worry about nothing. Just give us a chance." The conspirators then arranged a code to communicate the amount of heroin found in each shipment.

"Whenever you get this trunk in, I want to know," said Agueci to Palmeri. "I am going to call you up and you got to tell me how much narcotics you find in the trunk. I will explain it to you. I am going to ask you how old was the little boy with the passenger. When I say that, you tell me how old. For instance, whatever narcotics you find in the trunk, whatever number you find, you tell me, like, 'The boy was 5,' 'The boy was 10.' " Palmeri understood. A 10-year-old boy was code for a 10-kilo shipment.

At the end of May, it was trunk time. Palmeri had received a letter from Agueci's brother, announcing an imminent arrival. Palmeri was shocked by what he read. Aboard the next ship, arriving June 2, was Salvatore Milana bringing a trunk, and another passenger named Graziano, coming with a suitcase.

Palmeri's trip to Pier 84 was routine now, but he was worried about meeting two passengers. He brought Rinaldo along to lend a hand. The collection went smoothly and the luggage was taken to the bakery, where they went to work on the trunk, discarding the clothes inside. The trunk was well made, however, and the pair bashed and pulled but could not disassemble it to reveal the secret compartment. They had to run to a hardware store to buy crowbars to break it open. As they tore the trunk to pieces, Palmeri stuffed the wooden shards into his bakery's oven. Inside the compartment were 10 thin packages of dope. The suitcase held another five. Rinaldo placed the packages in the bottom of a cardboard box, covered them with groceries and a newspaper, and left.

Agueci was pleased. Mauro, however, was in a sour mood.

"I want to talk to you," Mauro snapped to Palmeri when they met the next day. "Who told you to take Salvatore Rinaldo to the pier? What do you do, work on your own? Do you know that Salvatore Rinaldo might be followed by the FBI?" Palmeri said nothing; he had never seen Mauro so angry, and Mauro could brilliantly display his anger.

"I am sorry," Palmeri finally managed. "I don't mean it. After all, I had to pick up a trunk and a valise and I needed help."

"I don't care," said Mauro. "Don't take Rinaldo to the pier anymore."

Palmeri did not dare mention it to Mauro given his mood, but the baker had a beef. When Agueci next visited New York, Palmeri pulled him aside. "I thought I had to pick up only a trunk, but now I pick up a trunk and a valise. Don't tell me you are keeping on giving me the same price?"

"Oh, don't go into that again," Agueci answered. "Vinnie told you all about this. You will get your money when the time comes. I might as well tell you everything. We need money at the present because I am trying to put a deposit on 300 kilos of narcotics in Italy. So we need all the money we can get. So let's forget about it for the time being."

Agueci was not spinning Palmeri a line. Getting the 300 kilos became an obsession. It was a deal that would guarantee a steady supply at cut rates and a chance to crush their competition. But they needed that cash first. Rinaldo was called to a meeting at Yonkers Raceway with Johnny and Caruso. Johnny said he came to New York to collect the money. Rinaldo said he had $14,000 at home from sales.

"Well," said Johnny matter-of-factly, "you will have to give it to me. I want as much money as I can get to keep the shipments going." Johnny said they would all go together to get it. The gangsters waited outside in the car while Rinaldo nipped into his house. He retrieved the cash and handed it to Johnny. Johnny took it, divided it into two equal piles, put one into each inside pocket of his trench coat, and headed back to Canada.

On Agueci's next visit to New York, he visited Mauro at his apartment and they walked onto the terraced balcony to talk.

"Albert, why do we have to pay more money than them?" Mauro asked, concerned about his competition.

"You know why," replied Agueci. "We discussed that before. Until you give me the money to put the deposit on 300 kilos, there is nothing that I can do about the price. But when that is done not only the price will come down, but we put them out of business."

In striking back at the competition, however, Johnny and Mauro had a little help. One of their competitors was Agueci's old bakery partner Benedetto Zizzo. Johnny brought this to the attention of Magaddino, mentioning how Zizzo's operation was cutting into the don's profits. The Buffalo boss ordered a financial penalty. To that end, five kilos of heroin were obtained from Zizzo on consignment and never paid for.

Hitting the competition made Johnny and Mauro happy.

Their mood would not last.

12

All it takes for a thriving scam to crumble is a screw-up and a rat. Johnny Papalia's dope ring had several of both.

"That morning I ran into a lot of trouble," Matteo Palmeri later told police, when thinking back to September 2, 1960.

The day started as had each of the five previous trips to the New York City pier to meet an immigrant from Italy who was unknowingly smuggling heroin. This time, however, at the gate to the pier, Palmeri hit a snag. On each previous visit the same customs officer had easily handed him a pass to get on to the dock after Palmeri told him—without a word of a lie—that he was there to meet a passenger and help with his luggage. This time, however, a new officer was at the gate and he was a stickler for regulations. The officer refused to let Palmeri on the pier until the passengers had disembarked. While Palmeri was stuck at the gate, the passenger he had come to meet, Vincenzo Randazzo, was already leaving.

Randazzo had just completed his first year of high school in San Vito Lo Capo, Sicily, when he made the move to America with his father, Girolamo. Since Randazzo had been a little boy, he remembered seeing Salvatore Valenti walking grandly through the streets of his village. The night before the Randazzos left Sicily, Valenti came to young Vincenzo and told him of a trunk he would like him to take to America. Once in New York, the young Randazzo was met by his aunt and uncle, but no one came for the key to the trunk or the baggage claim slip needed to collect it. By the time Palmeri got on to the pier, Randazzo had already left. He spotted the trunk, but when he moved towards it, another man beat him to it. His heart raced; it was a customs officer. Palmeri casually walked by, turning to note that on top of the trunk was scrawled the word *Randazzo*. Palmeri called Vinnie Mauro from a pay phone.

"Give me a chance, 10 minutes, until I locate Albert Agueci and I will tell you what to do," Mauro said. A few minutes later Palmeri called back.

"Get off the pier immediately and as soon as you get outside, get in touch with Albert and he will tell you what to do," were Mauro's frantic instructions. When Palmeri reached Agueci by phone at his home in Toronto, the mobster did not have much to offer. The problem was worse than Palmeri had thought. As it turned out, the Canadian crew who had arranged the shipment with the Sicilian *mafiosi* had failed to note the address where the passenger was staying in America.

"There is nothing that I can do for the present," Agueci told Palmeri. "My brother Vito is trying to send a telegram to Italy to get some information about this mess-up. Call me back every couple of hours." Palmeri made numerous calls, and even directly called Vito, who wasn't very helpful.

"I would like to know how you find yourself in such a mess," Vito said. "You couldn't locate the passenger. You didn't have any trouble before with the valise or with the other trunks. How come now all this trouble? How will you answer to my brother and Vinnie Mauro about this?"

Palmeri was not intimidated.

"I don't have to worry about that because you're the one who has to answer," retorted Palmeri.

"Why?" Vito asked, taken aback.

"Because you went to Italy and you sent the first trunk, you didn't tell your people to put the address on the trunk. So you are to blame, not me."

Vito weakly replied: "Well, I can't be there all the time." "Anyway," he said, cheering up, "I made a few telegrams to Italy. I am waiting for an answer to clear everything up. I will let you know as soon as I get the telegram."

An hour later Palmeri called Vito again. Still no word from Italy. Palmeri returned to his bakery to find Rinaldo anxiously waiting. Pumping coins into pay phones, they kept calling Canada. Six calls, seven calls, eight calls. Still no telegram.

"Things are in confusion," Palmeri finally sighed to Rinaldo.

On September 3, at 5:51 p.m., a telegram arrived in the Toronto office of the Canadian Pacific Railway. The message, from Trapani, Sicily, was addressed to V. Agueci and read: "You can find Vito at Salvatore Palmeri's, 147 Monroe Street, Airfield, N.Y." The message was passed on to Mauro, who was meeting with Caruso, Rinaldo, and Palmeri in a New York diner. Mauro came away from the phone booth with the name and address scrawled on a slip of paper. He passed it to Rinaldo, who passed it to Palmeri, who passed it back to Mauro. The fact that the last name of the family with whom the passenger was staying was the same as that of Palmeri the baker was pure coincidence. The bigger concern was the name of the town where they supposedly lived; no one had heard of a town called Airfield. Another flurry of phone calls followed. No one could solve the mystery. Rinaldo and Palmeri headed for the Lower East Side of Manhattan and drove slowly up and down Monroe Street. There was no #147.

"Why don't you call the New York operator? Maybe this might be in Garfield, New Jersey. Take a crack at that," Mauro ordered. Palmeri discovered there was, in fact, a 147 Monroe Street in Garfield, New Jersey. He dialed the number. On the other end of the phone was Vittoria Palmeri, wife of Salvatore, who was named in the telegram from Italy. Salvatore and Vittoria were Randazzo's aunt and uncle. Palmeri asked her about the trunk, and Randazzo retrieved the key and claim slip from his pocket.

"I will come right away," Palmeri said. Elated, the gang piled into a car and drove to Garfield. With the slip and key they hurried to the pier, but were too late—it was past 5 p.m. and the customs office was closed.

Early the next morning, Palmeri left to collect the trunk, but this shipment seemed fated. He noticed the signal lights on his truck were broken. In a panic already over the mix-up, he felt it unwise to drive the heroin around New York in a truck that could attract police attention. He remembered something Agueci had told him: "If you run into any trouble, the only person you can run to in Brooklyn would be Filippo Cottone. He is a friend of mine. He is also a friend of yours." Cottone, then 44, was known as "Fifi." Born in America to Italian parents, he returned to Italy when he was just two years old and grew up there, meeting Agueci before returning to America as a young man. Palmeri called and told him his troubles.

"What about this trunk?" Cottone asked.

Resenting how he had been first duped into smuggling dope under the guise of it being diamonds, Palmeri came clean with Cottone about the drugs. Cottone was still prepared to help, and picked Palmeri up in his station wagon.

When they arrived at the pier, Palmeri found the trunk in the customs office and handed over the claim slip. He unlocked the trunk for the inspector, who looked through the clothes and blankets inside and quickly cleared it. In a wry flourish, Palmeri signed a false name on the claim form—"Palermo." Cottone and Palmeri were met at the bakery by Rinaldo, who asked about the stranger.

"Let's stop the stalling," Palmeri said, "and let us get this thing over with."

Dumping out the shirts, quilts, and towels, the trio ripped open the false bottom and were relieved to find 10 bags of dope still there. Palmeri thanked Cottone and said his work was finished. Cottone eyed the discarded pile of clothes.

"What are you going to do with all this clothing?" Cottone asked.

"If you want it, you can have it."

Cottone filled up a large box from the pile. Palmeri still had two quilts that came out of the trunk.

"Could I have one of them?" Cottone asked.

Palmeri passed one over, and Cottone gathered up his haul and left. Palmeri later gave the other quilt to his landlord's daughter. Agueci called that evening.

"How old was the boy?" he asked.

"Ten years old."

"Oh, no," said Agueci, "that boy is bigger than that."

"Well, it is ten years old. That's all there is to it."

"No, that boy is sixteen years old," Agueci insisted, with a rising sense of panic. "You don't know what you are doing. You better look good. Did you see two blankets?"

"I saw them," Palmeri answered.

"Why, in those blankets there's three kilos each."

"Well, I am sorry. I will call you back." Palmeri broke out in a sweat and frantically searched Brooklyn for Cottone, spotting him on Central Avenue.

"Give me that blanket back," Palmeri said anxiously.

"What happened?" Cottone asked.

"In that blanket there's three kilos of narcotics." Amazed, Cottone retrieved the quilt and returned it undamaged to Palmeri, who then fetched the other from his landlord's daughter. Things had not gone smoothly, but the ring's largest shipment yet, a full 16 kilos, was now safely in their hands.

The bosses gathered at a diner on Lexington Avenue to discuss the screw-up. Johnny and Agueci traveled to New York to meet first with Mauro and Caruso and then with other members of their ring.

"I want to know about what happened on September 2nd with that trunk on the pier," Caruso said to Palmeri. "I know what happened, but I want to know from you."

Palmeri told of his ordeal. Caruso then turned to Agueci.

"Albert, you have to go to Italy and straighten everything up. I don't want anything like this to happen anymore."

Johnny then headed for Buffalo to brief Magaddino on the situation. This was not Johnny's first report. He and Agueci were personally bringing almost weekly updates—with cash payments—to Magaddino. Some months earlier, however, the overweight Buffalo don suffered a heart attack and was hospitalized. Magaddino left Freddie Randaccio in charge. Back in early August, Johnny and Agueci met with Randaccio at a racetrack in Fort Erie, just inside the Canadian border. Johnny was chipper from good news: their Canadian Mafia colleague, Rocco Scopelliti, had successfully brought over 10 kilos, the ring's fifth shipment, from Sicily to New York.[1] This visit to Buffalo, however, was not as cheery. Randaccio updated Magaddino, and the don said Vito Agueci must go to Italy to personally caution Valenti and his cohorts against future mistakes. Johnny said the elder Agueci was a better representative, but Magaddino was adamant it be Vito; Alberto Agueci was needed here, he decreed.

The Buffalo bosses were not happy with the mix-up but were not so upset with their Canadian boys as to snub them. On September 18, 1960, Alberto Agueci was celebrating the baptism of his daughter. Randaccio had agreed to be godfather and was at the celebration in Toronto, along with his wife. Johnny was there also, with his girlfriend Mollie McGoran. It was shortly before Vito was to leave for Italy, and as if he were not already under pressure from Johnny, he was pulled aside by Randaccio and reminded that Magaddino himself had chosen him for this task.

The gang was now breathing a sigh of relief. The 16 kilos were selling well. The New York end alone had accumulated more than $130,000 in pure profit, and the next shipment had already been paid for. They were a heartbeat away from scoring the 300-kilo master stroke. Everyone just needed to be a little more careful, Johnny said. Mauro had a carpenter build a secret trap in Rinaldo's home—in the closet of his children's playroom—where he could hide heroin and money. They felt they had regained control.

In reality, cracks were forming everywhere.

Surprisingly, it was not the missing trunk flap that attracted police attention. It stemmed from the one very real problem with running a dope ring: you are surrounded by drug dealers.

1 Scopelliti added a new twist to Johnny's scheme, using both willing mob accomplices and unsuspecting immigrants as drug mules. The mix was so hard for police to crack that, years later, secret police files show that officers were not always certain who was a dupe and who was in on the plot.

EVOLUTION

John Joseph Papalia: The Enforcer, Johnny Pops, Godfather—he went by many names during his more than half a century as a player in the underworld. He moved from the shadows, as seen in one of his first surveillance photos (bottom), through centre stage, when this mug shot caught him in his prime (below, left), to old age, seen in the last known photograph taken of Johnny while alive (below, right).

Brothers: Frank Papalia (left) often appears glum as he runs the family business; Rocco Papalia (right) is said to be light-hearted. Both had minor brushes with the law and remained close to Johnny to his end.

Busted: "Watch it with that camera, creep," Johnny warned a photographer in 1961 while being arrested for the beating of Maxie Bluestein. In the above photo, Johnny hides his face with a handkerchief while being escorted down a Hamilton street by Detective Mike Pauloski, to Johnny's left, an early police nemesis of Johnny's. The gangster's loyal brother Frank (wearing a dark suit and sunglasses) lends support and leads the way. In the photo to the left, Johnny is still determined to hide his face as he is hustled into a police car for his trip to a Toronto jail.

Rocco Perri: Bootlegging king and mob pioneer

Calogero Bordonaro: Black Hand bombing

Joseph Scibetta: Family had influence in Ontario

Roy Pasquale: Johnny's early gangmate in Toronto

Paul Volpe: First a friend, then Johnny's mob rival

Norman Yakubovitch: Took a bullet for Johnny

Red LaBarre: Johnny's affable bookmaker

Freddie Gabourie: Late-night crap games

Frank Marchildon: In Johnny's inner circle

Jackie Weaver: A master "mechanic" for Johnny

Hilton Harmes: Watched Johnny's local operation

Danny Gasbarrini: From gambling to business

James McDermott: One of the "Three Thieves"

Vincent Feeley: A lady's man and gambling king

Maxie Bluestein: Would not give in to Johnny

Giacomo Luppino: The wise old man of the mob

Bruno Monaco: Decades at the Papalias' side

Carmen Barillaro: Shot right after Johnny

JOHNNY'S AMERICAN CONNECTIONS

Freddie Randaccio:
Johnny's Buffalo mentor

Stefano Magaddino:
Johnny's top authority

Antonio Magaddino: The
don's brother and ally

Vinnie Mauro: Partner in
the French Connection

Anthony Strollo: Mauro's
New York *capo*

Carmine Galante: Pegged
for 80 murders

Joe Valachi: Dope ring
partner turns informant

**Frankie "The Bug"
Caruso:** Heroin partner

Benny Nicoletti: Monitored
gambling network

JOHNNY'S MONTREAL CONNECTIONS

Vic Cotroni: Threatened Johnny without fear

Paulo Violi: Moved from Hamilton to Montreal

Frank Cotroni: Last of the old Montreal gang to die

Under surveillance: Johnny (left) walks away from Paulo Violi's café in Montreal, leaving one of his brothers, Dominic (seen waving), and one of Violi's brothers, Rocco, in the mid-1970s. When Johnny traveled, police were often secretly watching.

Steve Koaches: Loyal
Papalia lieutenant

Howard "Baldy" Chard:
The Enforcer's intimidator

Enio Mora: Johnny's fearsome man in Toronto

Sheldon (Sonny) Swartz:
Extortion plot turned sour

Réal Simard: Hitman sent
from Montreal

Domenic Racco: His slaying upset Johnny

Benedetto Zizzo: From
old friend to heroin rival

Nick Rizzuto: Outlived
Violi for sway in Montreal

Lucky Luciano: Legendary
boss linked to Johnny

Charles Shiffman was a man of note to police. Whenever Shiffman was released from prison he immediately ferreted out another drug ring to latch onto. When a pair of alert deputy sheriffs noticed some heavy and careless betting at Yonkers Raceway, they decided the gamblers deserved further investigation. They asked undercover drug officers to look the men over, and one recognized Shiffman—dressed in rumpled street clothes but peeling off $100 bills like a millionaire. The officers then watched Shiffman meet with strangers in the racetrack's bleachers. Each lead was followed. Officers noted Salvatore Rinaldo's presence and learned of his contact with Vincent Mauro, whose name none of the officers needed to ask about, and this Canadian hoodlum known as Johnny Pops.

On December 1, 1959, the telephone in Rinaldo's home and the switchboard in the apartment hotel where Mauro lived were tapped by police. It was the first real crack in the ring.

Joe Valachi was also a dangerous man to have around. The U.S. Bureau of Narcotics had been keeping an eye on him since the 1940s. In 1956, he was sentenced to five years for a bit part in a heroin deal, but his sentence was overturned on appeal. In 1959, his associate Ralph Wagner was caught carrying heroin. In a bid to reduce his sentence, Wagner ratted out Valachi. Valachi was released on bail and looked to Mauro to help him flee the country. Mauro turned to his Toronto comrades, and Agueci helped Valachi across the Canadian border. Both Agueci and Toronto mobster Paul Volpe looked after Valachi until his boss, Anthony Strollo, demanded he return to New York, where he surrendered to authorities. In an effort to obtain leniency for himself, Valachi took the opportunity to return Wagner's favour. He ratted Wagner out to narcotics agents for his involvement in Johnny's dope network. Wagner was re-arrested.

Valachi had introduced another man into the heroin conspiracy who was not helping matters. Michael Maiello was anxious to unload his product, and on September 8, just two days after the wayward trunk was recovered, he sold 240 grams of heroin to a new acquaintance who haggled a little over price and then produced a $2,000 down payment in $50 bills. Maiello turned over the heroin—now only

72-percent pure—and was given another $1,900. Earlier in the day those very bills had had their serial numbers carefully noted before being dispensed from U.S. government funds. Maiello had just sold a chunk of Johnny's heroin to an undercover police officer, and some of the bills would soon surface in a very incriminating place.

It was not only on the U.S. side that slip-ups and loose tongues brought police attention. In Toronto, a personal friend of Johnny's—in a moment of weakness—set off a chain of events that would make both of their lives miserable. Myer Rush was a pal of several members of Johnny's inner circle and a man who made millions in stock swindles on two continents. But before he found his true calling in the financial markets, he was a thief who made a decent living using master keys that gave him access to every room in several of Toronto's poshest hotels. The keys allowed Rush, with his box-like build, to seem like a nimble bandit—able to whisk valuables away from guests, who then typically pointed an accusing finger at surprised maids and bell hops for their losses. Rush's good fortune unravelled, however, when, in a fit of despair over her husband's infidelity, his wife called a pair of officers from the Toronto police's robbery squad and arranged a secret, late-night meeting at Exhibition Place. There she told incredulous officers of Rush's master hotel keys. They soon arrested him, confiscated the keys and threw him in jail. Not long after the pinch, however, the officers were approached by senior detectives who insisted the officers withdraw their theft charges against Rush, a police officer involved in the case said. The detectives said that Rush was willing to provide important information against a big fish in return for the favour. In the end, in exchange for walking free for his hotel crime spree, Rush tipped police to Johnny's involvement in the heroin conspiracy in New York. It was a decision that would come back to haunt him in a significant way.

If all of that was not enough to doom the ring, police were also piecing together the supply side of the operation.

In April 1960, the RCMP nabbed Agueci's Sicilian colleague, Rosario Mancino, after he arrived in Canada at Dorval airport in Montreal. After eight hours of questioning by the RCMP, he decided to return to Italy rather than pursue admission to Canada. Perhaps interrogators should have gone easier; police had decided to let him stay to see if he contacted Johnny or Agueci.

An international police effort was rising to meet the global drug network. The RCMP and U.S. police were following up on each other's information, the French Sûreté was probing the activities of the Marseilles dope merchants, and Italian police were making inquiries at their end. The Italian government had already given the Americans a photograph of Rocco Scopelliti, taken from his Italian passport application.

Ignoring all warning signs, the ring pressed ahead, and on October 21, 1960, Palmeri was again heading to the pier, this time to meet Pietro Torrente, a fisherman from Marettimo, Sicily.

The trunks would no longer be taken to Palmeri's bakery, Mauro had decided. The woman who owned the bakery was getting suspicious. Rinaldo agreed the trunks could go straight to his house. Rinaldo said he would wait outside the pier, and Palmeri could get the trunk and then follow him to his house.

At 11 a.m. Rinaldo arrived at the pier's gates, but Palmeri was not there. He could see passengers were already leaving and he was worried he was about to miss another trunk. Ignoring his orders to stay off the pier, he went to find the trunk himself. Palmeri, however, was not late. In fact, he had arrived especially early to ensure there were no problems, and had already found the passenger. When Palmeri emerged from customs he was aghast to see Rinaldo skulking about the pier.

"What are you doing here?" he hissed. Rinaldo tried to explain.

Palmeri loaded the large, grey trunk onto his truck, and the two of them drove to the parking lot, where Rinaldo had parked his car.

"Follow me," Rinaldo said to Palmeri, and roared off in his own car towards his home. Palmeri followed, but was suddenly forced to a halt. Police were everywhere. The men were arrested at gunpoint and the trunk seized. Searching Rinaldo's home, police found $21,450 and 340 grams (12 ounces) of heroin in a hidden household compartment. In that stack of cash were eight $50 bills earlier marked by police for a heroin buy from Maiello.

Palmeri and Rinaldo were busted.

13

Nobody thought for one minute that this hapless baker and unemployed construction worker had masterminded the heroin ring. Federal narcotics agents now wanted to dismantle the ring from top to bottom, and pounced on Salvatore Rinaldo and Matteo Palmeri with unwavering vigour.

The two smugglers were quietly tossed into separate cells at Westchester County Jail, and on more than 20 occasions officers from various agencies pummeled them with questions and worked to convince them a deal was their only option. Interest in Palmeri and Rinaldo extended all the way to senior government officials in Washington, D.C. Robert Kennedy, the U.S. attorney general, took an immediate interest in the case and sent two attorneys from the Department of Justice's Organized Crime and Racketeering Section to New York City; every day, all day, for more than two weeks, one worked on Palmeri and the other on Rinaldo. Meanwhile, police scoured their homes and interrogated their families—Rinaldo's wife was even arrested and threatened with charges, based on the discovery of dope in her home. That could have meant losing their children to the state, a particularly ominous threat.

Investigators already knew a great deal about Johnny Papalia and his co-conspirators. What they needed now was testimony to convict them all.

Few records exist documenting how members of the heroin ring reacted when Rinaldo and Palmeri went missing with the trunk that October morning in 1960. It could not have taken long for Vinnie Mauro and Frank Caruso to figure out that things had gone awry and to alert Johnny and Alberto Agueci.

If they feared a sudden police sweep for the rest of the gang, they did not realize how painstakingly slowly the authorities were working. If the gang members recoiled after the seizure, they relaxed again in short order. Whether out of boldness or stupidity, Johnny still marched into the Town Tavern in March 1961, exactly five months after the heroin seizure, and beat the daylights out of Maxie Bluestein. That sent Johnny into hiding as a wanted man, and police digging into his affairs. On May 5, 1961, Agueci was plucked from the street by Toronto police, who found him carrying two capsules of heroin and a baseball bat. It is said that Agueci demanded Johnny turn himself in lest the hunt for him uncover the heroin operation. It was even reported in Toronto newspapers that Johnny was hiding in fear of gangland reprisals rather than from police. Police said publicity over Johnny's elusiveness placed him in "great disfavour" with key underworld figures. Said one police officer: "Some of them are pretty sore and it could be that he's afraid to come into the open." Whether Johnny listened to Agueci's demands, or possibly to orders from Magaddino—who could not have liked the prospect of being tied to the dope ring if an extensive police search continued unabated—or merely felt the time was right, he eventually surrendered to Canadian authorities. He might have acted differently had he known what was brewing south of the border.

Johnny's two New York underlings, Rinaldo and Palmeri, were charged with feloniously possessing a narcotic with intent to sell, which carried a minimum five-year prison term. A promise was made: if they gave up the rest of the gang, the charge would be withdrawn and replaced with conspiracy to sell a narcotic, which carried no minimum sentence. Palmeri and Rinaldo went from low-level smugglers to top-notch informers.

On May 22, 1961, in the United States District Court, Southern District of New York, a grand jury returned a true bill of indictment. Signed by the jury foreman, Indictment No. 61 CR. 527 laid out the essentials of the case: "On or about the first day of September 1958, and continuously thereafter ... [the accused] unlawfully, fraudulently, wilfully, and knowingly did combine, conspire, confederate, and agree together and with each other to ... import and bring large amounts of narcotic drugs into the United States from and through Italy and other countries."

Below that introduction were 30 specific counts under indictment; above were the names of 20 men.

Alphabetically arranged, Alberto Agueci, from Toronto, topped the list, ensuring notoriety when the case was from then on officially known as *The United States of America vs. Albert Agueci, et al.*

The others charged were the Mafia ringleaders Johnny (Pops) Papalia, Vincent (Vinnie) Mauro, and Frank (Frankie the Bug) Caruso; the middlemen and couriers Vito Agueci, Rocco Scopelliti, Luigi LoBue, and Filippo (Fifi) Cottone; the mid-level distributors Joseph (Joe Cago) Valachi, Salvatore (Sheer, The Little Guy) Maneri, Charles Shiffman, Arnold (Wash) Barbeto, and the unknown New York heroin distributor called "Andy," named John Doe in the indictment; as well as low-level distributors Robert Guippone, William (Shorty) Holmes, Michael Maiello, Mathew Palmieri, Anthony (Porky) Porcelli, Charles Tandler, and Morris Taubman.

Two days later, police staged pre-dawn raids across New York, arresting 12 of the accused. All pleaded not guilty. Mauro and Caruso had their bail set at an astounding $250,000 and were tossed back in jail.

Around 10:30 that same morning, while U.S. District Attorney Robert M. Morgenthau announced the arrests and the dismantling of an international conspiracy that had smuggled $150-million worth of heroin into the U.S. from Italy and Canada, the RCMP and Toronto police made simultaneous raids on the homes of Agueci and his brother Vito. Shortly before midnight that same day, Scopelliti was arrested as he arrived at his Toronto home, which police had been staking out all day. Just weeks later, U.S. Department of Justice requests for the extradition of the Aguecis and Scopelliti were all granted. Canadian authorities dropped Agueci's Canadian drug and weapons charges to clear the way for his trip to the United States.

Reminiscent of the situation just one month earlier, when police went looking, Johnny was nowhere to be found. A dragnet was launched; all railways, airports, and border crossings in the country were notified.

On June 12, with an extradition warrant from the U.S. and an arrest warrant for the Bluestein beating both hanging over his head, Johnny was moved to the top of the RCMP fugitive list, making The Enforcer Canada's most wanted criminal. That day was a busy one for the Bluestein Squad. They chased several tips on where Johnny might be hiding and that night raided a party in a swank Avenue Road apartment in Toronto. Johnny was not there, but it was not a bad tip— the gangster had left the party just an hour before. Shortly after midnight, Detective Sergeant Alvin Sproule was crawling into bed when he received a telephone call.

"Pops may be around Crescent Road and Yonge Street about 2 a.m.," an anonymous tipster said.

Sproule dressed, hurried downtown to pick up two other officers, and slowly drove up Yonge Street. Johnny was spotted where he was supposed to be—sauntering down Yonge, apparently window shopping—and offered no resistance. He carried no weapons or drugs, less than $100, and steadfastly refused to say where he had been hiding. He spent the night in police custody. When Johnny appeared in court, his lawyer, Frank Nasso, tried to have him released on bail. Senior County Judge Robert Forsyth did not fall for it, saying: "He knew we were looking for him last time and we weren't able to find him." The extradition case against Johnny was based on affidavits sworn out in the U.S. by Palmeri and Rinaldo as part of their plea deal; Palmeri's implication of Johnny was somewhat vague, Rinaldo's quite damning.

The second week of July 1961 was not the best of times for Johnny. Inside of three days he was found guilty of assaulting Bluestein and ordered extradited to the U.S. Johnny was relying, however, on having to finish his Canadian sentence before being sent south.

126 · ADRIAN HUMPHREYS

14

The massive indictment of Johnny Papalia, his Mafia colleagues, and their co-conspirators in the French Connection was—reported United States Attorney General Robert Kennedy, to his brother, President John F. Kennedy—"the deepest penetration . . . ever made in the illegal international traffic of drugs."

Despite the grandeur of Kennedy's words, it was not a particularly auspicious group of men facing trial. Of the 20 men charged under the indictment, only 11 stood trial that year. The Mafia contingent was largely missing and none of the ringleaders were before the courts. Johnny, of course, was still cooling his heels in a Canadian jail. Several others, including Vinnie Mauro, fled the country; others were killed.

"This," complained Joe Valachi, "made me the main guy."

Alberto Agueci was in the Federal House of Detention on West Street in New York awaiting trial in September 1961, and having a rough time of it.

After paying regular tribute to Magaddino when the heroin operation was in full swing, now that he was in trouble he was expecting cooperation from the Buffalo don. He was expecting help with his bail money, promises to look after his family—the kind of stuff mob tradition called for. Agueci waited day after day for word of Magaddino's assistance. From Buffalo there came only silence. Worse than silence, in fact. A Hamilton lawyer, Ignazio (Harold) Bordonaro, son of the old Mafia don Charlie, seemed to throw up roadblock after roadblock to Agueci's bid for release, the imprisoned mobster told his family. Bordonaro was close to Magaddino and Freddie Randaccio, and this fueled Agueci's anger towards Buffalo.[1]

Valachi, jailed with Agueci at West Street, offered a glimpse into Agueci's mental state: "Some guys just can't take being in the can, and I could see right away Albert Agueci wasn't going to last long. All he talked about was getting out on bail. He kept telling me his wife was raising the money to get him out and how he was going to declare himself if Steve Magaddino don't get his brother out, too—meaning he would tell everyone that Steve, his boss, was in on the deal, which he was . . . I said, 'You want my advice? You've been sending out too many messages . . . and you ain't getting no response. It's bad sending messages out like that. You're going to get into trouble.'"

Agueci would have done well to heed Valachi's words. Instead, his resentment grew daily. When he finally made bail by selling his home and borrowing from a friend, he is said to have had a heated argument with Bordonaro about his lack of assistance. In the heat of the moment, Agueci slipped in a threat—that he would rat out others' involvement if things were not settled. It is thought Bordonaro was the first to alert Magaddino to Agueci's instability. At any rate, threatening a boss of Magaddino's stature and demeanour is never wise.

On October 8, 1961, Agueci left his wife, Vita, and daughters in Toronto, telling them he was off to New York for a court appearance, which was scheduled for the next day. The next time Vita saw her husband, he was a charred, rotting corpse on a slab in the Monroe County medical examiner's office near Rochester, New York. On November 23, 1961, hunters stumbled upon most of Agueci in a cornfield in the town of Penfield, New York—although it was difficult to identify the

---

1 Harold Bordonaro was convicted of fraud in 1983, after a sophisticated land development scheme, and sentenced to 3½ years in prison. Strangely, he gave the Law Society of Upper Canada a written undertaking in 1980 not to practise law, and has been suspended as a member of the bar since 1981 for non-payment of dues. He has not appeared before a disciplinary committee.

body at the time. The man's face and hands had been burned beyond recognition. He had been beaten extensively, up and down his body, with enough force to break his ribs, fill his chest and abdominal cavity with blood, knock out more than half a dozen teeth, and fracture the back of his skull. He had been trussed up with barbed wire and eventually strangled with a rope. While he lay in the field, animals feasted on his flesh, consuming large portions of his beefy thighs. He had likely been dead for two weeks, declared the medical examiner.

A picture of what is believed to have happened slowly emerged. Magaddino ordered Agueci's elimination, both out of fear he would turn informer and out of retribution for his impertinent words. A Buffalo mobster close to Johnny is said to have personally dished out the contract. Sources say the instructions were specific: "Burn his face until he has no face; burn his hands until he has no hands; do it even if you have to use a blowtorch." According to police reports, a day after leaving Toronto, Agueci was seen with Randaccio near a Buffalo gas station owned by his close associate Fred Mogavero. No charges were ever laid in connection with Agueci's slaying.

When Agueci's case came up in court, nobody knew his body was being nibbled on in a cornfield, and the court deemed him a fugitive from justice. A warrant was issued for his arrest and his bail money was seized.[2]

There were others forced to miss their court appearance. Arnold (Wash) Barbeto was a slightly built man who, just a few years before his arrest, required electroshock therapy for chronic depression. His impending trial severed his already tenuous grip on stability. Two days after the jury was selected to hear the case against him, Barbeto threw a birthday party for one of his children. While the guests sang "Happy

2 Even after his death had been confirmed, the court still found he violated the conditions of his bail and refused to return the $20,000 to his family. The decision left his wife and daughters destitute as well as fatherless.

Birthday," they heard a loud *thump* inside the house. When the family went to investigate they found Barbeto near death on the bathroom floor, having tried to hang himself from the shower curtain rod. If not for the rod snapping from his weight, he would surely have died that night. He was sent to a psychiatric hospital rather than to trial.

It is to the eternal misfortune of William (Shorty) Holmes that the source he found for dope was Johnny. Because he was black, Holmes was no *mafioso*, and was deemed a weak link by the ringleaders. When he suddenly changed lawyers in July, it was seen as a sign he was about to join the rat patrol. It was a sound call; the federal prosecutor later said Holmes had indeed "made overtures to cooperate with the government." On August 9, 1961, his body was found on a Bronx street. The autopsy report notes the cause in one simple line: "Gunshot wound on the head, penetrating the brain."

The man who first brought Holmes into the ring, Ralph Wagner, fared no better. After being found guilty for narcotics offences at a separate trial, he was sentenced to five years in prison. Just two weeks after his parole, he disappeared forever under the most mysterious circumstances. And before Johnny and Mauro came before the court, Mauro's boss, Anthony (Tony Bender) Strollo, was taken for a ride. He left his New Jersey home on April 8, 1962. His wife's last words to him: "You better put on your topcoat, it's chilly." Strollo replied: "I'm only going out for a few minutes. Besides, I'm wearing thermal underwear." Rubber might have been more appropriate; he has not been seen since.

Mauro, Caruso, and Maneri, meanwhile, manoeuvred their case to appear before a New York City judge who was notoriously soft on drug traffickers, and argued their bail down from $250,000 to $50,000. Once out of jail, the three New York gangsters called upon their Canadian connection. Police believe a Hamilton lawyer arranged for false Canadian passports through a travel agent in Toronto. Mauro and his two colleagues then fled the country in an early example of identity theft, masquerading as three legitimate Hamilton citizens: Mauro using the name of a variety store owner; Caruso, the name of a cigar store owner; and Maneri, that of a steelworker.

Even with most of the big names absent from the courtroom, prosecutors pressed ahead, putting their two star witnesses, Palmeri and Rinaldo, on the stand with dozens of corroborating witnesses. For 18 days the government presented its case to the jury. The defence team attacked the credibility of the government witnesses, calling them "rats," and "scum of the earth."

On Boxing Day, the jury heard the judge's lengthy charge and then began deliberations. At 10:05 the next morning, the jury reached its verdicts: all guilty on all counts. Sentencing was stiff. Cottone was handed 5 years; Scopelliti got 10 years; Vito Agueci, Maiello, Tandler, Porcelli, and LoBue each got 15 years; Palmieri, Valachi, and Guippone, who each had a prior narcotics conviction, were given 20 years; and Shiffman, with his deplorable criminal record, was handed 25 years.

While federal prosecutors were laying bare the narcotics enterprise, Mauro, Caruso, and Maneri were living high and loud in Nassau, Bahamas, where they flew with their bogus passports. Flashing money and chasing women, their behaviour was so outrageous that they were noticed by other tourists. When three Canadian women returned home after their holiday, they recognized the photographs of the three fugitives splashed across the newspapers as being of the "Canadian" men who had lavished affection upon them in the Caribbean. The RCMP alerted U.S. authorities, who now had somewhere to begin their search. One step ahead of police, however, the gangsters jet-setted through the Bahamas, Venezuela, England, France, and finally to Spain. Once in Europe, they did not exactly hide. They stayed at the best hotels, gambled heavily in fancy casinos, and—as final evidence they were begging to be caught—placed direct phone calls to the one person in Europe who was guaranteed to be under police surveillance: Lucky Luciano.

Although banned from the U.S., Lucky maintained some control over La Cosa Nostra while in exile in Italy and claimed no important decision was made without his input. Regular visitors, letters, and telephone calls kept Lucky in the loop, bringing news to the hotel suites he made his home, and taking away his advice. The couriers also brought cash, averaging $25,000 a month, as his take on the American enterprises. Police were tracing the source of the heroin used in Johnny's and other Mafia drug schemes, and were convinced they bore the mark of Lucky. In fact, when Mauro first jumped bail, Lucky was summoned to Naples police headquarters for questioning. It was even suggested he fronted the money for Mauro's bail. Despite known rules in underworld circles against phoning Lucky at his apartment, on January 14, 1962, and again the next day, Mauro placed just such calls. Mauro made no attempt to hide his identity, and openly stated he and his colleagues had come to Europe to offer their services to Lucky, since he was "moving big into the junk business." Lucky slammed the phone down and suffered an angina attack. Less than a week later, Italian police again hauled Lucky in, and this time questioned him about his involvement in Johnny's and Mauro's drug ring. He was released, but police decided to arrest him in two days' time. They would not get their chance. The next day, January 26, Lucky made his way to the airport to meet a Hollywood producer writing a movie on the mobster's life. After greetings were exchanged, Lucky sagged to the floor, his eyes rolling back as he struggled to breathe. Lucky's heart would pump no more.

After such foolhardy phone calls, it took only days for Mauro, Caruso, and Maneri to be arrested in Spain. Mauro was carrying almost $12,000 with him, and police found another $48,000 in a safety deposit box. Under heavy guard, the mobsters were brought back to New York, where a battery of reporters and photographers awaited them. Mauro, copying Johnny's brand of press relations, lunged at the media. Handcuffed between his two colleagues, he dragged them all down when he suddenly head-butted a CBS cameraman and all four tumbled into a heap.

Perhaps fearing gangland retribution for their stunt with Lucky, or perhaps anxiously eyeing the death toll among their former dope ring colleagues, the gangsters did not request bail.

"You mean he is satisfied in jail?" an incredulous judge asked Mauro's lawyer. "Yes," he answered. The press went wild.

Most of their co-conspirators had already been found guilty on their narcotics charges, and a new trial was convened for the three stragglers. There would still be one more accused—an unexpected one—joining them in the prisoner's box.

Three days before Johnny's 38th birthday and without any advance warning to his lawyer, his family, or the press, an order was signed on March 15, 1962, by the Governor General, commuting Johnny Papalia's sentence for the Maxie Bluestein assault. With no more sentence to serve in Canada, it suddenly cleared the way for his swift extradition to the U.S. Johnny was transferred without warning from the provincial maximum security reformatory at Millbrook to the Don Jail in Toronto, and then, under an escort of RCMP officers, taken to Malton Airport for the short flight to New York. Johnny, not happy at this unexpected turn of events, foiled the flight in a very ungangsterish way: kicking, screaming, and shouting that he was being kidnapped in such a temper tantrum that airline officials refused to allow him on the plane. Officers were forced to drive him to the U.S. border at Fort Erie, with Johnny lying on the floor of their car, shaking, doubled over, and vomiting from anxiety. At the border, he was handed over to Bureau of Narcotics officers and formally charged with three counts under the original New York indictment: unlawfully conspiring to violate narcotics laws, and two counts of unlawfully importing heroin into the United States.

Debate raged in Canada over the legality of the move—lawyers noted it was the first time a Canadian's sentence had been remitted to allow him to stand trial in another country—but in the U.S., Johnny quickly appeared in a New York courtroom, where his bail was set at $250,000. Assistant U.S. Attorney Edward Brodsky asked for Johnny's bail to be set high because he was "in this conspiracy at the highest level." Johnny pleaded not guilty and was returned to jail.

"In the States, everyone called him 'Canadian John'; they didn't call him 'Johnny Pops,'" said James Roxburgh, a Canadian who found himself with Johnny in New York City's West Street jail while Johnny awaited his trial.

"They knew who he was and that he ran the locals up here. I didn't really know anything about him, but I walked over to him and said 'I hear you are from Hamilton,' and he said 'Yeah.' Then I said, 'Well, I was born and brought up in Simcoe.' John just looked down at me and said: 'Who the fuck cares?' He was close-mouthed and didn't really want to get to know me. He was anything but a gentleman. I knew some other people that knew him, acquaintances of Carmine Galante, and those guys were class acts in comparison."

Johnny learned to play chess in prison and spent hours poring over a chess board learning the moves and studying strategy. It was a habit he kept long after his time in jail ended.

"The people like myself—just the walking around criminals [in the West Street jail]—respected him because they knew he had some power. To the little guys there, Canadian John was given a lot of space, but to the bigger guys, Canadian John was just another prisoner," Roxburgh said.

Wouldn't you know it? Just when the prospect of prison re-appeared, so did Johnny's tuberculosis.

In jail, Johnny was not a healthy man. *Mafiosi* rarely are. There is a durable tradition in the underworld of bosses who feel fine enough to kill, maim, and cheat, but the moment they are under indictment their frail condition, dodgy hearts, or ailing organs flare up, requiring the court to show tremendous leniency on humanitarian grounds.

Johnny does seem to have had a more convincing case than many, but most involved in the proceedings approached Johnny's health complaint with healthy skepticism. His lung problem was inflamed by the dank conditions and regime of jail house life; he fell ill, coughed up blood, and lost considerable weight. He looked bad enough to prison officials in the infirmary at the Federal House of Detention in New York that they transferred him to the prison hospital in Riker's Island Penitentiary. If Johnny really was sick, he certainly needed better treatment than he was going to get on Riker's Island, and if he was faking it, his ruse worked. His bail was reduced from $250,000 to $75,000, a sum the Papalias managed to muster.

Out on bail in New York City, Johnny prepared for his legal defence by heading straight to a doctor.

15

"The name of the play is *A Funny Thing Happened on the Way to the Forum*," Johnny Papalia told his brother Frank, while the two were in New York City. "This is a stage play. It's very nice. You'll get a lot of laughs there."

While Johnny was out on bail in the United States awaiting his trial for masterminding part of the French Connection, his loyal brother Frank shuttled back and forth between Manhattan and Hamilton for discussions of family affairs. The brothers would eat together at favourite New York restaurants and grab morning coffee at The Stage, a café on Seventh Avenue. One evening after dinner, when Johnny was feeling weary and planned on going straight back to the hotel room to lie down, Frank said he would slip off to catch a movie. Johnny chastised him, saying there was much more to do in New York than see movies; this was the home of Broadway and big stage extravaganzas. He recommended Frank spend his time at the award-winning musical that had just opened at a theatre around the corner. Johnny had already seen the screwball, historical comedy and had enjoyed it.

Johnny and Frank always stayed at the Papalia-preferred accommodations in Manhattan: the Park Sheraton Hotel. The elegant and expensive hotel has a bloody history. It was in the barbershop of the Park Sheraton, on October 25, 1957, that fellow Calabrian, Albert (The Mad Hatter, Lord High Executioner) Anastasia, was gunned down by masked men while having a shave and a haircut.

Despite the idyllic sound of a luxurious hotel, Broadway plays, and fine restaurants, there was a lot on Johnny's mind. He seemed argumentative, was easily agitated, and showed signs of stress. When Frank tried to discuss problems in the family with Johnny, he got no response.

"I feel I could never talk with John when he was nervous and depressed. I could never talk to him. And I would go back home and discuss the matter with my family," Frank later said.

Frank did make arrangements, through the Papalia family's criminal lawyer, Clive Bynoe, to hire a New York City attorney to represent Johnny. At least once Bynoe traveled to New York with Frank to meet with Harris Steinberg, who agreed to take on the high-profile case. Bynoe also arranged for the American legal team's bills to be paid.

Johnny started making regular visits to Dr. Clara Gross, a New York doctor and professor of medicine at Columbia University, for treatment of his TB. He was placed on a regime of isoniazid, known as INH. Johnny visited Dr. Gross eight or nine times, and on four occasions was prescribed mitt fulls of the pills, almost 350 in total. Any visit to Dr. Gross was an occasion to grab more pills. On December 19, 1962, shortly after 1 p.m., Johnny came to her office without an appointment.

"A squirrel bit me in the park," he complained, producing a bloody index finger on his right hand. It was true; Johnny had been feeding peanuts to the squirrels in New York's Central Park when one took some offence at the mobster. Dr. Gross cleaned and disinfected the wound and bandaged him. Johnny took a new prescription for TB medication away with him. After each visit, Johnny would take his prescription to the pharmacy in the same building and have the pharmacist load him up with pills.

"Immediately after taking such drugs I started to notice that I would get a feeling of giddiness for certain stretches of time, sometimes lasting one or two days, and that when the giddiness disappeared I would feel as if I had a hangover," Johnny later told the court. When he complained of this to Dr. Gross, he was given a second drug, para-aminosalicylic plus ascorbic acid, known as PAS-C, to take as well. But Johnny was skeptical. He figured the euphoria and depression was what made INH work on his lungs—and he did feel better—so he skipped the new drug altogether.

The euphoric effects of the drugs helped him cope with his depression, Johnny said. He was worried about his mother. About 10 years earlier, she had suffered a brain hemorrhage, and had recovered. She was now very ill, however, and Johnny was convinced he would never see her again. His fear was misplaced. It was actually his father who would die while Johnny was in jail. Maria Rosa Italiano went on to see her son's eventual release, and died some years later, on July 27, 1970, at the age of 80.

With the capture of Vinnie Mauro, Frank Caruso, and Salvatore Maneri, there were now four men from the original indictment ready to stand trial, three of them the ringleaders of the $150-million heroin trafficking ring. Each defiantly pleaded not guilty.

The escapades in a previous Mafia heroin case, that of Johnny's mob mentor Carmine Galante, were still fresh memories for New Yorkers. Galante and 20 others were arrested after members of the narcotics ring were caught buying 160 kilos of heroin. William Tendy, a New York prosecutor, led the attack on Galante in the courtroom. In *Connections*, a ground-breaking and highly publicized television exposé on the sprawling ties of Canada's *mafiosi*, Tendy spoke of the unusual experience: "Some of the most bizarre incidents that have ever occurred in a courtroom happened. Many of those defendants as a result of their behaviour had to be gagged, shackled. One witness threw the witness chair at the attorney who was helping me try the case, and since that date, every witness chair in that courtroom is bolted to the ground. They had phony suicides, lawyers were beaten up, allegedly by individuals who apparently had nothing to do with the case. A number of potential witnesses were, in fact, brutally murdered . . . after 10 or so months in a courtroom, despite all of these obstacles, we were able to successfully complete this prosecution."

Johnny's heroin case would eventually spark another great court battle, reminiscent in some ways of his Bluestein ordeal. It featured an obstinate and feisty Johnny, trying to get out of paying for something he clearly was a part of. That courtroom confrontation, however, was more than a year away.

On March 4, 1963, Johnny Papalia, then 39 years old, and his three co-accused, gathered in court with their lawyers. Two hours after the jury was selected and was about to be called into the courtroom to hear the prosecutor's opening statements, the court was surprised to hear that all four defendants were prepared to change their plea to guilty. With an eye on the earlier press coverage of Johnny's TB—and with an obviously shrewd mind—prosecutor Gilroy Daly asked the defendants to state for the record how they felt physically, and whether this in any way influenced their decision. Johnny's lawyer, Harris Steinberg, quickly replied that his client "feels badly but knows what he is doing."

Johnny's guilty plea surprised many, especially his brother Frank.

"Before I knew it, John was pleading guilty to something," Frank later said. In the hallway afterwards, an incredulous Frank asked Johnny why he had taken the plea.

"John, what did you do? All along you was telling me you were not guilty. What did you plead guilty for?"

"Well, leave it as it is," Johnny replied. "The lawyer knows what he is doing."

"You pleaded guilty!" Frank continued.

"No, I never pleaded guilty; it was adjourned for a week," was Johnny's reply, Frank said later.

After the guilty plea, Johnny was allowed to remain free on his bail, pending sentencing. The two brothers shared a cab back to their hotel. All the way, Frank said, Johnny was "tinkering with his fingers now and then. He had something on his mind. You just couldn't talk to him."

Back in their room at the Park Sheraton Hotel, Johnny sat in silence. Meanwhile, in Hamilton, news of Johnny's guilty plea was filtering into the city. The news wires carried a story out of New York City, and several Canadian newspapers had reporters on hand for what was thought would be the opening day of a lengthy trial.

Don Johnston, the news director of CHML, a radio station in Johnny's home town, was looking to confirm the story and get some reaction from the source.

"I asked the Park Sheraton switchboard operator for the room of Mr. John Papalia," Johnston said. "The operator rang the room and a man answered. And I said, 'John Papalia?' and he answered, 'Yes.' "

Johnston asked the notorious home town boy if it was true he pleaded guilty. Johnny repeatedly asked him what he was talking about, and Johnston, growing frustrated, read to him the full wire story. Johnny looked up at Frank in astonishment and, pulling his mouth away from the phone, asked Frank if he knew what the reporter was talking about. Frank just shrugged his shoulders.

"Somebody's been pulling your leg," Johnny replied to Johnston. "I don't know anything about it. I must have been drunk. I don't remember nothing. Goodbye and good luck to you. . . ."

Frank left the room, preferring to drink alone in the hotel bar.

"The first thing that I remember after the time I am alleged to have pleaded guilty was being contacted by a news reporter from Hamilton," Johnny later said of the radio interview. "I could not remember anything about taking a plea. However, I do recall having taken rather large doses of this drug . . . I had what might be considered a terrible hangover when I spoke with the news reporter and I [thought] I had been drunk for two days in my hotel room."

The stiff sentencing on March 11, 1963, of Johnny, Mauro, Caruso, and Maneri might have sobered him up. Johnny's health was taken into consideration by Judge Thomas Croake as was his status as an alien who would be deported upon conclusion of his sentence. He was given 10 years on each count to be served concurrently. His three co-accused were given 15 years each and another 5 years for jumping their bail. There was a Canadian contingent in court for Johnny's sentencing: two Hamilton police officers who had chased Johnny for years, Staff Sergeant Albert Welsh and Staff Sergeant Mike Pauloski; two of Johnny's brothers, Frank and Rocco; and a coterie of reporters.

The *Toronto Star*'s coverage was particularly interesting, quoting a variety of opinions on Johnny, now a convicted drug smuggler. The poll provides an interesting insight into Johnny's conflicting personas.

"In the 15 years I've known him, I've never known him to engage in a legal activity," one police officer said. He is "a cop-hater, a primitive. He got where he is through fear. He's hard, hard, hard." Another cop said: "A real deadly man who would crush you without thinking. No regard for anyone or anything, neither for the criminal laws nor the laws of the underworld." Said a Toronto gambler: "A moody person who would just as soon spit in your eye as look at you."

"One of the most gentle and generous men I've ever known. He was always a gentleman, nice spoken and courteous . . . one of the nicest persons I've ever met," said Helen Kublis, a Hamilton resident. A Hamilton lawyer, who knew him as a kid, said Johnny was "the softest touch in the world. He'd travel 500 miles to see a sick friend, or hand you $9 out of his only $10 if you needed money." Clive Bynoe, the Papalias' lawyer, described him as "a gentleman, polite, cordial, and thoughtful of others. I can only speak of him as a client, and that's how I found him."

"He always attended mass," said his older brother Angelo, "donated money to the church and to the Italian community and gave handouts to families in the North End of Hamilton who were down on their luck."

Everybody, it seemed, knew what was happening but Johnny, Frank later insisted in court.

"He didn't believe it. He didn't believe that he was actually sentenced for 10 years. He thought it was an adjournment. He was going to come up, or something else was going to come up in the future." Frank tried to change Johnny's mind, but Johnny told him to butt out.

"Leave it as it is. It's the lawyer's work. It's up to the lawyer. I don't want to hear no more. This don't mean nothing. This don't mean nothing," Johnny said.

When he got back to Canada, Frank reported what had happened to his parents and the rest of the family.

"My parents told me that John must know what he's doing and just leave it as it is," Frank said. "I got so upset at home, they didn't like the way I was talking; and they said 'Leave it the way it is, John knows what he's doing.'"

Frank obeyed. He spoke to no one outside the family—"it was always a family affair," he said—about the circumstances surrounding his brother's sentencing, until he was asked to by Johnny almost a year later. Then he approached his long-time legal counsel, Clive Bynoe.

After several months in the federal penitentiary in Lewisburg, Pennsylvania, Johnny had a change of heart over his legal defence. He fought all the way to the Supreme Court of the United States to have his guilty plea withdrawn and to face a new trial on the narcotics charges. It was rather late in the process, but Johnny was finally in fighting form.

The crux of Johnny's appeal was his claim of mental incompetence when making the plea because he was under the influence of his TB drugs.

"Since he was feeling so elated and in such high spirits from taking this drug, everything, no matter what was said to him, seemed to be correct or all right," said Edward Bobick, Johnny's new lawyer.

On March 19, 1964, the day after Johnny turned 40—and faced turning 50 behind bars—Bobick appealed Johnny's guilty plea. Since it was difficult to say with certainty what his client's mental state had been more than a year earlier, Bobick argued, the defendant's rights were best protected by allowing him to withdraw his plea.

"For the two years prior to taking his plea of guilty," Frank said in a sworn affidavit, "my brother had always insisted to me that he was innocent, and I cannot comprehend his pleading guilty to charges which might result in imprisonment for him . . . This is especially so since he knew that if this would happen he would never again see his mother, who was gravely ill."

Johnny did not come to his senses until he was imprisoned and stopped taking his medication, he claimed. But even then he did not contact his lawyer for almost a year. Frank, then living on Wellwood

Street in Hamilton and saying he was a real estate manager, took the stand to defend his brother. He said there "was a big difference" in the way his brother looked between the time he was first jailed and the time his case finally went to court.

"When John was out on bail his appearance, and I seen John on the street, knowing John as I do, as his brother back home . . . his difference in his appearance was he was always twiddling with his fingers. He was nervous. He was always scratching his head. He was upset. His tie was always upset. He was always moving his tie with his fingers. He was always doing something with his fingers . . . Every time I would discuss something with John he would get emotional. He was always upset about something. He was very nervous."

Dr. Gross testified that the drugs could have the effects Johnny claimed, but admitted that in the several thousand other patients she had administered the drug to, she had never seen a psychiatric disturbance result from standard doses, such as the ones she was giving to Johnny. She also admitted that her statements in her files about Johnny being depressed were often accompanied by a question mark.

"I put in front of it a question mark because you cannot always tell from one time or two times whether a patient is depressed," she said.

She also denied that Johnny had complained to her about feeling "giddy" from the drugs, despite his swearing to that in his affidavit, and said he had not complained to her about itching.

Two other doctors were called to the stand by Johnny's lawyers, both citing knowledge of the drug he was on and its side effects, and concluding it was possible that Johnny was telling the truth about his memory lapses and mental disturbances. But even then, the odds seemed long. Neither doctor had directly examined Johnny, a point not missed by the state attorneys fighting to deny Johnny's request.

Johnny took the stand and, under questioning by Bobick, got right down to business.

"Are you guilty of any crime of which you are now doing time?" Bobick asked as his opening question.

"No, sir," came Johnny's reply.

Under cross-examination, Johnny and Martin R. Gold, an assistant

U.S. attorney in Robert M. Morgenthau's office, sparred acrimoniously. The cross-examination spiraled. The judge interceded, saying it was all repetitive. At one point in their testy exchange, Gold had to be warned by the judge not to argue with the witness. At another, when Johnny was scolded for dodging a question, he turned to the judge and said: "Your Honour, I'm not familiar with the rules." The judge assumed his ethnicity played a role.

"You don't understand English?" the judge asked.

"I'm ignorant to the question. I do understand English perfectly," Johnny replied. Well, he may have overstated his expertise. Later in the cross-examination, Gold was having trouble pinning down exactly when Johnny met with his lawyer.

"Subsequent to that date did you speak with Mr. Steinberg?" Gold asked him.

"I don't know what 'subsequent' means," Johnny replied. Later Gold asked how many times he discussed his case with his lawyer:

Johnny: I don't remember how many occasions.

Gold: Approximately how many occasions?

Johnny: I have no idea.

Gold: Did you go more than 20 times?

Johnny: I couldn't tell you.

Gold: Did you go less than once?

Johnny: I wouldn't know; I don't remember.

Gold: Did you go at all?

Johnny: I think I did; I am not sure.

Gold: You are not sure that you ever went to the offices of Mr. Steinberg between those dates?

Johnny: Mr. Steinberg or Mr. Kasenof [Steinberg's assistant]?

Gold: The offices of Mr. Steinberg and Mr. Kasenof are the same or were the same between those dates, is that not correct?

Johnny: I don't know.

Gold: They were in the same building, isn't that so?

Johnny: I don't know.

Gold: Do you recall going to visit either one of them?

Johnny: I believe I went to see Mr. Steinberg. . . .

Gold: Did you discuss the facts of this case with them . . . ?

Johnny: He's my lawyer . . . What would he come for, to see if I'm a good looking guy or something? What, are you, kidding . . . ?

Gold: Do you recall speaking with Mr. Steinberg during March of 1963?

Johnny: No.

Gold: Do you recall anything that happened during February of 1963?

Johnny: In regards to what?

Gold: Do you have any recollection of any portion of your life during that period?

Johnny: 1963?

Gold: February.

Johnny: February? I remember a few things . . .

After two-and-a-half hours of testimony, the judge was clearly unimpressed with Johnny's evidence.

The government barely presented a rebuttal. Gold said simply, "None of the side effects claimed by Papalia actually occurred; he knew precisely what he was doing at all times when he pleaded guilty and was sentenced." He moved to dismiss the motion on the grounds that the burden of proof had not been met by Johnny's lawyers.

Judge Lloyd F. MacMahon immediately agreed, and was equally terse when he ruled: "The case is a tissue of lies from A to Z."

Johnny's lawyer jumped up. "Your Honour, is that comment on the record?"

"Yes," said Judge MacMahon.

Undeterred by the summary dismissal, Johnny appealed to the Second Circuit U.S. Court of Appeals and was refused, and, finally to the Supreme Court, before the motion died on October 12, 1964, leaving Johnny in prison.

Everyone was asking the same question: If Johnny was so messed up and he and his brother and others knew it, then why did they not try to do anything about it for close to a year? Why did Frank not talk to Johnny's lawyer about it? Presumably, Johnny would be champing at the bit to get out of the "big house" if he really thought there had been such a serious miscarriage of justice.

"The sole evidence of the appellant's alleged incompetency at the time of his plea and sentence came from the testimony of the appellant and his brother, Frank," summed up the attorneys in Robert Morgenthau's office.

Credibility was an issue.

16

"**I**s it because of my name, my last name?"

Frank Papalia was standing at the side of the road in a well-appointed Hamilton neighbourhood, staring into the eyes of a uniformed police constable. He was angry. It was close to 2 a.m. in the summer of 1979, and the police cruiser's flashing lights reflected off Frank's shiny Cadillac, which had just been pulled over by Constable John Harris.

"You're only stopping me because of who I am and the family name," Frank complained.

In many ways, Frank was right. It was no accident or random check that brought him to the side of the road with a police car behind him. It was part of a concerted effort—one step in a plan concocted earlier that summer by members of a special police unit targeting organized crime.

Frank's older brother Johnny was in jail. Despite the absence of the acknowledged Mafia chieftain, police attention focused on Frank, whom officers suspected was the head of the family when Johnny was away. Members of the Papalia family were always eyed suspiciously by law enforcement officers as they watched all of Johnny's brothers become involved, in some capacity, in illicit activity.

Johnny spent far more time with his three younger brothers, Dominic, Frank, and Rocco, than he did with his older half-brothers, Angelo and Joseph. He was, however, generous to them all.

"Angelo was ostracized," a retired police officer said of the eldest brother. "He was looked after but wasn't really involved." Despite early brushes with the law in the family's gambling joints, both Angelo and Joseph worked as labourers for Hamilton companies such as Gartshore-Thomson Pipe and Foundry, Pigott Construction, and Canada Iron. They also both died in the same year, 1983—Angelo on May 21 and Joseph on Christmas Eve.

The lives of Johnny's younger brothers seemed to revolve, to a great degree, around their imposing older brother.

"John was the boss," said a former associate of the Papalias. When it came to the business side of the Papalias' affairs, "nothing went down without him knowing. The impression I got was everyone answered to Frank and then Frank would answer to John."

Dominic was five years younger than Johnny, and a partner with him in early ventures.[1] In 1952, he started driving a taxi for Crown Cabs in Hamilton, and in just a few years he was co-owner of the taxi firm, with Johnny peripherally involved at the company's James Street North office. The cabs were used as much as a front for illicit activity as for ferrying passengers, and probably helped in distributing Sylvestro's heroin and in Johnny's fledgling extortion and bookmaking activities.

Dominic was an affable man with prematurely white hair and a chunky build. At the Town Manor hotel bar, one of his regular drinking spots, he would even share a drink with cops who knew him from years of chasing Johnny. That fraternization abruptly ended, however, when his brothers heard of it. One day the officers sat down and ordered a drink for Dominic. He got up to leave, apologized, but said firmly: "I just can't."

"Dominic was strictly a watchdog," said a retired police officer. "He had a booze problem. They put Dominic in the house next door [to the Railway Street office] to keep watch over it. His house was the meeting spot for people; when something was going down they would

---

1 There is some confusion over the correct spelling of Dominic's first name. His death notice reads "Domenic," but his tombstone, "Dominic." I ran with the 'i' spelling, because that one, after all, is carved in stone.

meet up at Dominic's, but because of his drinking, they had to be a little careful with what they told him."

Dominic would later travel to Mexico to launder some of Johnny's proceeds of crime. On a visit there in February 1988, he was in a serious car crash.

"As far as I can put it together," Dominic's son, Tony, said shortly after the accident, "he was riding in the Jeep with three other people. The Jeep was cut off by another vehicle and hit the side of the road and rolled over." Dominic was trapped under the Jeep and badly injured. After days in a Mexican hospital, he was flown aboard a private jet to Hamilton, where he was admitted into St. Joseph's Hospital. On April 6, he died of his injuries. His brother's death hit Johnny hard, and the mobster worked to make Dominic's widow and children as comfortable as he could. He acted as a father to Dominic's children, always making time for them—whatever else he was involved with at the time—and ensuring Dominic's family always had a home on Railway Street.

Frank was less flamboyant than Dominic, and Johnny gravitated to him as a steady hand to run the family's businesses. Six years younger than Johnny, Frank was prepared to quietly listen and glumly do as he was told. He was also looked to for leadership when Johnny was in jail. Like Dominic, Frank had an early business venture—as Frank The Hatter, he established a hat shop in 1954, right next to the Crown Cabs office. Over the years, he has been a proprietor of many companies operating out of 20 Railway Street.

"Frank was like his partner, Rocco was like his gofer," said an old family friend. "Frank was as miserable as John, maybe more so because he worked at it."

Frank has obsessive-compulsive tendencies, showing themselves through his fierce aversion to germs and obsession with cleanliness. He would tell a woman to shower before he would even contemplate sex, ask dinner companions not to sneeze, cover his furniture in plastic, and repeatedly take showers. It was one of the motivating factors in his fleeing the industrial area of his birth for the cleaner environs of the Hamilton Mountain. Today, he remains polite, quiet, and often glum. When police were searching his home during one of his legal problems, an officer pointed out that his Christmas lights were sagging into a puddle of water, which could be dangerous. Frank politely thanked the officer for bringing it to his attention, and sat placidly while police went about their work.

Rocco was the baby of the family, a full 11 years younger than Johnny. Perhaps because Johnny and Frank did most of the important work, he was known more for his sense of humour, charm, and generous nature. Old newspaper articles report that, at the age of 18, Rocco walked into a Hamilton police station with a lawyer to tell officers that an 18-year-old woman, who had been a passenger in his car, was now dead. The body of Shirley Telfer was found on a railway track near Dundas. The young woman had arrived in Hamilton just two days earlier and had been a passenger in a car with Rocco and two family friends, Joseph and Guiseppe Fazzari. The trio were originally held as material witnesses to the girl's death and were later charged with criminal negligence causing death. One of the lawyers representing the trio was Harold Bordonaro. They claimed the girl jumped out of the car and ran into the path of the fast-moving C.N.R. express train.[2]

"Rocco was a sweetheart. He had no right being in the business. Rocco said, had his circumstances been different, he wouldn't have been in that position," said a long-time friend. Rocco, like Frank, moved with his family to the newer, larger homes on Hamilton Mountain, where neighbours enjoyed watching his Victoria Day fireworks displays and local children made sure to visit him on Halloween for the best candy giveaways in the area.

Rocco often drove Johnny about, acting as chauffeur. He seemed to accept his role with a shrug, and enjoyed the life of relative leisure that being Johnny's brother could bring. Rocco's day-to-day schedule was hardly a taxing one. He started his day late, around 11:30 a.m., and rather than head to an office would often go fishing or play a round of golf. The recreational time also often doubled as an opportunity to talk business with those accompanying him. By early afternoon he

2 Some members of the Fazzari family remain close to the Papalias and the Musitanos to this day.

would appear at the Railway Street office and stay for a few hours, then head to meetings in certain bars and restaurants around Hamilton or Toronto.

"I never saw them actually work," said a former girlfriend of Frank's and Rocco's. "They had people that did that for them. They were raised as the Papalias. Their oldest brother [Johnny] set the rules, and they just went along."

"John was very generous to his family," said a family associate. "He was very generous to his brothers. John would pick up most of the bills. I can never remember John being anywhere that he didn't pick up the bill. He either picked it up or would say to Rocco—never to Frank—'Rocco, pick up the bill.'"

Although all the brothers were loving and loyal to Johnny, their relationships with each other at times seemed strained. Frank would often be seen with Bruno Monaco, a long-time family business partner and a man whom police regarded as the family's *consigliere*; Rocco would be seen with Monaco, but rarely would Frank and Rocco be seen together, apart from business meetings and family gatherings, unless Monaco or another associate was with them. Customers of the Papalias' vending business know Monaco as the friendly, neatly dressed manager who is quick to respond to their business needs. One client remembers him most for the case of Canadian Club whiskey he brought to the arcade's office each Christmas and for sometimes having a large man, who was never properly introduced, stand silently behind him during business meetings.

Frank, Rocco, and Monaco would frequently eat together in restaurants in Hamilton, Burlington, and Oakville. They particularly enjoyed the food at Switzer's Deli in Hamilton's Westdale neighbourhood, Clancy's in Burlington, and the Aquarium in central Hamilton. A Cadillac would pull up in front of a restaurant or bar, and Frank and Monaco would hop out and head inside. Frank might stop to make a phone call at a pay phone along the way. Rocco would park the car and join them.

Police showed an interest in each of the brothers. The police code name for Frank was "Fredericton"; Rocco's was "Rochester." Getting nearly equal attention from police, Monaco was code-named "Michigan." It was part of the police plan, called Operation Fredericton, that led to Frank being pulled to the side of the road in the wee hours of the morning in the summer of 1979, answering police questions about whether he had been drinking.

The goal of the operation was to plant a bug—an electronic listening device—in Frank's Cadillac, because police believed conversations dealing with criminal activity were taking place inside. Police had twice before tried to bug the car, but failed. This time, their idea was to stop Frank's car, demand a breath sample to test for alcohol use, and hope he would refuse—which was a pretty good bet. Then the officer could arrest Frank and have his car towed away by police. If that happened, the car was destined not for the privately owned, commercial car lot where impounded vehicles were usually taken, but for Hamilton's central police station where a team of specially trained RCMP technicians would be waiting.

On the day of the operation, Frank's Cadillac was put under surveillance early in the morning. That night, officers watched Frank enter the Gold Key Club, an exclusive nightclub and piano lounge opened in 1975 and owned—on paper—by Papalia hanger-on Harry Apigian and Johnny's brother-in-law Domenic Pugliese. Apigian also owned Trade Wind Travel, a travel agency a dozen or so blocks west of the club, and was loyal to the family, despite being treated poorly. Called "Coke Bottle" by many because of his thick glasses, he later got into serious trouble when arrested in 1992 after a multimillion-dollar marijuana pipeline was smashed.

The Gold Key Club, inside a large, converted house on Wentworth Street South, at the corner of Main Street East, was the Papalias' club, and it attracted a diverse clientele, from street-smart rounders to some of the city's élite. Members included career criminals, defence lawyers, at least one judge, and Papalia associates Art Tartaglia, Domenic Longo, Louie Nickiluk, and millionaire Oakville businessman George Clinton Duke. Also mingling at the club were citizens not involved in crime but trusted to not blab to police. Members were given a plastic, machine-readable membership card that registered who came into the club. All non-members were screened before signing in, and entry to the club was tightly controlled by hostesses watching the doors.

Frank left his club at around 1:30 a.m. and headed west. By the time he was stopped by police, an officer said, Frank's car had weaved up Queen Street and had passed through a red light. Frank was asked to walk in a straight line and was told he looked inebriated. At first he agreed to provide a breath sample, but then declined. Frank asked the constable to explain what would happen with the breath test. He later claimed the officer said that if his reading showed he had more than the legal limit of alcohol in his system, he would be charged, and if the reading showed less than the legal limit, he would still be charged.

"You mean if I blow over I'm charged and if I blow under I'm charged?" Frank said to him. "I'm damned if I do and I'm damned if I don't."

Frank assessed the situation perfectly. He was charged with impaired driving and refusal to give a breath sample, and put in the back of a police cruiser. Within two minutes of his being pulled over, a tow truck was already at the scene to take his car. While Frank was phoning lawyer Michael Baker, his Cadillac was being worked on by the RCMP.

It was not the only sneaky plot the police employed. In the middle of the night, officers picked the locks and circumvented the alarms at 20 Railway Street and spent more than two hours wiring the place for sound. Bugs were also placed at two other businesses. Monaco's car, while it was parked at Toronto's Pearson International Airport, was broken into and bugged. In total, 13 wiretaps were running, each hooked up to two tape recorders.

Court authorization to allow the wiretaps came on June 21, 1979, after RCMP Corporal James Euale swore out allegations—that would later be called into question by the court—of a criminal organization running an extensive gambling and loan-sharking operation where repayments, with exorbitant rates of interest, were enforced by threats and actual violence.

At Frank's 1981 trial, defence counsel Ross MacKay was clearly agitated. Judge Michael Cloney demanded he stop his "histrionics" and stop conducting his cross-examination like a "Shakespearean drama." MacKay contended the drinking and driving charges were bogus and only part of a larger police plan to plant the bug. Crown Attorney Dean Paquette did not dispute the police operation, but argued that it did not take away from the strength of the evidence for the charges. The judge split the difference: guilty of refusing to take a breath test, not guilty of driving while intoxicated. Frank was fined $150 and forced to surrender his driver's licence for three months.

While the driving charge seems petty in the big scheme of the fight against organized crime, Ken Robertson, the recently retired chief of the Hamilton police, who was a young sergeant at the time and involved in the car bug sting, later cooed about the operation. He said it showed that gangsters were not invincible.

"Their rise to prominence was partly because of the community putting them on a pedestal and because the police didn't take enough action against them as they were coming up from being street hoodlums to become organized crime figures," said Robertson. "When Frank Papalia was arrested for drunk driving, and convicted, that was one of the things that caused some of the most significant criticism against that organization. They had a reputation that they controlled the police and controlled the judges and it was totally fictitious and a myth. And, of course, here was the guy who supposedly had everyone in his pocket, and he couldn't even drive his own car because he had his licence suspended. That kind of put it into perspective."

The bug in the car would also later lead to one of the most embarrassing incidents to hit the Papalia family—even without Johnny there to act as a lightning rod. At about the same time as Frank ran into driving trouble, the family found itself at the centre of two very different scandals—one, a low-brow sexual indiscretion, and the other, an allegation of a large, sophisticated fraud. First, the sex woes.

Just as things were starting to heat up for the mob in Ontario in the 1960s, the Papalia family's sex life was likewise starting to sizzle—or what passed for sizzle in the bedrooms of these straight-laced, old-school *mafiosi*.

In 1962, while Johnny was awaiting trial in the French Connection case, Shirley Ryce, an attractive Hamilton housewife, first met the mob. How the bedroom antics and sexual mores of the Papalia family came to be a matter of public record is a story in itself, one that comes from police notes, court records, and the tell-all words of Ryce herself, who dropped the secrecy from her nearly two decades as a mob mistress, first on television and then in a popular book.[3] Ryce caused the family much more than embarrassment.

Ryce, a wife and mother, started moving in mob circles when she had an affair with Donny Buckle, a well-known Hamilton rounder. Through Buckle, she met Rocco Papalia, and by her third date with him, in his brother Dominic's apartment, they became lovers. Ryce was 23; Rocco, 27. As James Dubro documents in *Mob Mistress*, his book on Ryce and her dalliances with the Papalia clan, Rocco "was following the conservative, Italian-mob convention that said it was perfectly all right to have a mistress, as long as you did not flaunt her in front of your family or have her in your home. The mistress was to be part of Papalia's outside social life with the mob family, not a part of his personal family life at home." Rocco's position within the underworld impressed Ryce. One night she and a girlfriend were unable to get into a popular bar at the Royal Connaught Hotel because it was filled to capacity. She called Rocco, who made a brief appearance, and two patrons quickly and conveniently left, making room for Ryce and her friend.

3 In 1986, CBC-TV's *the fifth estate* first aired Ryce's story in a segment entitled "Mistress to the Mob." That was followed up two years later by *Mob Mistress: How a Canadian Housewife Became a Mafia Playgirl*, by James Dubro.

"I was 23 years old and all of a sudden there I was with people waiting on me and taking care of me," Ryce said. "Being Rocco's best girl
opened doors for me. I never had to wait for a drink. Everywhere I
went I was treated as somebody special. I loved it. Rocco projected
power and over the years some of it rubbed off on me . . . You need
help? They got it for you. You know you didn't have to give them anything back. They were generous that way. Once you became their
friend and earned their respect, and you were loyal to them, you didn't
have to worry . . . There was no limit on what they spent. Money was
no object. They spent money like water."

In mid-1972, Rocco passed Ryce over to his older brother Frank.

"Frank Papalia also introduced me to friends of his," Ryce said.
"Usually he was setting me up to 'entertain' them." It was a role she
became familiar with, and she was sometimes given $100 and told to
entertain a friend or ally of the Papalias, she said. Her instructions
meant dinner, drinks—and a romp in the sack if the man was still
able after a night of hard drinking. For the *mafiosi*, oral sex was
strictly taboo.

Police interest in Ryce was not one of voyeuristic fantasies. On September 5, 1979, she became the focal point of a large police investigation.

Frank Papalia was heard, through the bug planted in his car, discussing
with his Toronto lawyer the procuring of a woman for the lawyer to
have sex with. Although he may have felt lucky at the time, the unfortunate recipient of Frank's largesse was long-time Papalia criminal
lawyer Clive Bynoe, a prominent and respected bencher with the Law
Society of Upper Canada. Bynoe had represented the family on several
occasions, including working on Johnny's assault charge for beating
Maxie Bluestein and arranging for Johnny's legal team in New York for
his French Connection defence. A room was arranged for the tryst at
the Hamilton Holiday Inn by Apigian, through his travel agency.

Police secretly listened in as Frank railed against the immorality of
young people—"They all come down on Railway Street, these kids . . .
They're all smoking grass on your lawn and everything"—and then

watched as he handed Shirley Ryce a $100 bill and the number of the hotel room where Bynoe was waiting. Police also got a good look at the couple by having one officer dress as a waiter to deliver drinks and a cheese tray the couple had ordered from room service.

In April 1980, Bynoe was identified by police as the "john," and asked to come to OPP headquarters for a chat. He asked what it was about and was told he would find out when he got to the meeting. A few minutes later, lawyer David Humphrey phoned the OPP, asking what they wanted to speak with Bynoe about.

"Are you his lawyer?" an OPP officer asked. "I guess so," came the reply. "Then why don't you come in with him." Bynoe shamefacedly admitted to police his part in the sexual encounter. A month later, officers identified Ryce. During her interview with police, she admitted she was paid $100 by Frank to provide sexual favours to Bynoe. Bizarrely, she agreed to cooperate with police and even agreed to be wired up with a tape recorder inside her purse.

After her talk with the cops, loyal Papalia lieutenant Steve Koaches picked Ryce up for a chat. The conversation was recorded, and Koaches was heard chastising her for talking to police. He told her to recant her statement and then go away for a while, all expenses paid, plus $100 a week. The next day Koaches took Ryce to see the Papalia family's Hamilton lawyer, Michael Baker, who was on retainer. The conversation was again secretly recorded by Ryce. Koaches told Baker there was no sex, Frank did not pay her, and Ryce's statement to the cops was made in a state of shock. Ryce said that was a lie. Baker said he was in a conflict of interest because he represented the Papalias, and made an appointment for the pair to see another lawyer that night. Koaches went early and told the new lawyer the same story he had tried to peddle to Baker. When Ryce arrived she stuck to her version of events, and was advised to keep telling the truth. A visit to a third lawyer brought similar results.

Koaches was not happy, and when his insistence grew, accompanied by unexpected visits to her apartment, Ryce asked for—and received—police protection.

With Ryce's evidence and Bynoe's admission, Frank was charged with procuring a prostitute, which gravely offended his stern sense of morality; the charge made him out to be a pimp. Frank, Koaches, and their associate and Gold Key Club regular Alfonso (Al) Franco, were charged with obstructing justice and conspiring to obstruct justice. (The charges against Franco were later dropped.) At their bail hearing, Frank told the court he was "a businessman" working out of a Railway Street address that was "the family estate." He said he owned one-seventh of the property. His business interests, he said, had included Monarch Vending, A-1 Fibrequeen Home and Industrial Insulation Co. Ltd., and Queen-York Motors, a Hamilton car lot. His sister Antoniette Pugliese posted a $25,000 surety for his bail. Koaches said he had worked for Frank at each of those businesses and was now working on the docks as a stevedore.

On June 8, 1981, the trial began. Dean Paquette represented the Crown; Ross MacKay, Frank; and Brian Jones, Koaches. Frank and Koaches both pleaded guilty to obstructing justice, and in return, charges against Frank of procuring a prostitute were withdrawn. Koaches's criminal record, entered as Exhibit #1, was three pages long, starting with an auto theft conviction in 1943 when he was just 17 years old. In a bid for leniency, MacKay pointed out Frank was 50 years old, separated from his wife, and had an 11-year-old daughter to worry about. Frank was fined $2,000; Koaches was jailed for four months.

Judge Michael Cloney was very pointed in his worries over Ryce's safety. Frank and Koaches, he said, "should pray every night before they go to bed that this girl doesn't stumble over a cobblestone and break a leg or smash her nose up against a telephone pole or something like that in the course of idle walking."

"They do these things for a reason," a veteran police officer said of the Papalias' shenanigans with Bynoe. "They do it for the future. They're setting people up to be compromised. Here is a Law Society bencher, he's likely going to become a judge, or if he goes into politics, he'll become the attorney general. They are always looking to compromise people who might help them, even if it is years and years down the road."

Frank Papalia's other legal hassles were not as salacious, but charges stemming from police allegations of defrauding the government were potentially more serious.

This trouble also started in the summer of 1979, when police launched an investigation into an alleged fraud involving members of the Papalia family, their associates, and the Canadian Home Insulation Program. Rocco Papalia described the government's program this way: "It's like someone throwing a whole bunch of money on the floor and you have so many seconds to pick it up." The allegation was that Papalia's company, A-1 Fibrequeen Home and Industrial Insulation Co., of 20 Railway Street, was charging the government for more foam insulation than it was really pushing into people's attics under the government assistance program to encourage better insulation of homes. Police suspicions were piqued when Johnny's old friend, Frank Marchildon, and Koaches visited Sam Shirose, an associate of the late Toronto Mafia boss Paul Volpe. Volpe was notorious for pulling swindles in construction. A long-time Papalia associate and construction contractor, Vic Mancini, wrote a qualifying examination to obtain a licence for the company to install the insulation. Also working with Fibrequeen were Frank, Rocco, Monaco, Koaches, Ed Fisher, who was a Hamilton alderman, Leo Cavasin, who was a disbarred lawyer, and Marchildon.

At the end of November 1979, 15 police officers raided various homes and businesses, carting away files and arresting Frank, Rocco, Koaches, Monaco, Fisher, and Cavasin. All were charged with conspiracy to defraud the federal government. Police alleged that over five months the government was short-changed more than $50,000.

The case was unusual right from the start. The involvement of the family of a notorious Hamilton mobster with a city alderman and a former lawyer caused a sensation in the press. And a rarely used legal move—a preferred indictment signed by Ontario Attorney General Roy McMurtry—did away with a scheduled preliminary hearing, sending the case straight to trial. The hope for swift justice dissipated, however, as the case bogged down in a legal quagmire. The defence questioned the validity of wiretap evidence gathered by police from bugs in Frank's and

Monaco's car. After 10 weeks in late 1981 and early 1982, the trial was halted when Ken Robertson, then a staff sergeant, said during testimony that there were ongoing police investigations of some of the defendants.

"This trial seems to have been doomed from the beginning," Judge Thomas Quinlan said in court when declaring a mistrial. A second trial the next year saw all six of the accused acquitted. The Crown successfully appealed that verdict and a retrial was ordered, but in October 1990, more than 11 years after the police raids, the charges were withdrawn. Crown Attorney David Carr said a recent court ruling that disallowed the recorded wiretap evidence "left the Crown with very little evidence."

In throwing out the wiretaps, Justice David Watt said the police allegations were "more the product of over-active imagination and speculation than it is rooted in the sources identified." He went on to call the police action "a reckless disregard for the truth." Ironically, given the nature of the allegations, Justice Watt said the officers were approaching "outright fraud," in the sworn affidavits used to obtain the wiretaps.[4]

The news came too late for Koaches. He had missed several of his court appearances because of advancing cancer, and the career criminal, who once said he would give his life for Frank, died in August 1990. His final years were not peaceful ones, his painful illness aside. His arrest in the insulation fraud came the same year he was released from Kingston Penitentiary after serving an eight-year sentence for bank robbery, and he was a spokesman in the violent dispute over control of union work on Hamilton's docks.

Docks have always been important to the mob. They are where shipments of all sorts come in, and in an industrial city such as Hamilton, controlling the docks meant a degree of control over a huge patch of the city's economic activity. In cities such as New York, the mob held a notorious iron grip on the dockworkers—the stevedores who

4 Frank Papalia and Bruno Monaco sued police for "malicious prosecution, negligence, and false imprisonment." The lawsuit was mysteriously settled out of court some years later. One source said the wiretap evidence that was deemed inadmissible in their criminal case could surface again—publicly—in any civil case stemming from the arrests, giving Frank, as well as police, a reason to let the case go away quietly.

load and unload cargo—and gave final say on who got work and who did not, what ships got unloaded and how fast, and what secret contraband was brought ashore and what was dumped overboard. Koaches was a long-time member of the International Longshoreman's Association, and took up the cause of 21 dockworkers fighting a lifetime ban from the union. In Hamilton, the dispute got nasty, sparking numerous firebombings, several beatings, and at least one murder—the 1989 beating death of a burly dockworker named Jimmy Smith. In the end, the banned workers felt the association with the Mafia that came with Koaches was not helping their cause.

Johnny was not the only Papalia dealing drugs and achieving underworld glory for his family name. The Papalia clan remains one of prominence and power in Italy and elsewhere. When Tony Papalia emigrated to Canada, he left behind the thriving family that had first initiated him into the ways of the *Picciotteria*. As Johnny went on to underworld prominence, so too did certain of his kin who remained behind.

According to Italian magistrates, Domenico Papalia, Johnny's first cousin, was a boss of the *'Ndrangheta* throughout the 1980s. He was involved in the planning of at least five kidnappings, using the home of his sister Marianna Papalia. Domenico and Johnny shared many qualities—among them ruthlessness, power, and a craving for respect. Domenico, however, had something Johnny could never quite muster in his life: great influence in very high places.

Domenico was convicted of murdering rival mobster Antonio D'Agostino, and sentenced to life in prison. It was quite a blow to the family, but, like Johnny, he did not give up fighting for his freedom. Domenico, however, met with far greater success than did his Canadian cousin; thanks to his strong connections to respectable society, including court magistrates and other officials, he was able to obtain a judicial review of his case. He was the first Mafia boss ever to be granted the rarely exercised reversal of a conviction, and it was a striking display of his power and influence. Even the judge at Domenico's preliminary hearing, Ferdinando Imposimato, who is now an Italian senator, had a shocking change of heart on the evidence against Domenico. At the trial he was a strong advocate for seeing Domenico imprisoned; afterwards, however, he went on television pronouncing that there was insufficient evidence to convict him. It is widely believed in Italy that the judge received a credible threat from the Papalia clan for his role in their boss's conviction.

L'Inserto di Calabria, a newspaper in the Calabrian province of Cosenza, also took up Domenico's cause, and started agitating for his release. A committee was established to free him, claiming an injustice akin to the imprisonment of the legendary *Picciotteria* founder Giuseppe Musolino. Luciano Violante, the former head of Italy's parliamentary anti-Mafia committee and now speaker of the Italian equivalent of the House of Commons, said Domenico Papalia's case destroyed the view that the Calabrian Mafia was a second-rate power within the underworld.

"Only one boss obtained a review of his trial," Violante said, "a boss of the *'Ndrangheta.*"

In the 1970s, a branch of the Papalia clan relocated from their family home in Platì to the area surrounding Milan. There they formed a stronghold in the city of Buccinasco. According to informer Saverio Morabito, who testified before magistrates in 1988, two more of Johnny's first cousins, Antonio and Rocco Papalia, along with Pasquale Violi, used ransom money from kidnappings in Calabria to buy large shipments of drugs for export. The Papalias and Violi were well positioned for such a scheme, with their rich contacts in the south and their new base of operations in northern Italy. Police thought so too, and the trio was arrested in Operation Nord-Sud. In 1993, using the state's "proceeds of crime" legislation, authorities seized a house, factory, land, cars, and businesses, all belonging to Antonio and Rocco Papalia, worth more than $40 million. A year later, a report of the *Direzione Investigativa Anti-Mafia,* an Italian police service akin to the FBI in the U.S., named the Papalia group as one of the most powerful Mafia organizations in the country. According to Italian police over the years, Papalia had been a leading *'Ndrangheta* family in the Calabrian towns of Sinopoli, Platì, and Delianova.

Johnny did not have the kind of direct contact with his cousins abroad that he might have liked; he was incapable of visiting Italy. Just five weeks after Johnny's sentencing in the United States in the French Connection case—an investigation aided by Italian authorities—he had a charge of Mafia association and trading in narcotics registered against him in his father's homeland. Johnny was sentenced, *in absentia*, to 10 years, a sentence he would only face if he set foot in Italy. Canadian authorities made note of the conviction, but the government was unwilling to extradite a Canadian citizen to face a charge that did not exist in Canada's *Criminal Code*.

When Johnny's father left Italy for Canada, other relatives emigrated to Australia. Today, there is a branch of the "Platì Mafia" in Griffith, New South Wales, a small village in the desert north of Melbourne.

The Australian branch was involved in converting money from Mafia kidnappings into drugs; this time, rather than running north-to-south across Italy, the scheme ran west-to-east between nations. From Platì to Griffith, friends and relatives wired large amounts of cash to be invested in Australia's burgeoning marijuana industry. After trafficking the pot on and off the mainland, the substantial profit on the investment—estimated at $60 million—was sent back to Italy, where it was invested in restaurants, hotels, and other tourist ventures throughout Calabria. It was a simple arrangement, but one that eventually raised the suspicions of police who watched supposedly poor retirees constantly calling and transferring money like professional money-market managers.

Members of the Mafia in Australia have been implicated in—but not convicted of—high-profile murders. Two of the country's most scandalous slayings have been blamed on the Platì Mafia. Donald MacKay was a crusading politician from Griffith who called for a crackdown on organized crime and drug trafficking. He led the Sydney Drug Squad to an enormous marijuana plantation just south of Griffith, where officers seized $80-million worth of pot. That was in 1975. Less than two years later, he received an anonymous telephone call from a man purporting to have crucial information to pass on to him. He went to meet the caller, and promptly disappeared. Two years after his presumed slaying, the investigation concluded it had been carried out on the orders of the Platì *mafiosi* in Griffith.

Colin Winchester, assistant commissioner of the federal police, was killed in January 1989, in Canberra, the nation's capital. Winchester was an effective cop, crushing both organized crime's gambling dens and marijuana plantations linked to the Platì *mafiosi*. Although a former civil servant was convicted of the crime in 1995—a conviction currently under appeal—several police reports suggest the root cause of the murder was the Platì *mafiosi*.

Although the place of the Papalia clan in the hierarchy of Australia's Platì Mafia is unknown, in September 1989, in Sydney, Filippo Papalia, and in May 1987, in Victoria, Domenico Papalia were slain in apparent Mafia disputes.

Other members of the Papalia clan also helped prove that the Mafia can be hazardous to your health.

Angelo Macrì was a mobster based in Delianova known to most residents as "The King of Aspromonte," a nickname suggesting he was a man not to mess with. In 1951, that appears to have been a message ignored by Francesco Papalia, 47, a relative of Johnny's who remained in their Delianova homeland. Francesco is thought to have tipped police off to the whereabouts of Macrì's brother, Giovanni, who was a wanted man. When police arrived at Giovanni's hideout to arrest him, there was a shootout in which the King of Aspromonte's brother was killed rather spectacularly.

Whether Francesco was the source of the tip or not, the elder Macrì certainly placed the blame directly on his head and decreed revenge was necessary, personal—and urgent.

Francesco Papalia was having dinner outside with friends when Angelo Macrì arrived. Francesco invited him to join them, an offer Macrì declined, reportedly saying: "No, no, please, finish your dinner. I can wait." When the meal was done Francesco went to see what Macrì wanted. The answer came not in words—Francesco was mercilessly killed on the spot. Macrì then turned to the terrified witnesses and said: "I am sorry if I disturbed your dinner, but I did what had to be done and I couldn't wait any longer."

17

Cigarette machines, coffee machines, pinball machines, video arcade games, pool tables—if you can put a coin in it, chances are the Papalias have tried to get a piece of it. It is whispered that a portion of every dollar stuffed into every pay-to-play pool table in the cities from Niagara Falls through Hamilton and Burlington to Oakville goes to the Papalias.

In the vending machine and amusement arcade game business, Johnny Papalia perfectly blended legitimate business with his underworld activities. Vending is a cash-only business, and customers do not get receipts; the government cannot track how many coins are stuffed into the machines, or where the materials come from that come out.

"Taking care of business" has long been an underworld euphemism for any number of illegal and legal activities. Not all of Johnny's business was criminal, although it often became difficult to separate the man from his business, and the criminal from the man. In any transaction, Johnny's name was a commodity in itself.

In 1958, Johnny had an interest in Star Vending Machine Company in Toronto with Alberto Agueci, and Monarch Vending Machine Company in Hamilton. Monarch was set up with Art Tartaglia, a man with a talent for getting Papalia machines into almost any location—even city-owned properties. His successful sales pitch is remembered, not so fondly, by one business owner.

"Your cigarette machine's in pretty bad shape," Tartaglia said to the restaurant manager. "How would you like a modern machine?" When the manager said no, he was offered $100 to put a Monarch machine in. A further rebuff brought an intimidation. One restaurateur who completely refused needed hospitalization after the beating he received.

"His head was bandaged for weeks, a walking advertisement of the advantage of doing business with the Papalias," recalled a Hamilton detective.

Out of the business office and warehouse at 20 Railway Street, Johnny's brother Frank and long-time associate Bruno Monaco became the named principals of Monarch Vending, a company that placed thousands of cigarette and food machines around the region. Two more of Johnny's brothers, Rocco and Dominic, were also Monarch employees. The names of the companies operating out of that small building have changed over the years—Monarch, Galaxy, F.M. Amusements—but business always revolves around finding busy places to put in machines that take people's money in return for some product or service. Another company, Beer Magic, had a lock on beer dispensers in the province for years, with taverns leasing the taps and purchasing maintenance contracts as well. Today, their businesses still boom.

Johnny became involved in business opportunities early in his criminal career, largely because they provided a front behind which his criminal activities could flourish undetected. In the mid-1950s, he established a short-lived auto repair company, called Ben's Garage, at 26 Railway Street, the former home of Silverwood-Burke garage, from where the licence plates used in Bessie Perri's 1930 slaying were likely stolen. As Johnny's notoriety grew, however, his name disappeared from the corporate records of the Papalia family's business interests.

Johnny's association with his brothers' business was always open to much debate. Although not a corporate officer, even when Johnny was in jail he was associated—at least in the minds of the police, most customers, and municipal employees—with the businesses. Johnny was employed by his brothers over the years and often spoke of the generosity of his family when asked what he did for a living. In the 1980s, Johnny variously described himself as a supervisor of an amusement arcade on a $500 retainer, an employee of F.M. Amusements working for $250 a week, and unemployed.

Johnny even joked about his reputed role in the vending machine business. When Johnny was asked in 1986 what he did for a living, he smiled and said: "I go into a bar and I tell them my name and I intimidate people into taking our equipment. That's what the police tell you, isn't it?" It *was* what police said. But it wasn't just police saying it.

In the *Connections* television exposé, a Toronto mobster spoke anonymously about the Papalia vending machine operation: "Various types, all types of them, cigarette machines, pop machines, candy machines, soup machines, just every type of machine that vends. He [Johnny] doesn't show anywhere in the operation. A lot has to do with unions, etc. He's involved in unions and his men know where to place the machines. They know who to approach. They know what new structures are going up, what structures that are busy. They just know where to put them, that's all." When asked by series producer Bill Macadam what would happen if someone refused to take a Monarch machine, the mobster answered: "Eventually, they would come to him for his machines. Now, firms that just couldn't meet their commitments, he might just cut into a piece of their business . . . it winds up he's a 50-percent partner."

The Papalias like to deal with competition head-on.

When a young, Hamilton street-gang leader was stealing pinball machines, stripping them of all serial numbers, and recirculating them to other businesses, he made the mistake of making off with a couple of the Papalias' machines. Stealing from the Papalias is rarely a good idea, and it was not long before agents of their vending company paid the street tough a visit with a message from their boss: "You step on our grass once more and we'll step on your heads."

An even shrewder business ploy took place in 1979. The Papalias sold Monarch Vending to Toronto-based Allind Distributors. The sale included the cigarette machines and vans, but not the pinball and amusement machines. Several Monarch employees also went to the new company, which continued to operate under the name Monarch Vending. As part of the arrangements, a noncompetition deal was signed, saying Frank and Monaco could not involve themselves in any way with cigarette or food vending machines within a 322-kilometre radius of Hamilton for the next five years. Police knew of the impending deal and paid a visit to Allind, making sure they knew what they were getting into. The company said everything was fine and pointed to their noncompetition agreement. Police officers just shook their heads and left.

Allind soon found the name Monarch Vending brought with it some heavy baggage. Said Rick Page, Allind's general manager: "We were being shut out of a lot of places, especially government spots. They weren't even sending us the tender. Every time one of the trucks was parked it was ticketed. It didn't matter whether it was on delivery or not."

A memo from a senior police officer to all patrolmen was needed to stop the harassment of Monarch vans under the new owners. Meanwhile, Rocco and Dominic Papalia—who were not named in the noncompetition agreement with Allind—soon set up shop as Galaxy Vending, and the pair returned to many of Monarch's old customers and started replacing Allind machines with those of the new company. Sometimes Allind would find their machines dumped outside in a back alley, sitting in the rain. Allind was understandably upset. Stepping deftly around the issue, Page said business was lost because of the "familiarity of the Papalia family in the Hamilton area," and because their "personalities are well known." Asked if his company was somewhat naive in purchasing a company like Monarch, Page replied: "Yes, we knew the connotations, yes, we were naive. We thought we had a noncompetition agreement. I think it is unethical as hell."

When police started investigating Johnny and his family, they followed Monarch collectors on their routes, watching them empty the machines of all the coins. That was often the job of Johnny's brother, Dominic, and police secretly watched as he went to the many hotels, restaurants, and bars. Monarch Vending was supposedly splitting the take 50/50 with the proprietor of the business where the machine was located, but no one from the establishments was usually present to even guess how much money was being removed. Police wanted to learn everything about the vending business, and interviewed competitors, machine manufacturers, and businesses where Papalia machines were located. An undercover officer even participated in a large pinball tournament to get a feel for the industry. The cop was a natural and came within a paddle thrust of winning the top tournament prize.

One thing they learned was that Monarch was bringing in a ton of cash; police estimated in excess of $12,000 a day. Police asked competitors around Hamilton to come into the city and do business. The response was a unified one.

"No, no, no. You don't go to Hamilton. Do you know who runs that?"

One lone operator did come to the city. He placed a few machines in an east-end mall, but his office was paid a hasty visit by unknown assailants, and he was escorted out of town.

Police were determined to see if free enterprise really flourished in the vending industry, and went into the vending business themselves. Undercover police rented a small office and warehouse on the Hamilton Mountain and stocked it with a number of arcade games borrowed from sympathetic competitors. With a supply of Pac-Man and Galaxia games on hand, they started drumming up business by banging on doors. Never disclosing who they really worked for, the police officers offered businessmen a deal to put their machines in instead of Monarch's. After 200 sales calls, they had no takers. Officers then sweetened the deal. Rather than the 50/50 split offered by Monarch, the cops offered the proprietors the lion's share of a 70/30 split. Owners were still unsure.

"Do you know who you are dealing with?" some owners asked.

In a final bid to make an impact on Monarch, police offered a 70/30 split plus 100 percent of the take for the first three months of the contract. The new deal finally attracted some takers—and attention. Some of the police-placed machines were tossed out the back door of their new premises, and a pair of musclemen visited the company's office. They looked around, they asked questions, they offered a few suggestions. And then they left, wishing the company good luck. Perhaps they smelled a sting; or perhaps they figured the business was so small that it was not worth flexing muscle over. For whatever reason, the sting was a bust.

Johnny kept an unwavering eye on even the smallest competitor in the vending business. Perhaps fearing government intervention if he held an utter monopoly, he allowed a few to operate unfettered. One independent operator received a surprise phone call from Johnny at his home soon after his video games went into a few stores in Burlington. Johnny wanted to know how many machines the man had. He answered, 24.

"Good, I like the competition," Johnny said. A few weeks later, while repairing one machine in his living room and setting up another in his home, the man received a second phone call from Johnny.

"You told me you had 24 machines—how come you only have 22 of them out there?" Johnny wanted to know. The fledgling vending operator went white.

The Papalias may hold a virtual monopoly on coin-operated machines, but vending has not held a monopoly on the family's business interests.

A Hamilton company on Queen Street North, for years carrying on business as Central Body and Paint, was incorporated shortly before Christmas 1954, and from 1968 on had Rocco Papalia as an officer and director.

Car repair is another perfect cash business with plenty of room for quiet—and largely untraceable—adjustments. At the end of the 1990s, the old Central Body and Paint premises was used by Northgate Collision, an auto body shop notorious for hiring motorcycle gang members, former convicts, and intimidating musclemen. Tow truck drivers with frightening features and mammoth dimensions arrived from Northgate at accident scenes and aggressively solicited business. Sometimes victims were pushed around, or rival tow truck drivers chased off. Victims were sometimes offered amazing deals and waived insurance deductibles—even gifts of karaoke machines—to let Northgate take their damaged cars in for repair. Once in the Northgate lot, however, trouble often started. Cars were dismantled before estimates were given, parts were ordered but never installed, stolen parts were put into cars and car owners billed for brand-new equipment. Unexpectedly large bills, including previously unmentioned "storage fees," were handed out. Police were often called by intimidated customers. One man was surrounded by five burly men when he tried to get his car out of the lot. Police tried to help, but some officers appeared also to be part of the problem. In 1996, after a six-month probe, police charged two Hamilton constables with criminal breach of trust after allegations they were sending business to an auto body shop associated with Northgate in return for favours. One cop was found not guilty in court, and the other was found not criminally responsible because of a psychiatric disorder.[1]

Northgate defaulted on federal tax arrears of $90,000, closed, then reopened for business the same day under a new name. The tax address for both companies was 20 Railway Street.

After Johnny's slaying, the curb-side shenanigans lulled. Many of the prime muscle-bound offenders shifted allegiance from a Papalia-associated company to one associated with another family in Hamilton with a deep Mafia tradition: the Musitanos.

---

1 His bizarre behaviour included driving his car into a bridge abutment at 135 kilometres per hour to find out if the airbag worked.

18

Looking rumpled and tired—for once not wearing a suit and tie—and carrying his meagre belongings in a small kit-bag, Johnny Papalia walked back across the Canadian border looking like a shadow of his former self. Out of prison after five years for his role in the French Connection heroin smuggling ring, Johnny had lost considerable weight, but none of his notoriety.

"Look, fellows," he wearily told a reporter and photographer there to greet him with flashbulbs and questions, "I've had enough. I'm a sick man. I've been aggravated for years. It's over now. Why this? I'm nothing now. I'm not even a spit in the ocean." With a fedora pulled down tight and his trademark dark sunglasses, he asked that his picture not be taken.

"You've got the Korean War," he added, suggesting there might be more important things to write about than a sick gangster. This comment, perhaps more than anything else, suggested just how out of touch Johnny was after his stint in prison; the Korean War had long since ended and it was the Vietnam War eating up newspaper space.

The day before—January 25, 1968—after serving almost half of his 10-year sentence, Johnny was released from the federal penitentiary in Lewisburg, Pennsylvania, into the custody of U.S. Immigration officers, who flew with him to New York City as the first step in the deportation order that accompanied his sentence. There he was reunited with his brother Frank, and then spent one final night in an American cell.

Early the next day, immigration officers and the two Papalia brothers headed for LaGuardia airport and boarded a plane to Buffalo, touching down at 11:21 a.m. From the plane Johnny was escorted to a waiting patrol car and driven—just as he had been taken to the States, only far more quietly—to the border. It took only 15 minutes for Johnny to pass through the Canadian immigration office at the Peace Bridge in Fort Erie. All he had with him were a small prison-issue bag and some newspapers carrying word of his release. Once back on Canadian soil, Johnny was greeted by another brother, Rocco, his loyal lieutenant Red LeBarre, and an unidentified man of about six feet tall and 230 pounds.

Frank Papalia told reporters his brother wanted to slip back into life in Canada quietly, and that the reception at the border was not appreciated.

"His mother is sick and this thing killed his father. His father died of a heart attack on May 14, 1964," Frank said. Johnny's tuberculosis was bothering Johnny greatly, Frank said, he had lost weight, and he would be going to see a Hamilton doctor as soon as possible.

The three Papalia brothers, LeBarre, and their bodyguard all clambered into a large, late-model car and drove back to Railway Street, where The Enforcer was given a hero's welcome. Cadillacs and Lincolns jammed the tiny street—one of them brand-new and a "welcome home" gift for Johnny Pops, the returning *mafioso*.

Despite Johnny's humble words at the border—"I'm nothing"—he returned to Canada with big plans. Although he wanted the public attention to fade away quickly, within the narrow clique of the underworld, he refused to let people forget about his time in the can.

"We all knew he did go to jail for the French Connection," said an old underworld associate of Johnny's. "The fact that he was mixed up with New York and such heavy connections there helped build his reputation a lot. He traded on that very heavily. John would bring it up years and years later. He would sit down and say: 'Time here is nothing. You wanna talk about doing time, when I did my time in New York . . .' or 'These guys are nothing. You should see the guys I dealt with in New York . . .' He would make sure that if anybody didn't know about it that they did know, and for those of us who were already aware of it, that we knew it that much stronger.

"He built his own legend to some degree and did it very well."

Johnny got right down to business. Within months he had made his presence felt in the province and let it be known that he planned to pick up where he had left off: The Enforcer was back. Johnny met with Giacomo Luppino, an old-world Mafia don who emigrated to Hamilton from Calabria and immediately formed a close relationship with Stefano Magaddino, to discuss the state of underworld affairs. Johnny heaped respect on Luppino and discreetly pledged his allegiance to Magaddino—no doubt still thinking of the smoking corpse of his friend Alberto Agueci. He also attended an important international organized crime summit meeting in Acapulco, representing his own organization and, more importantly, the entire Magaddino organization. If anyone wondered whether Johnny was still tight with Buffalo, that meeting was a not-too-subtle display that Johnny was still Magaddino's man. The meeting in Mexico, in August 1970, brought close to 100 mobsters together from Canada, the U.S., and France to carve up underworld interest in Quebec's planned gambling casinos and to create a cross-border money-laundering scheme. The meeting was in vain, however. The Quebec government dropped its plans in October when the terrorist activities of the *Front de Libération du Québec* brought tanks to the streets of Montreal, fear into the hearts of politicians, and a whole lot of unwanted scrutiny of criminals in a renewed push for provincial law and order.[1]

Johnny also started meeting regularly with mobsters from New York at Turkey Point and Port Rowan, two small Ontario resort communities along Lake Erie. If U.S. mobsters wanted to meet with Johnny, now they generally traveled north, as Johnny's drug conviction removed his freedom to legally visit the United States.

---

1 The names of some Canadians allegedly attending the summit were released in 1974 in the Ontario legislature by MPP Morton Shulman. They included Red LeBarre, Domenic Pugliese, Richard Perrin, Dominic Ciarillo, Jack Donnelly, Jack Pettigrew, Frank Gabarino, Vincent Cossini, Armand Cossini, Frank Pasquale, and Albert Moretti. An unfortunate Canadian of Italian heritage who happened to be innocently staying at the same hotel was also named by Shulman. The MPP later apologized.

As quietly as Johnny slipped to Mexico, he tried to slip into the sub-urbs, moving into a modest bungalow on Inverness Avenue, in a peaceful Burlington neighbourhood, where he lived with Red LeBarre. Two bachelors with big things on their minds and big cars in their driveway were at odds with the hardworking neighbours who took great pride in their properties. Johnny didn't like to cut his grass, he didn't trim back his shrubbery, he left newspapers gathering on his porch for days, and—what is more—he certainly did not wash his windows. On Inverness, this was scandalous behaviour.

"I don't know what goes on there," said one neighbouring housewife. "All I know is there's this one man with a hooked nose and a second, very big man. They never seem to eat there. I've never seen any food or groceries go in, only supplies from the liquor store." Neighbours called their city councillor about the untidy state of affairs, and the councillor in turn contacted police. Police told neighbours to just take it easy.

"I don't know and I don't care who he is," said another of his neigh-bours. "All I wish is that he would put his garbage out like anyone else and get his lawn cut now and again." The nosy response from neigh-bours drove Johnny back to the people and area he knew. He moved into a sixth-floor apartment at 255 Bold Street in central Hamilton, a building owned by a company over which Danny Gasbarrini presided. Johnny's apartment was leased under the name "Miss Jones," a woman he lived with until she moved out when their relationship fizzled.

The situation with his suburban neighbours typified Johnny's exis-tence throughout the 1970s. While Johnny tried to keep quiet, the public was not prepared to let go so easily of their favourite bad guy. The more he tried to keep his head down, the more he was drawn into the spotlight. While the 1950s and early 1960s were marked by Johnny looking for trouble, in the 1970s trouble came looking for him.

On June 4, 1970, Dr. Morton Shulman, a New Democratic Party member of the Ontario parliament, rose in the legislature and deliv-ered a very unusual speech.

"The specific case that I want to discuss at some length today, because it does involve the Mafia, is a case that has been discussed in the House at some length before but without this particular aspect being known, and that is the Clinton Duke case," Shulman began. Drawing on information and allegations leaked to him from several sources—and leaning heavily on the legal protection against slander that is given speeches inside the legislature—Shulman talked at length of inappropriate relationships between high-ranking members of the Ontario Provincial Police and known members of the criminal underworld.[2]

"The Enforcer for the Mafia in Canada is one Johnny Papalia. And Johnny Papalia, and his bodyguard, Red LeBarre, has [sic] attended several garden parties at Clinton Duke's home—this is recently. And just to explain who Johnny Papalia is, he was in charge of the heroin branch of the Mafia for many years," said Shulman. The maverick MPP explained how Johnny and Clinton Duke both had apartments in one of Gasbarrini's buildings. "Gasbarrini," Shulman said, "is a keypin in the Mafia in this country." Shulman was a master of the dramatic. Eloquent, dedicated, and gutsy, he carefully laid out the criminal past of Johnny and Gasbarrini.

"I do not wish to draw any conclusions . . . but there is an obvious conclusion which is a frightening one to me. In October 1945, Gasbarrini was charged with receiving stolen bonds. The case began with the arrest of a Hamilton man, Paul Donat, who tried to cash one of the stolen bonds at a Hamilton bank. Donat told police he did not realize the bonds were stolen and he agreed to give evidence against Gasbarrini, who was charged with receiving these bonds. On the day of Gasbarrini's trial, Donat failed to show up, so the charge against Gasbarrini was dismissed. Donat has never been seen since."

After Shulman's speech, Gasbarrini denied the allegation of his being involved in the Mafia. "Sure, I speak with other ex-convicts, with ex-gamblers, ex-bootleggers and ex-bookies. I sometimes play a

---

2 Much of his information came from investigations by *Hamilton Spectator* reporter Gerry McAuliffe, who had been called by a *Spec* official saying he was a friend of Duke's and did not want the man's name in the paper in connection with any charges. The call backfired, only alerting McAuliffe to a story he had not known about.

round of golf with John Papalia, who has had his troubles just like I have had mine. But the fact is, there is nobody else for people like us to associate with. We can't get into the Lions Club or the Rotary Club or the Kinsmen Club . . . there is this small, self-righteous group in control which intends to keep ex-convicts in their place."

Shulman painted a shocking picture of OPP Commissioner Eric Silk and others who socialized with Duke—an Oakville businessman who, in turn, was pals with Johnny. The speech was particularly galvanizing as Silk was appointed in 1963 in a shake-up of the force after the Roach commission took issue with some members of the provincial police. Silk was supposed to be the new broom—the one to put everything right.

Duke himself was a swashbuckler of a man. Born on the last day of the year in 1905, near Belleville, he started racking up criminal charges at the age of 20, and found himself holding the bag for a $400,000 jewel heist in Buffalo in 1930. After serving 12 years in prison, he was deported back to Canada, became sales manager for a lawn mower manufacturer, and married a widow with two children, Marguerite Helen Nolan, whom he had known since his school days. When the company he worked for collapsed, he accepted lawn mowers in lieu of missed paycheques and started a modest lawn mower sales and service company of his own. Apart from running afoul of the tax department in 1961, the company was a model enterprise, and the Dukes showed the fruits of their labour through large, lavish parties and barbecues at their imposing mansion on Lake Ontario. But Duke's personal life never seemed to escape the bizarre. He was a man who had two conflicting passions: alcohol and guns.

Duke had registered 79 restricted weapons. He built an air-raid shelter at his home, and had a machine gun mounted on a golf cart. Once, he roared along his property line in his cart, firing the machine gun furiously into the lake during a neighbour's garden party to which he had not been invited. He had extramarital affairs, and after drinking too much became abusive to his wife. In the summer of 1968, his wife met with Hamilton Police Chief Leonard Lawrence. She was fearful for her life because of domestic troubles and Duke's friendship with Johnny. It was two years after she went to the Hamilton chief that

Shulman made his speech, and a provincial inquiry, headed by Campbell Grant, was called, with Johnny named in the commission's frame of reference. Johnny, however, had sadder news to deal with. The inquiry was called the day after his mother died.

In August 1970, OPP Staff Superintendent Jack Kay interviewed Johnny about Shulman's allegations. The interview was pure Papalia: flippant, witty, slang-filled statements that had the air of honesty but ultimately showed an utter lack of cooperation. Duke had told police he did not even know Johnny, a remark the mobster said was silly. If Duke had told the truth from the start, Johnny opined, there would not have been an inquiry.

"If the truth comes out, there will be no problems," Johnny said.

Johnny was irked by Shulman's suggestion that he and Duke lived in the same apartment rather than in the same building. Johnny told Kay he might be living with "a broad," but definitely not with a man, because he was "not a queer." He referred to the OPP as "the pros," and described Shulman as "deranged." In a rare bout of sympathy for police, Johnny said he felt sorry for the two officers whose careers would be ruined for having a drink with Duke. As for Johnny, he was not concerned about having to testify at a public inquiry.

"I am ruined so I don't care," he said. When it came time for Johnny and his friends to testify, they came bearing lawyers: John J. O'Driscoll representing Johnny, N.D. McRae for LeBarre, and future Supreme Court of Canada justice John Sopinka acting for Gasbarrini.

Johnny's testimony was a media spectacle. Outside the Old City Hall Court in Toronto, news photographers snapped pictures of Johnny draped in a dark trench coat and wearing a fedora, lighting a cigarette that he sucked heavily, and looking brutish and sombre. But inside, fashionably dressed in a grey business suit, blue shirt with stylish long collar tabs, and a maroon tie, Johnny was debonair and polite. He said he had first met Duke about 20 years earlier at his Porcupine gambling club, and "bumped into him in the garage of the building" on occasion. He said he renewed his acquaintanceship with Duke in February or March of 1968, when both were looking at cars at Hamilton Motor Products. He said LeBarre was a very dear friend and that in

1968 the pair, along with Gasbarrini, had gone to Duke's estate, where Gasbarrini had talked with Duke about high-rise apartments.

"I just went along for the ride," Johnny said. In 1970, he again met Duke and went to Duke's home for drinks and Chinese food. Later, Johnny visited Duke at his office. Remembering the fuss his neighbours had made over the state of his lawn on Inverness Avenue, he said he needed something to take care of the grass.

"I asked Duke what was cheaper, a lawn mower or a goat, but I bought neither," Johnny said. Johnny denied visiting the Duke estate to frighten Duke's wife, as Mrs. Duke had suggested. "No way," he said.

In the end, inquiry commissioner Grant did not much like what some police officers were up to. He gave Silk a slap for not checking on Duke's background before exchanging gifts with him and giving him an OPP tiepin. Two police officers were disciplined for continuing a relationship with Duke after they were ordered not to. But Grant found no evidence of improper relationships between the OPP and the gangsters. He rejected the allegation that the mobsters gained access to top OPP brass through Duke. Ultimately, his report suggested Shulman had all the right dots, but he had connected them poorly.

After the inquiry, Duke receded into obscurity until he died quietly in 1994 in a Burlington nursing home.

Johnny's soft-spoken approach to the Duke commission amused the audience, but belied his seething temper.

At the end of August 1971, Len Joy, a court employee in Hamilton, cautiously approached the Papalia enclave on Railway Street. He did not have an enviable task: serving The Enforcer with a summons. After a knock at the door of the house next door to Monarch Vending, Joy pushed the summons into Johnny's hands. Johnny exploded with rage and literally threw Joy off the veranda. Joy was not amused and, to everyone's surprise—especially Johnny's—filed assault charges against the gangster. One month later, Johnny sat in the second row of seats in a Hamilton courtroom, wearing a conservative grey suit and listening intently as a written apology from him to Joy was read aloud. Crown Attorney Cameron Gage read from the letter how Johnny had "been under a great deal of pressure at the time," and the incident had resulted from "a conflict of personalities." Gage told Judge Ross Bennett he was satisfied "as well as I can be, that no undue influence" had been exerted on Joy not to press charges. Johnny's lawyer Clive Bynoe demanded it be put on the court record that Joy's decision was "completely voluntary [and] not the result of any threat, intimidation, or coercion exercised on behalf of my client." The assault charge was withdrawn, but The Enforcer got more bad press.

It was the same thing when Johnny showed up as a spectator at the trial of Peter Demeter, who was accused of hiring a contract killer to bump off his wife. The 1974 trial was already a media circus, and Johnny's appearance was another sensation, with television crews and newspaper photographers crowding him. At first he held up a warning finger against taking his picture; then he scuffled with photographers, shoving and pushing as he stomped through the scrum with two companions at his side. A television cameraman had his camera stuffed into his face, cutting him above his eye. Johnny got more headlines.

And again, later that year, when the Waisberg commission commented on mobsters' involvement in the construction industry, Johnny's name appeared.

Not everything Johnny did during this period became public knowledge, however. In 1971, when Toronto mobster Remo Commisso became involved in a power struggle in his Italian home town in Reggio Calabria, it upset other leaders of the Calabrian Mafia in Canada. Johnny interceded on Remo's behalf, mending the rift—and furthering his own position within the underworld as a powerful ally and valuable statesman.

If Johnny's name was associated with petty criminal activities for most of the 1970s, that was about to change. He was to find himself again facing serious charges and—worse—a very credible death threat.

19

"I know you'll kill me, Vic. I believe you'll kill me."

Such simple, meek words, coming from the mouth of The Enforcer.

Poor Johnny had stumbled into a bad scene while swindling a Toronto stock broker and had inadvertently upset Vic Cotroni, the Godfather of the powerful Montreal Mafia. And now he had to face the music.

On April 30, 1974, Johnny traveled to Montreal at the behest of Cotroni, whom he had worked with under Carmine Galante two decades before. Cotroni was older, more experienced, well respected, and extraordinarily well connected. He had a powerful organization, with Paolo Violi as his right-hand man. Violi, a former Hamilton resident, also knew Johnny personally. In fact, it was Violi's father-in-law, Giacomo Luppino, the wise old don in Hamilton, who sent Violi to Montreal so he would not butt heads with rising star Johnny in Ontario. And now, here they were, meeting together in Violi's Montreal bar to discuss a most serious matter: money.

Listening in—although the gangsters did not know it—were Quebec police officers who had wired the Reggio Bar in the city's north end.

Cotroni and Violi were upset. Johnny had used their names in a swindle that netted $300,000. Unfortunately, the Montreal mobsters caught wind of it, and for this breach of mob etiquette they now wanted what they saw as their rightful share of profit from the swindle—half of the total.

"I don't want chicken feed," Cotroni said. "He used our name. Half."

"That's it," answered Violi. "He got to this person because he used our name. Not because he used his name. The guy was afraid of us and he paid. People [who] use our name pay."

The swindle itself was simple, but the many layers of duplicity gave it a labyrinthine quality that confused everyone, it seems—including Violi at the time, and the courts some years later.

"Look, I don't remember if that guy swindled this guy or this guy swindled that guy," Violi said, getting flustered by Cotroni's quick explanation of what Johnny was involved in. Cotroni tried to make it simple.

"This guy brought the $300,000 to Johnny . . . so he could fix the deal that no one would touch him anymore."

Well, yes, that did happen, but the swindle that brought Johnny before both the fearsome Godfather and the Canadian courts started years before Johnny collected that pay-out.

In 1971, a tall, skinny, pock-faced Sheldon (Sonny) Swartz first met Stanley Bader, and the pair started a rather shady moneylending and stock sales business. It was an odd mix. Swartz's father, an old-time racketeer whose nickname was "Schwaby," was very close with Johnny from years back. Johnny always took an admirable interest in his associates' children and he kept in touch with Swartz. Swartz, however, was a bit of a goof-up. He was incompetent when it came to making money. His partner Stanley Bader, on the other hand, was a genius at it. Bader wheeled; Bader dealed.

"Stanley couldn't help screwing the people he did business with, because that was Stanley's nature," said an old friend of the broker. "Stanley was a stock salesman in Toronto and a very good one. A very successful one. And a thief. Whoever Stanley was dealing with, Stanley just couldn't help stealing off of. It was how he did business."

What Swartz and Bader set up was a little business in the Bay Street office of Sydney Rosen, a businessman who agreed to be the pair's "banker." Rosen lent them money at 2 percent-per-month interest and they lent it out on the street at rates of between 4 and 7 percent per month. Swartz was finally making a bit of cash, but not nearly as much as he was spending. Bader, however, seemed to want for nothing; he dressed well, drove a big car, lived in a nice neighbourhood. Swartz jealously watched Bader amass a small fortune from various swindles and financial fast plays. One day, in the summer of 1973, Bader confided in Swartz about one of his better scams. He told Swartz he had made a big score by ripping off some people in Montreal on a phony stock deal. Some time later, Swartz mentioned this to Johnny, and Johnny's quick mind immediately whipped up a plan to get some of that money for himself.

"Let's tell him that you found out that it was really Cotroni's money that he took and then bring him to me for verification," a source recounted Johnny saying to Swartz. The plan developed. They would have Johnny take the money from Bader to "return it" to Montreal to make sure he remained safe from the Quebec mobsters' vengeance. The money Bader made in Montreal could then secretly be split between Swartz and Johnny, and no one would be the wiser.

Swartz was not much of an earner, but he was a heck of an actor.

On August 26, 1973, Swartz phoned Bader and said he had to see him right away about something "very urgent." Swartz arrived at Bader's home, frazzled, unshaven, and looking rough. He broke to Bader some very grim news.

"There is going to be trouble for you," Swartz said. "Some people are mad and looking to get even."

Between gasps of breath, Swartz explained to his business partner and supposed friend that word had gotten out about his Montreal stock swindle. He said he had heard from Johnny Papalia in Hamilton that mobsters in Montreal were livid about losing their cash and had arranged for Bader "to be maimed so [he] couldn't work." There was a way out, however, Swartz told his shaken partner. Johnny could get the Montreal thugs off his back, but he would have to return the money. Swartz said he had already given Johnny $100,000 from their joint business capital and now Bader had to come up with another $200,000—in a hurry.

Bader was an easier mark than Swartz probably imagined. He

Pondering his fate: The strain shows on Johnny as he sits with his head in his hands at his extradition hearing in 1961. He was ordered to stand trial in the United States for his leadership role in the notorious French Connection heroin smuggling ring.

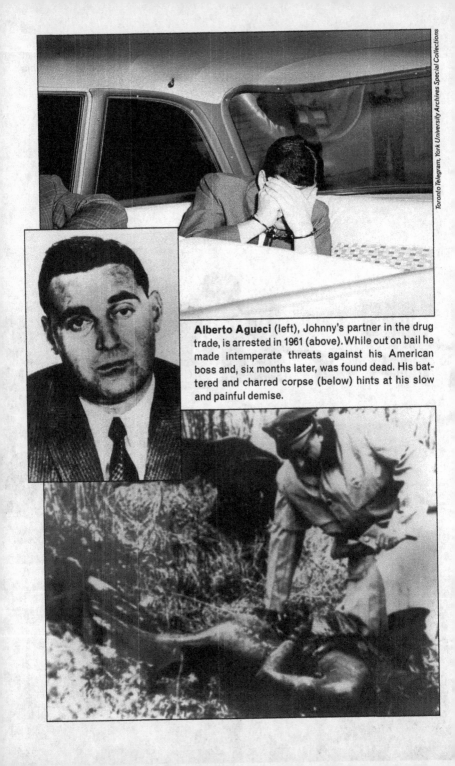

Alberto Agueci (left), Johnny's partner in the drug trade, is arrested in 1961 (above). While out on bail he made intemperate threats against his American boss and, six months later, was found dead. His battered and charred corpse (below) hints at his slow and painful demise.

Free at last: Johnny (middle) is escorted back across the Canada-U.S. border in 1968 after doing hard prison time for the French Connection heroin smuggling ring. He is accompanied by his closest brother, Frank, who is carrying his suitcase. "I'm nothing now. I'm not even a spit in the ocean," Johnny told a reporter while keeping a straight face.

Making headlines: Johnny, gasping for a cigarette, leaves a Toronto courtroom during the Duke inquiry in 1970 (left). At right, he greets the press with his lawyer after making bail in 1974 on his extortion charge. Despite the smile, his mood—and mouth—were foul. As always, his brother Frank lurks quietly in the background.

Candid call: Hitman Réal Simard (left) calls his Montreal mob boss from a Hamilton pay phone in 1983 to show Johnny (right) he really is connected. Frank Majeau watches.

Carmine Galante: Johnny's early Mafia mentor meets an end not unlike Johnny's—gunned down outdoors. A man rarely seen without a cigar, Galante died with a lit stogie still clenched between his teeth.

AP Wide World Photos

Murder scene: Johnny was gunned down in the parking lot of his family's vending machine company on Railway Street. Although police flooded the area and tracking dogs were quickly brought in, the hitman was already far away.

Visitation: Pat Musitano (fourth from right), who was originally charged in Johnny's slaying, pays his final respects to The Enforcer at the Friscolanti Funeral Chapel. Private gatherings—away from the prying eyes of police and the press—were also held.

Sombre walk: Johnny's body is carried out in a cherrywood casket by his loved ones. With the Roman Catholic Church refusing him a funeral mass in a cathedral, his service was a small affair in a private chapel.

Johnny's final ride: A string of limousines and carloads of mourners snake through Hamilton's streets towards Holy Sepulchre Cemetery, where Johnny was buried in a grave that remained unmarked for two years.

Scott Gardner

PRAY FOR THE SOUL OF
A DEAR FATHER
ANTONIO PAPALIA
DEC. 14, 1894
MAY 14, 1964
BELOVED HUSBAND OF
MARIA ROSA ITALIANO
RIPOSA IN PACE

Adrian Humphreys

PRAY FOR THE SOUL OF
A DEAR SON
JOHN PAPALIA
MAR. 18, 1924
MAY 31, 1997
BELOVED SON OF
ANTONIO & MARIA ROSA
RIPOSA IN PACE

At rest: Johnny was buried in his family's plot in a wooded, picturesque section of a large Catholic cemetery in Burlington, just outside of Hamilton (top). The family tombstones match each other and are set into the ground at the base of the cross. Johnny's stone (bottom, right) lies beside his mother's and his father's (left). Family members, including his brother Dominic, are buried nearby.

immediately became paranoid and jumpy—saying he now remembered seeing strange cars parked outside his house at odd hours of the night. Bader called Rosen that night to arrange a large and urgent loan. Swartz and Bader went to the basement of a bank in Toronto and collected the money in $100 bills, packed it into a suitcase, and the last Bader saw of it was when Swartz and his girlfriend were leaving for Hamilton to take it to Johnny.

"Sonny was in Seventh Heaven; he'd never seen that kind of money his whole life," said one of Bader's friends who watched it happen. "We are talking about some heavy dough. He'd never had it so good. He started to brag about it. He started to brag to people how they ripped Stanley off."

Rumours got back to Bader. He also noticed Swartz had suddenly started living a very expensive lifestyle. He grew suspicious about where his money ended up and started making inquiries. When he asked Swartz about it, he was warned he was just "stirring up trouble." Bader even asked Johnny, who shrugged it off by giving Bader the ubiquitous mobster line: "Forget about it."

A year later Bader asked some underworld acquaintances in Montreal about it, and it did not take long to reach Cotroni's ear. Cotroni beckoned Johnny to a meeting to settle things.

That is how Johnny ended up in the heart of the Montreal Mafia's turf, talking with Vic Cotroni and Paolo Violi about the swindle, with police listening in.

"You, Johnny, know these things, that [we] have to work all together, but instead you did it alone," said Violi. "You used our names. Didn't you want us to be friends? Bring the hundred and fifty thousand and no one will know anything.

"Be aware that we don't like crooked things. Beside our friendship, and what we say, we respect each other. But with us, you have to come straight."

Johnny said he did not know that Swartz had used their names to scare Bader or that $300,000 was the sum involved.

"He comes to me at the end. He's already got the score. I don't know nothing. He tells me, 'I'm going to take out a hundred thousand,

I already took the score and this guy owes me,' Right? 'You know I'm going to take out a hundred thousand and I'll split it with you fifty-fifty!' But he gave me forty thousand," Johnny said.

Cotroni accused Johnny of pocketing the entire $300,000. "You see, the guy, he gonna say 'I gave this money to Johnny,'" Cotroni said.

"He can say he gave it Jesus Christ! I don't care what he says," protested Johnny. "He didn't give it to me, Vic."

"Let's hope not because, eh, we'll kill you," Cotroni casually said.

"I know you'll kill me, Vic."

It was a rare instance of The Enforcer's humility and a recognition of Cotroni's superiority in the Canadian Mafia. Cotroni, after all, had been a rising boss under Carmine Galante in the mid-1950s when Johnny was just one of Galante's foot soldiers. Had it just been Violi making the threat, Johnny's reaction might have been different. Interestingly enough, when Johnny bowed, it was directly to Cotroni—by name. At any rate, if Johnny was not legitimately nervous of Cotroni's intent at that point, he very much was later on.

After listening to the *mafiosi* talk of this scam, Montreal police suddenly had an interesting case on their hands—one that involved three of the country's top Mafia chieftains. They had listened in on the three mobsters talking before, including an important summit meeting that same year in which Johnny, Violi, Cotroni, and Joe Gentile, the Mafia boss of Vancouver, planned an international money-laundering scheme to recirculate their ill-gotten gains through a bogus drapery company. But this time, the police wire picked up something solid and specific that could result in criminal charges. Montreal police contacted the OPP and Toronto police, and the three forces worked closely to try for a mob-busting hat trick. In the summer of 1974, Bader was involved in a tax evasion hearing, and he was approached in court by an RCMP officer about the extortion. Bader unraveled when he heard of the con that his conniving business partner had pulled. Not fully realizing he was implicating three of the most powerful *mafiosi* in the nation along with Swartz, he told police everything he knew about the plot. A few months later, police seized Swartz's bank records.

These showed that the man who claimed to be unemployed on his tax returns and who was collecting welfare had deposited more than $120,000 in the bank and had another $5,000 in $100 bills stashed in a safety deposit box. In fact, Swartz's bank account was severely overdrawn the day before the extortion, and flush immediately afterwards.

In September of 1975, RCMP Inspector James McIlvenna asked Violi about the payoff. Violi said he had "never heard of" Swartz or Bader, and knew nothing about a $300,000 extortion. He did admit he knew Johnny. If Violi did not realize he was in trouble then, he certainly knew on November 6, 1975, when he was arrested while eating dinner in Toronto with a Montreal lawyer and John Luppino, another of Giacomo's sons. Cotroni was arrested in Montreal and put on a plane to Toronto. Swartz was grabbed in Toronto, and Johnny in Hamilton. All were charged with conspiracy to possess money obtained by the commission of an indictable offence, a rather cumbersome way of saying extortion.

Wearing handcuffs, dark glasses, dark blue suit, blue shirt, and tie, Johnny was pulled into Toronto police headquarters. He raised his $50,000 bail in short order—with the money quietly being fronted by a bank in Hamilton where Johnny had done business for years—and left that afternoon in a sour mood. On his way out of court he shouted obscenities at reporters and made threatening and obscene gestures. His lawyer, Clive Bynoe, grabbed him by his right elbow and coaxed him away, saying, "Take it easy, take it easy."

Prosecutors were in a better mood. What a haul they had. Clay Powell, a rather chipper special prosecutor from the attorney general's office, wore a button in court reading: "Fight organized crime."

The pride and good cheer of government prosecutors belied the simple fact that despite the immense efforts by police to bring charges against Johnny during the almost eight years since he walked out of a U.S. prison, it took a fluke chat caught by Montreal cops to see Johnny in handcuffs again.

It took almost a year for the extortion case to come before the courts, and despite the testimony of Bader and the tape recordings made in Montreal, it was not open and shut. Bader was the first witness, and boldly declared on the stand that Swartz said Johnny was taking care of his problems in Montreal and that the money was said to be going "to Hamilton."

"Hamilton *is* Mr. Papalia," Bader said.

"We are dealing with a group of people who operate as a matter of course outside the law," said Crown Attorney Dave Doherty, and "that creates a tremendous danger to all of us. This type of offence by this strata of society is rarely before the courts. It is hard to detect, hard to prosecute. It operates and is fed on by terror. It is hard to get witnesses to testify." While Doherty called the crime "an affront to the citizenry of Ontario," Bynoe, Johnny's lawyer, said the Crown's case was such a fairy tale, it could have been authored by Hans Christian Andersen. Lawyers for Cotroni and Violi contended their clients were simply doing Bader a favour by trying to get his money back for him. During the judge's instructions to the jury, he reminded them to consider only the facts of this case rather than the reputations of the men on trial.

"They are not guilty of being what they are, they can only be guilty of what they did," Justice Peter Wright said.

After three hours and 40 minutes of deliberations, the jury returned its verdict. All four were found guilty. The word "guilty" quite literally echoed through the courtroom as it was repeated 48 times when defence counsel asked for an individual poll of the jurors for each of the four defendants.

Before sentencing, Justice Wright called the four "hardened and successful criminals living off the terror, fear, and vices of others.

"The evidence in this case is grim and appalling. It exposes a world of big money grabbed and held by the exercise of brute power. You did not fear the laws of this country and you have chosen to live your lives in a sub-strata of society that operates beyond the rule of law. You must be stopped and stopped in your tracks . . . Let this be a lesson to you and all those like you that this society is neither powerless against nor blind to your actions."

Johnny's lawyer said his client's TB would make incarceration difficult for him, adding that fresh air, a good diet, and exercise were crucial to Johnny's health.

"Do not crush this man with an oppressive sentence," Bynoe pleaded.

Wright then sentenced them each to six years in jail. They appealed, but Johnny's fight all the way to the Supreme Court was in vain. At the end of May 1977, however, Cotroni and Violi had their convictions overturned by the Ontario Court of Appeal. The appeals court deemed the Montrealer's actions a swindle-within-a-swindle not covered by the original extortion in Toronto—and Johnny and Swartz clearly did not have one purpose with the Montreal mobsters, which is the basis of a conspiracy charge.

Johnny—as well as Violi and Cotroni—breathed a sigh of relief. When police arrested all three *mafiosi*, Cotroni placed the blame squarely on Johnny—despite the fact that it was Violi's place that was bugged.

"This was a period in John's life when John was afraid," said Ron Sandelli, the retired head of the Toronto police's intelligence unit. "Through sources, we were told that Cotroni said to Papalia, 'If I go down on this, you're done.' He wasn't convicted in the end but was very embarrassed by this play by John Papalia."

Johnny avoided Cotroni's wrath but was again behind bars, and this time he was no longer a young, tough mobster. He was 53 years old and thoroughly unhappy.

Ontario's Mafia chief remained in Ontario's prison system for four years. Mafia leaders often have an easier time in prison than do regular cons. They tend to be treated well by other prisoners, who are reluctant to upset, and quick to curry favour with, these kings of crime. The respect accorded by other cons usually means *mafiosi* are able to complete their sentences without behavioural infractions that could lengthen their stays. They have money that can sometimes gain them special treatment or creature comforts such as smuggled cigars and fine cognac. Even so, jail can be a hard place for a man nearing retirement age, especially one with legitimate health complaints.

For Johnny, it was an ordeal.

Not everyone gave Johnny an easy ride behind bars, and he endured three separate attempts on his life—all of them coming far too close to succeeding for his comfort.

One came when Johnny was in the lunchroom at Collins Bay Penitentiary, in Kingston, Ontario. His apple came to him with an unnoticed but significant modification—pieces of a razor blade had been pushed inside by an unknown enemy. Poor Johnny bit down hard on the fruit, slicing himself badly. With blood dripping from his mouth, Johnny was helped to the prison infirmary by Big John Akister, the stepfather of Ken Murdock, the man who would later shoot Johnny dead. From then on, Big John acted as Johnny's jail house enforcer—a job not without some dangers. A second crack at Johnny also drew blood from the don, this time from his throat.

"He was in his cell, it was the old cell that if you accidentally closed the door, you would get locked in," recalled Robert (Rosie) Rowbotham, now a contributing editor with CBC radio's popular morning program, but a man who in a previous incarnation spent 20 years in prison for trafficking marijuana. Two of those years, in the late 1970s, he spent with Johnny in Collins Bay, where the two socialized, smoked pot together, and talked about everything but business. There was someone else behind bars with them, however, who had a few, very pointed, problems.

"This individual was a paranoid schizophrenic and somehow in his mind he thought there was a hit out on him from the Mafia," Rowbotham said. Because of Johnny's infamous status within the mob, this troubled prisoner focused his fearful delusions on the aging don. "So he sneaks onto Three Block, on the range, steps inside Johnny's cell and cuts his throat. While in that scuffle, the door closes behind him [and locks]." What happened next is hard for those not schooled in the underworld code to understand, but for Johnny, cooperating with any authority—be it police or prison guard—is never an option, and the only thing he detests more than a man trying to kill him is a guard wearing a uniform. When the scuffling prisoners heard a guard approach, Johnny's actions were automatic. He stopped fighting and hid the man—knife still in hand—under his bed inside the cell. He then covered his wounded throat with a towel, turned away from the cell's door, whipped out his shaving tackle, and appeared to be casually shaving when the guard opened the window in the door and looked in. When the guard had left, Johnny asked his attacker why he was trying to kill him.

"You had a contract on me," he said.

"I don't even *know* you," Johnny replied. For 40 minutes Johnny and his would-be assassin peacefully shared the cell until the guard came back and unlocked the door. Johnny let his attacker safely creep out and off the range before walking up to the guard's station to tell them: "I accidentally cut my throat while I was shaving."

On another occasion, Johnny and a number of other *mafiosi* gathered in the commons room to watch *Connections*, the CBC's documentary on the Mafia. While the show was on, a couple of prisoners started roughhousing nearby, raising a dreadful clatter. One man in particular was extremely large.

"Johnny came out storming, called him a punk: 'You got no respect. What are you doing up on this range?'" Rowbotham remembers. "And before Johnny got another word out, the guy had put a hand on his throat and lifted him about a foot-and-a-half off the ground. His feet were twitching, his veins were popping out as well as his eyes. I happened to be standing there at the time and this guy intimidated me as well, so at a real long arm's length I was touching his shoulder, saying, 'You're killing him . . . Let him go, let him go.' And he was [killing him]; he was finally going under. The guy looked at me and I gave him that very neutral look from my eyes—because I didn't want no part of it at the same time. I said, 'You're going to get charged, you're going to kill him.' He let him go and he collapsed on the ground and, of course, all the air came back in 10 or 15 seconds."

Johnny was not used to being on the receiving end of such treatment.

20

Reporters were not there to meet Johnny Papalia in October 1980. This time, his release from prison, after serving time for the extortion swindle, went largely unnoticed by everyone but his family, the criminal establishment, and police. Had reporters witnessed Johnny climbing out of the passenger seat of the car sent by his family to collect him, there likely would have been shock expressed on their faces and in their timely prose.

Seeing Johnny again after four years in the can was a shock to everyone who had not visited him in prison. He had aged terribly. His hair, which had started thinning and greying when he left for prison, was now almost white, and a huge swath on the top of his head was essentially bald. He needed glasses to see clearly; his cheeks were jowly; his brow furrowed with thick wrinkles when he frowned. The Enforcer looked old.

After arriving back in Hamilton, Johnny was in a reflective and introspective mood. It was the start of a new decade and as the conspicuous consumption of the 1980s was forming a new *zeitgeist*, Johnny had much on his mind.

Shunning his usual bodyguard and driver, he climbed behind the steering wheel of a car soon after his return to Railway Street, and drove to Holy Sepulchre Cemetery, a massive Catholic graveyard in Burlington. Driving to the rear, east section, he parked and walked slowly towards a large black cross at the edge of the gravel laneway, then stopped, head lowered. At the base of the cross two stone angels sat in prayer and a sculpture of St. Anthony of Padua stood serenely. Carved into the base of the cross, in swirling script, was one word: *Papalia*. Set into the grass were two flat stones, one bearing the words "Pray for the soul of a dear father, Antonio Papalia," and the other "Pray for the soul of a dear mother, Maria Rosa Italiano." For long, silent minutes, Johnny stood at his parents' grave. Alone. Thoughtful. Sad.

It was not long before Johnny again left the city by car, alone. A police surveillance unit scrambled to keep an eye on him as he drove north along Ontario's highways. Johnny drove past Toronto, past Barrie, past Orillia. Somewhere between Orillia and North Bay, where Johnny had many friends and business associates, police realized this was no ordinary trip for the mobster. They envisioned a crime summit, a meeting of the newly free boss with key members of his gang in the wilds of northern Ontario, away from the prying eyes of police. One officer on the surveillance team even suggested this might be "our Apalachin," referring to the ill-fated meeting of La Cosa Nostra leaders in rural New York state decades before. Undercover police raced north. Johnny did not stop long in North Bay, continuing on, farther north, along the scenic Frontier Trail. He cut off the highway left and drove towards the rustic beauty of Lake Temagami. There, he stopped the car in front of a modest cottage on the shore.

No other vehicles were in sight. There was no barbecue pit with smoking mounds of meat; no welcoming crowd of hoods.

Police scrambled to rent a cottage nearby, set up surveillance gear, and waited to learn what this strange ploy was about.

The next morning, officers watched as Johnny walked out of the cottage carrying a box and a fishing rod. He climbed into a small boat along a wooden pier, pushed away from shore, and paddled out into the lake. The boat drifted to a stop, and Johnny lowered a line into the deep waters and sat clutching a fishing rod. Police watched and waited. And waited. Day after day, Johnny followed this tranquil routine. A couple of officers even rented fishing gear and a boat to get a closer look. They paddled near Johnny's boat and dropped lines of their own. Johnny would not talk to the other "fishermen." He was not there to socialize. He wanted nothing but to be left alone. Each day for a week, Johnny sat in solitary silence in the middle of the lake.

Johnny, it seemed, was doing a little post-prison soul-searching. It is understandable; he had a lot to deal with. Much had changed in the underworld since he had been sent away.

The police were now taking careful aim at mobsters and had developed several new weapons to get at men such as Johnny. The first successful prosecution using Canada's new wiretap law made it especially dangerous for crooks to talk on the phone. And police had established specialized units in Toronto and Hamilton for the sole purpose of knocking out organized crime. The efforts hit close to home for Johnny; while he had been in jail, his brother Frank had been arrested twice.

Johnny's Calabrian colleague in Montreal, Paolo Violi, faced—and lost—a bloody war with Sicilian rivals. The war stretched from 1978 until 1981, bringing a body count of more than 20 mobsters in Montreal and Italy—Violi and his three brothers among them. In New York City, Johnny's powerful, early mob mentor, Carmine Galante, was also gunned down, further evidence of the rapid changes in the gangland Johnny knew.[1]

And a highly publicized television series, *Connections*, had exposed hidden details of the Mafia in Canada, and showed an embarrassing scene of Johnny swearing a blue streak at the camera crew.[2]

Johnny could no longer kid himself that he was a young man; he looked and felt old. His health was getting increasingly problematic. What would his role be in the coming decades? Was he considering dropping out of the underworld? Was he planning bigger and better scores? The answer to what had gone through the keen but weary mind of Johnny Pops on that northern Ontario lake died with him, but

[1] Galante set an example for Johnny even in death. Although Galante considered himself a good Catholic, the church disagreed and—as with Johnny—refused him a funeral mass, branding him a "public sinner."

[2] When Johnny was caught by the CBC film crew, he quickly decided to spew every foul word he could think of, mistakenly thinking it would render the footage unfit for broadcast. After much hand-wringing, the network decided to run the clip, after adding some background street noise to slightly obscure the profanity. Johnny was appalled.

signs of a thoughtful reorganization of his life were evident over the next few years.

Johnny was moving into a new stage in his life and taking on a role he had seen others such as Santo Scibetta and Giacomo Luppino assume before him. The Enforcer was morphing into that rarity in the underworld, the senior "man of respect."

In January 1981, shortly after his release from jail and after a lifetime of confirmed bachelorhood, Johnny stood at the altar to marry his longtime, on-again off-again girlfriend Janetta (Jan) Hayes. It was a very hush-hush, private ceremony. Hayes was some 15 years younger than Johnny, but they had known each other for years. Even while Johnny was in jail, she was often described as his girlfriend or, by people who did not realize that the greying Johnny had never married, as his mistress. She was auburn-haired and attractive.

"She was good-looking and a real nice girl," said a man who knew her when she married Johnny. "She was well-turned out, but not sluttish-looking. She was a bit glamorous but maintained some class."

Shirley Ryce, Frank and Rocco's former mistress, described Hayes as "a really nice personality and friendly as hell. I got along with her although she was a bit of a glamour girl." Hayes often wore false eyelashes and wigs.

Hayes was a singer and hostess—and eventually manager—at the Gold Key Club, run by Johnny's brothers, and her connection with the infamous mobster made getting performance gigs there a sure thing. One night, a group of young men were in the club, drinking heavily, and were more interested in swapping bawdy jokes than listening to the siren songs Hayes was performing. At one point the lads got a little too loud for the likes of some. Papalia lieutenant Steve Koaches walked over and leaned in to have a quiet word with them. Koaches simply let them know that the woman who was singing her heart out by the piano was Johnny Papalia's girlfriend. He needed say no more. For the rest of the night, Jan Hayes never had a more attentive and appreciative audience than the men seated at that table.

Whenever Johnny talked business with his brothers or criminal associates, Hayes discreetly left the room, striking up a conversation with the girlfriends of the men who had come to speak with Johnny.

One night in 1978, while Johnny was still in prison, Frank Papalia sent Hayes out to the police officers who were constantly watching the Gold Key Club, to invite them in for a drink. She approached OPP constables Jack McCombs and Ian Knox in their car.

"Frankie wanted to embarrass us," said McCombs. "He thought he was pulling one over on us by sending Jan out to our car to confront us and invite us in for a drink. We happily went in. She seated us near Frankie's table, where he sat with Stevie Koaches and Al Franco, and brought us over a couple of rye-and-waters. We toasted Frankie and we waved at Jan. She then dedicated her next song to 'our new friends Ian and Jack,' and then sang 'My Way.'"

Hayes was certainly not Johnny's first serious girlfriend. Decades before, Johnny spent years courting Mollie McGoran, the sister of his best friend, Toronto businessman David McGoran, who was a front man for many of Johnny's investments and a constant companion of Johnny's when he ventured into Toronto for his two or three-times-a-week visits; McGoran was even at the Town Tavern when Maxie Bluestein was worked over. Many felt Mollie and Johnny might get married—once she sorted out a faltering previous marriage—and Mollie considered that too. He trusted her enough to take her to some of his most important social engagements, including the baptism of Alberto Agueci's daughter, where Johnny's esteemed mentor Freddie Randaccio was named godfather.

"Mollie was very cynical, tough around the edges," said a long-time friend of hers. "It is fitting she came from that family with all of the boys, her brothers, because they made her tough—they were almost softer around the edges than she was. She was a tough cookie. The guys loved her because she was a guy's chick; not in a sexy, romantic way, but that she understood guys. She could also be a very funny lady." That Mollie stood just five-foot-four also pleased Johnny, who was sometimes sensitive about women towering over him.

Alas, Johnny's relationship with Mollie did not last. Despite the severing of their romantic ties, however, he remained fond of her. When Mollie, suffering from manic depression, killed herself in the winter of 1986, while her brother was vacationing in Australia, Johnny was exceedingly sad.

During the year or so after his return from the American prison system, Johnny became smitten by a waifish nightclub singer who fronted a band of mostly Toronto musicians. When he first saw her on stage in a Niagara Falls hotel he was mesmerized. Afterwards, with his suit jacket draped loosely over his shoulders, he introduced himself and bought everyone a round of drinks. The singer was unimpressed. Johnny did not give up, however, and followed the band from hotel to hotel around southern Ontario to watch her sing, and when he could not make it to a gig, he sent one of his henchmen to keep an eye on her. She never relented—"He gives me the creeps," she once said—but his unrequited crush gave her the unusual ability to slap Johnny on occasion, and even hit The Enforcer over the head with her shoe.

Johnny's interest in women not only led to his bout with syphilis back in his late teens, but also to an embarrassing passage in a newspaper profile after Johnny's 1961 rise to public prominence.

"His relationships with women provide the best clue to his character," wrote Peter Sypnowich in the *Toronto Star Weekly Magazine*. "Papalia had an inbred need to steal other men's women. They served as trophies. The women themselves were attracted by his money, but it was his muscle that won them (his last girlfriend was the wife of a major Toronto crook, who got beaten up when he tried to do something about it). And although Papalia had a succession of girlfriends, he was no lover. He used his women only as sounding boards, talking to them by the hour—about Johnny Papalia and his plans to become a big shot."

Either Johnny had matured by the time he was snuggling with Hayes, or she did not mind his bedroom patter. Or perhaps she did, for Johnny's union with her did not last long. By 1983 she had moved out of his apartment and into a relative's home in Toronto.

Some say it was Johnny's slovenly tendencies around the house; others noted the difficulty he had in suddenly sharing a life with a woman after 57 years of bachelorhood. Another friend said it was Johnny who did not take to married life, that he was bothered by having to say where he was going, what time he might be home, and whom he was going to be with. Perhaps Johnny and Hayes realized the difficulties their union faced before they tied the knot; a prenuptial agreement, in which Johnny acknowledged he had no claim to Hayes's furniture or other property if they split, was one of the few contracts Johnny ever signed. Her split with Johnny seemed amicable enough, however. She tearfully attended Johnny's funeral, and each year, on the anniversary of his death, she pays for touching advertisements in the *Hamilton Spectator* as a memorial to her slain husband.

"John, in loving memory of my beloved husband, who entered into eternal sleep, May 31, 1997," she penned the year after his death. "To some you may be forgotten, to others a part of the past. To me your name will ever be the key that unlocks precious memories treasured forever in my heart. As long as my life and memory last, I will always love and cherish thee."

In May 2004, Hayes again paid tribute to Johnny: "I love you for your total respect for family, the elderly—your belief in helping those in need, your love of nature, your laughter, your sense of fair play, your unfailing strength of character—walking always with dignity . . . How sad I feel for those with short memories . . . As you were you will always be—the greatest."

She is not alone in public displays of affection for Johnny. Sharing space in the classified section with Jan one year was another message for Johnny: "I'll never forget—Wild Heart."

A year after his wedding, Johnny tried to settle some other outstanding business. For years he had been scrupulously avoiding the tax man, as many good mobsters and other corporate masters are apt to do. When driving past the Revenue Canada building in Hamilton, Johnny once quipped to an associate: "They're the only people I fear." That fear was well-placed. The government wanted $39,000 from Johnny in back taxes—what Revenue Canada figured he would have had to pay if some of his ill-gotten gains had been duly taxed.

"Revenue Canada came to me with this debt," Johnny complained, yet "I have had no income for several years . . . I have never been in business."

On July 23, 1982, Johnny filed for personal bankruptcy. His only income, he swore, came from supervising an amusement arcade for a $500 retainer. He said he had no cash on hand, no furniture, no personal effects, no stocks or bonds, no property, no vehicles, and no recreational equipment. He might have had about $50 in his account with the Royal Bank at York and Bay streets, he continued, but had no safety deposit box and no credit cards. He requested a discharge from his debts of $43,920: $39,000 owed to Revenue Canada; $2,000 to his brother Rocco; $1,000 to his brother Frank; and $150 to William Momotiuk of James Street North, in Hamilton. At a meeting with his bankruptcy trustee, Johnny admitted he might have about $3,000 in assets from a 1971 Lincoln car he drove, although he believed it was owned by his brother's auto body shop, Central Body and Paint.

Shortly after filing his bankruptcy, Johnny started work at F.M. Amusements, another of his brothers' companies operating out of the family's Railway Street office, for $250 a week, he claimed. His monthly expenses were listed as follows: $400 for rent, $200 for food, $100 for clothing, $80 for cigarettes, haircuts, and entertainment, $50 for transportation, $20 for electricity, and $10 for his telephone.

Johnny's list of expenses was laughable, especially the $80 for cigarettes, haircuts, and entertainment in a month. The chain-smoking gangster was known for always pulling from his pocket a large wad of "browns and reds" ($100 and $50 bills) to pick up the dinner tab for anyone with him. He would spend more than his claimed monthly total on a single dinner, and lose more than that same amount on any given night when he went to the track at Toronto's Woodbine or Greenway raceways, or to Flamboro Downs, just outside Hamilton.

The following year, when he tried to win his bankruptcy discharge, his application was successfully opposed by Revenue Canada officials, who said they were quite sure Johnny had the means to pay his taxes.

As if a crumbled marriage, bankruptcy, and infamy were not enough, Johnny's first few years of freedom were also marred by the deaths of his older brothers, Angelo and Joseph, in 1983.

In that same year, Johnny tried to settle the brutal kidnapping of his long-time friend Pat Mancini, a millionaire businessman from North Bay.

Mancini, then 52, left his North Bay nightclub on February 24, 1983, and drove to a motel to meet a young woman who had previously approached him. Moments after entering her motel room, however, a man emerged from the bathroom and stuck a gun in his face. Mancini was bashed on the back of his head, tied up, and tossed into the trunk of his own car.

The next night, the kidnappers phoned Mancini's friend and lawyer Frank Falconi, and demanded $2 million for the businessman's safe return. After dismissing the call as a sick prank, Falconi sobered up when the kidnappers called back, this time playing a tape of Mancini answering personal questions and imploring Falconi to act as a friend, not as a lawyer. Police were called. That part of the kidnappers' operation seemed rather professional, but other shenanigans showed them to be rank amateurs. A ransom note, demanding "two big ones," had actually arrived three days before Mancini was even nabbed; luckily for the hoods, it was seen as a joke. Once the kidnappers had Mancini, the threatening and demanding phone calls were placed collect, allowing the calls to be easily traced.

Word soon spread among Mancini's friends, and two men stepped forward to help—Johnny and Danny Gasbarrini.

The Papalia, Gasbarrini, and Mancini families went way back. All were from Hamilton, and struck up friendships, if not business deals, long before Mancini headed north to find his fortune. Mancini's brother Vic stayed in Hamilton, and later worked as a lieutenant in Johnny's criminal organization. Vic was involved with a local racquet club that police were sure was being used for nefarious purposes. Police could never grasp the needed proof, although Vic was sentenced to more than seven years for cocaine and extortion charges for other activities. The extortion case was a particularly easy one to close. Police had Vic under surveillance and watched him enter a massage parlour he was trying to extort. A few minutes later they saw him emerge—wiping blood from his hands. Moments later, the surprised officers saw the victim stumble out, holding a towel to his bleeding head. When police pushed Vic to rat on others who might have been involved, perhaps Johnny or another friend, he refused, preferring to take his time in prison.

So when Pat Mancini was kidnapped and the Mancini family needed help, Johnny spoke up, offering to personally deliver the ransom money to Mancini's kidnappers. Police, who learned of the proposal surreptitiously, snickered at the prospect.

"I can just see John showing up at the rendezvous point to pay over that kind of money for the release of Pat Mancini," said an officer involved in the investigation. "We could see that just wasn't going to work. The great fear was, it would turn into the shootout at the O.K. Corral."

Before Johnny could take control of the situation, however, a police informant gave officers the name of someone thought to be involved, and police put him under surveillance. Between the collect phone calls and the surveillance, police became pretty certain Mancini was being held in an auto body shop in an industrial area north of Toronto. Six days after he was abducted, police used a battering ram and tear gas as they swarmed the garage, arresting four people and freeing Mancini from the trunk of his Oldsmobile. He was alive but physically and emotionally drained.

Three men and a woman eventually were sentenced to prison for the kidnapping. They are perhaps lucky that police, and not The Enforcer, solved the Mancini mystery. The businessman, however, went from being a victim to an offender in just four years. He pleaded guilty to defrauding creditors through a sprawling bankruptcy process that saw him cast off more than $1.5 million in property to friends and family while under a bankruptcy order. Mancini was sentenced to nine months in jail.

Johnny and Gasbarrini were not Mancini's only influential friends. While facing sentencing for the fraud charge, Mancini's lawyer presented a letter of support from Mike Harris, Progressive Conservative MPP, who went on to become premier of Ontario. Mancini was not a single-party kind of guy. One day when Mancini's car was stopped by the OPP, they found inside Mancini, Gasbarrini, and a man reluctant to identify himself, police sources said. He turned out to be John Munro, a prominent member of Pierre Trudeau's Liberal cabinet.

In 1983, yet another violent incident bothered Johnny greatly.

In December, the bullet-ridden body of Domenic Racco, 32, was found draped over railway tracks in Milton, halfway between Hamilton and Toronto. Domenic was the son of Michele (Mike) Racco, a very respected, old-world Calabrian Mafia boss who moved to Toronto and acted as a Godfather figure to many in Ontario. Domenic had found himself in debt to the wrong people.

Years before, Domenic—always a bit of a hothead—got himself into trouble when he shot and injured three young men at a shopping plaza over a perceived slight to his honour. To protect his son, Mike Racco called a meeting of key *mafiosi*. Johnny was invited, even though he stood out among the native-born Calabrians who spoke quickly in their regional dialect. Johnny could get by in Italian, but he was not fluent in the delicacies of the language. The men sat down and discussed who was to go after the jury, who would try to interfere with the witnesses, and who would hide Domenic in New York until he was ready to surrender. (Despite these efforts, in 1972, Domenic was sentenced to 10 years in prison for attempted murder.) That Mike Racco, the pre-eminent immigrant Italian criminal, invited Canadian-born Johnny to this important family meeting was a mark of great respect. An even greater mark of respect, and recognition of Johnny's power, came when the ailing Mike Racco asked Johnny to look out for his son when he no longer could. Johnny's bond with the Racco family had been strengthened by time he spent with Domenic Racco when the mobsters were behind bars together.

Johnny took his responsibility to Domenic seriously, taking him to boxing matches, and sitting and talking to him enthusiastically during the fights. They looked like a father and son, or an uncle with a favoured nephew. Johnny was also concerned about Domenic's nasty drug habit.

"The first time I ever saw cocaine was Domenic doing a line of it at Rooney's restaurant in Toronto," Johnny said in a private conversation a few years after Domenic's slaying. "I couldn't believe it. It's a dreadful drug. Everybody was doing it, but seeing Domenic doing it was awful. You just get hooked on these things. Cocaine's a terrible drug." When it was pointed out that this was an odd sentiment coming from a man who masterminded a massive heroin importation ring, he became angry and defensive.

"I had a relationship with Domenic. I was very friendly with his father. I gave my word to his father that when Domenic got out of jail I would look after him," Johnny said. "All they had to do was come to me and I'd have paid the money. What was it? Twenty, thirty thousand dollars? I would have stood good for Domenic. His father was dead and I was honour-bound to look after him.

"It's a terrible thing, he was killed for no good reason. They could have come to me; it was really a lack of respect. I'd have been good for anything that Domenic owed and they know I'm good for it. You may think I'm a tough gangster but when I heard he was killed, I was shocked," Johnny said.

Six men were eventually charged for the hit on Domenic. Johnny knew most of them very well; they were connected to the Musitanos, one of three centralized Mafia families in Hamilton. Anthony (Tony) Musitano, a man in prison for a Hamilton bomb spree, organized the hit from his cell and pleaded guilty to conspiracy to commit murder.[3] His brother Dominic Musitano pleaded guilty to being an accessory to murder after a police search of his Colbourne Street home found two loaded .38-calibre handguns under the basement staircase—one was the murder weapon. The Musitanos' nephew, Guiseppe (Joey) Avignone, who is treated by the family as an adopted son, pleaded guilty to conspiracy to commit murder and was handed a five-year sentence.

3 For more on the bomb spree and what it meant to the Musitano family, see Chapter 23.

Many in the underworld saw the shooting of Racco as a sign of disrespect towards Johnny. Murdering the son of Mike Racco was inconceivable until the old man died of cancer in 1980. Racco's slaying proved it was possible to slight Johnny and get away with it, but it certainly was not a signal that The Enforcer had lost his bite. If anything, it highlighted the fractured underworld in Toronto—a city chock full of gangsters all trying to do business. No one boss was able to bring it all under control, the way Carmine Galante and Vic Cotroni had managed to do in Montreal. Toronto featured a pantheon of powerful mobsters, and navigating successfully around them could be a difficult and dangerous endeavour. While Johnny was in prison, his mob rivals thrived. Paul Volpe rose to great prominence in Toronto as a leader within La Cosa Nostra, also answering to Magaddino. The Calabrian *'Ndrangheta* was also a force, not only because of Mike Racco, but because of Rocco Zito, Cosimo Stalteri, and the Commisso brothers. Sicilian Mafia members have also maintained an active role in the city, including Johnny's old heroin rival Benedetto Zizzo, and Volpe's former driver Pietro (Peter) Scarcella. Throughout the 1980s, Johnny would be seen meeting with each of these men, as well as with mobsters from Montreal and Buffalo.

It was an important time for Johnny. His fortunes soared when police action and gangland violence removed some of his rivals from the streets. Cosimo Elia Commisso and his brother Rocco Remo Commisso were jailed in 1981 for conspiracy to commit murder, and Paul Volpe was slain in 1983. Johnny's visits to Toronto two or three times a week became bankable rituals.

In the mid-1980s, Johnny again pushed for a lock on gambling and loan sharking in Toronto. Last time out it had meant locking horns with Maxie Bluestein. This time it meant going after the Greek gambling clubs that dotted Danforth Avenue. A major move by Johnny rarely came without some violence spilling over. A shot was fired through the window of one club; the ear of the owner of another was sliced with a knife. In December 1985, 10 men were arrested, but police could not pin enough on Johnny to lay charges. One officer said they refused to lay charges that he could likely beat, for fear of adding to his underworld mystique as had happened with New York City's John Gotti, who had earned the nickname "the Teflon Don" because charges could not stick. However, two of Johnny's close associates, Enio Mora and Carmen Barillaro, were among those charged with extortion. Mora was later murdered, just eight months before Johnny.

While police said Johnny's interest in Toronto was clearly related to the troubles on the Danforth, Johnny had another explanation. "I like being there," he said in 1986. His trips to Toronto were for pleasure, not business, because Hamilton had become "a dead place."

"Yeah, I know the people they charged, they're friends of mine. But that doesn't mean I was involved. I wasn't, because I wouldn't have anything to do with Greeks. I don't like them, I don't like their restaurants, I don't like their food." When he was asked why he hung around with so many mobsters, Johnny shrugged and said: "You go to Italian weddings, you meet people. I go to a lot of Italian weddings."

Shortly after Volpe's 1983 murder, Johnny went on yet another organizational drive. Individually, he met with virtually every *mafioso* of note in Toronto, Hamilton, and the Niagara peninsula, regardless of whether they considered Johnny a friend or foe. What he forged over the next year or so was a state of relative peace within the underworld. By 1986, Johnny and Vincenzo (Jimmy) Luppino had grown quite tight. The remnants of the Volpe group acquiesced to Johnny through the Luppinos, and other leading Calabrian and Sicilian gangsters had "walk-and-talks" with Johnny. Times seemed good for him. Several informants told police that any significant organized gambling in Toronto needed Johnny's blessing, regardless of its ethnic affiliation. In November 1986, Toronto police raided a high-stakes crap game, under Johnny's control, that had been held every Wednesday inside Toronto's Royal York Hotel. Each night's betting exceeded $160,000.

In the summer of 1983, Johnny was considered by the Montreal Mafia to be the man to meet with before moving into Ontario's underworld.

Réal Simard, a self-confessed hit man for the Cotroni family in Montreal, and his partner, Frank Majeau, started bringing Quebec strippers to Ontario bars, where the young women were greeted with enormous enthusiasm as they were the first to provide nude table dancing in the province. In July 1983, Simard arranged a meeting with Johnny *"per rispetto"* (out of respect), Simard told Johnny when the mobster arrived at Hanrahan's Tavern in Hamilton. "People have told me about you," Simard said.

"Maybe you have friends? In Montreal, for instance?" Johnny asked, using the strange mobster's way of saying something without actually saying it.

"Of course I have friends. Don't you?" Simard cockily replied.

"Maybe we have friends in common, like F.C.," Johnny continued, referring to Frank Cotroni, who had taken over as boss of Montreal following the death of his older brother Vic and the murder of Paolo Violi.

"Sure, F.C. is my friend," said Simard.

Johnny then dropped his challenge: "Can you get in touch with him? Now?" Simard, Majeau, and Johnny all traipsed out to a phone booth and huddled inside while Simard proved he was as connected as he claimed. Johnny then met with Frank Cotroni to discuss the move, and a week later, Cotroni met with Simard to see how things were working out.

"Have you run into Johnny Papalia?" Cotroni asked Simard. "Is he being polite at least?"

"Everything is fine. Papalia promised to help out if I needed anything in Hamilton," Simard replied. Claude Faber, Cotroni's right-hand man, then cut in with a statement suggesting how much he liked Johnny: "If he makes trouble, kill the fucker—he's old enough to die."

Always a shrewd man, Johnny seemed to hedge his bets on the power struggle in Montreal. The same month he met with Cotroni, he also met with his rival, up-and-coming mobster Vito Rizzuto. The two chatted quietly during a boxing match in Cornwall, Ontario, on July 29, 1983.

Johnny and Simard, however, were not at odds—in fact, they managed to work together rather nicely. Johnny solved for Simard and

Majeau problems that occasionally arose, and in return Simard let Johnny put Papalia pinball machines in his clubs, Simard said. When the young Montrealer was charged with murder after shooting two Montreal cocaine dealers—one of whom survived despite three bullets in his head—Johnny even helped out by collecting money for Simard's legal defence. The money made no difference. Simard went to Archambault prison for second-degree murder and turned informant as part of his rehabilitation. On the other hand, Majeau went to Ottawa to work as senior policy advisor to Roch LaSalle, a Progressive Conservative cabinet minister from Majeau's home town of Joliette, Quebec, who had been named minister of supply and services.

21

There are three kinds of citizens in this world: those who get a thrill
out of hanging around notorious mobsters, those who refuse to have
anything to do with them, and those who would rather steer clear, but

There are three kinds of citizens in this world: those who get a thrill
out of hanging around notorious mobsters, those who refuse to have
anything to do with them, and those who would rather steer clear, but
are forced by adversity to seek them out. This was a division marking
almost all of Johnny's relationships outside gangland as he settled into
his role as a senior man of respect. His response to each type of person
was capricious. Seemingly on whims, he alternated between acts of
mercy and merciless acts.

Johnny assumed a role that is often hard to grasp. For many people,
particularly in the areas of Hamilton heavily populated with Italian
immigrants, Johnny essentially replaced the village *signori* or *mercanti
di campagna*—"merchants of the countryside." For many in the community, Johnny was their mediator with the outside world—although
they rarely kidded themselves; he was always seen as a mediator of last
resort. Sure, he charged exorbitant interest rates and had a fearsome
reputation, but at least he knew where your home town was in Italy,
and was open for business in the evening when you finally got home
from work. There are hundreds of people throughout Hamilton who
attest to Johnny's helping hand. Some speak of Johnny readily flipping
them change when they were children running about the neighbourhood,
others of him sorting out misunderstandings between neighbours, still
more of him taking away threatening encroachments by unsavoury
figures from outside their neighbourhood. It was a role he was especially

adept at playing, as a Canadian-born Italian with an abundance of free time.

Johnny was cautious of whom he spent time with, but was not one to clutter his social schedule strictly with mobsters and hoods. Those not from Johnny's world, however—even those who thought of him as a great friend—could suddenly find themselves in very awkward situations.

Johnny's presence brought trouble in a variety of ways.

Donald Pressey, a Toronto businessman, is said to have loved the excitement that came with being around Johnny Pops. And, it must be said, Johnny did not mind traveling in the kind of circles that came with buddying about with businessmen such as Pressey.

"Pressey was one of these typical businessmen who prides himself on being able to sit down and have dinner with an organized crime figure; to say he was able to rub shoulders with him," said a veteran Toronto police officer. "Much like one of us might want to sit down with a well-known professional athlete and then tell people about it, there are people out there who feel that way about criminals."

Johnny was perfectly willing to have dinner with Pressey one night and orchestrate an out-and-out scam against him the next. Using a set-up remarkably similar to the one he used to swindle Stanley Bader, Johnny sent a pair of his key lieutenants to Toronto's waterfront, where Pressey owned a cruise ship that ran harbour tours. Gary Pine, from Welland, was Johnny's driver, bodyguard, and trusted confidant for many years. He had served a six-year term in Attica, N.Y., for a bank robbery in Buffalo. Another Welland man was an enforcer who filled the role vacated by prizefighter Baldy Chard after he was pushed from Johnny's fold. He was built like a brick outhouse, seeming as broad as he was tall. What's more, he possessed a particularly menacing skill that might have seemed quaint at cocktail parties but elicited shivers when seen on the street. While putting the squeeze on a target, he would talk calmly and politely, all the while flicking a penny about between his teeth, not unlike the way some people play with a toothpick. At just the right moment, when presenting an unpalatable payment option, he would clasp the penny between his teeth, reach up with one hand, and bend the coin to a 45-degree angle.

It was remarkably effective, and a skill that earned him the nickname "Pennybender."

Johnny sent Pine and Pennybender to Toronto one day to pull a fast one on Pressey. From a distance, the pair watched him go about his business at the harbour. Pressey knew Pine, so the Welland man stayed well out of sight. His only job was to point Pressey out to Pennybender, who then sauntered up to Pressey as he docked his ship. Pennybender cordially introduced himself as a representative of a group from Montreal, and explained that if Pressey wanted to continue operating on the Toronto waterfront he would have to make a peace offering to certain people. He mentioned the sum of $10,000 and—before Pressey could scoff—did his penny thing.

Pressey was understandably shaken, but felt he had an ace up his sleeve. He was, after all, friends with The Enforcer. Not realizing the threat was all Johnny's doing, he trundled off to Hamilton to bring his predicament to Johnny Pops. Johnny listened thoughtfully and then announced that Pressey would not have to worry.

"I'll look after this problem for you," the businessman was told. "Just go ahead and carry on with your business. It is going to cost you, but I'll look after it for you." Johnny then told Pressey to meet Pine in a little restaurant near the waterfront, and to bring $10,000—what it would cost to have Johnny deal with the heavies "from Montreal."

It was a frightfully simple scam, and an example of how Johnny's notoriety and network of friends were easily converted to cash. The Pressey extortion displayed Johnny's incredible duality: at times he was a friend and a godsend, at others an unshakable devil.

A now-deceased sports writer, for instance, had nothing bad to say about Johnny: "The writer, like so many of his vintage in the business, had a weakness for booze, fast women, and slow horses," said the writer's colleague, *Toronto Sun* sports writer Jim Hunt. "He was into the bookies for 10 grand, a lot of money on a sports writer's salary. They threatened if he didn't pay up, he would get a knee job . . . The writer put in a call to Johnny Pops, whom he had met on a few social occasions. The mobster told him not to worry, he would make a phone call. He did, and the sports writer never heard from the bookie again. He also took one bit of advice from Papalia. He stopped betting."

Vintage Johnny. Help someone in need, especially someone who may be in a position to return the favour. He used his considerable influence and tacked on some sound advice. Police note with some annoyance that about the time Johnny solved the sports writer's problems, he wrote two dramatic and enthusiastic profiles promoting Baldy Chard's boxing career.

Not everyone got the same treatment—not even all reporters. A writer at the *Hamilton Spectator* also found himself in Johnny's debt after a dismal performance at picking horses. This time, Johnny was not in a forgiving mood. In the newspaper's parking lot the reporter was slapped about by some of Johnny's boys, who demanded their several thousand dollars back promptly. He did not have a hope of paying, so he went to his bosses and explained his predicament. The newspaper had a solution; they flew him out to Edmonton and got him a job at the *Edmonton Journal*, a newspaper owned by the same company. Years later, when the reporter returned to Hamilton, Johnny still wanted his money. A Hamilton cop played middleman and arranged a payment plan.

Oddly, the best protection against Johnny's power seems to have been ignorance of it.

In the 1950s, Jackie Washington, a much-loved jazz and blues man from Hamilton, was a struggling young musician working as a men's room attendant at Duffy's Tavern. "There was a man who would always give me a good tip, real nice. One day he was in the men's room and two men started beating up on him," Washington said shortly after Johnny's death. Stepping into the fray, Washington grabbed one of the attackers and put him in a full nelson. Struggling in his powerful arms was Johnny Papalia. Such an encounter would likely doom a man who was a player in Johnny's world, but the gangster seemed to accept Washington's ignorance of who he had grabbed. "He took me aside some time later. He had his arm around my shoulder and said, 'It's okay, but next time you see me do that, turn the other way, alright?'"

Another of Hamilton's good citizens, a young man who spent as much time in church as Johnny spent in night clubs, blithely took his only suit to a dry cleaner that appears to have been a front to hide Johnny's illicit profits. The suit quickly disappeared, either through theft or sloppy shopkeeping. The customer was furious and demanded adequate compensation. Staff members tried to whisper sense into him, advising him not to push the matter, but the name Johnny Papalia—and, indeed, the whole existence of the mob—was foreign to him. Filled with righteous indignation, he insisted on seeing a manager. He threatened to call the police and to report the shop to the Better Business Bureau. He made a hue and cry the likes of which no one in the know would ever contemplate—and then promptly left his name and address. The next day a dark limousine pulled up outside his home and an associate of Johnny's hopped out, walked to the door and rang the doorbell. When the aggrieved suit owner answered, Johnny's man stuffed $600 into his hand—twice the value of the suit—and told him to find himself a new dry cleaners.

Even though his assistance was not always forthcoming, Johnny loved people coming to him for help. It was a pleasure he felt on many levels. Practically speaking, doing a favour meant he was owed a favour, and even as his brain aged he retained a keen memory for where people stood in his personal ledger. Far more esoteric, however, was his desire to be respected.

"John Papalia would like nothing better than to walk into a bar and have everyone in the room bow their head in respect," said a police officer who chased Johnny for years.

It was the classic role of the old-school *mafioso*, the century-old role played out in the Calabrian countryside and Sicilian villages. As a mediator, Johnny exuded power and was given respect. Everyone who came to him did so because they believed—they *knew*—he had the ability to help, and that bestowed prestige far beyond any financial deal. He maintained this "champion of the oppressed" image, one first cultivated by his *mafiosi* forefathers, and his populist background throughout his later years.

"John was revered on Railway Street," said an old associate. "I was standing there talking with John and this old Italian guy was walking by and the old guy bows his head to John and says, 'Ah, *compare* [Italian equivalent of "godfather"].' He was very good to all the kids and very good to all the people who lived in the area. If a guy needed a few bucks, John would give him a job taking the garbage out, or painting something, or whatever needed to be done. He would look after them. He wouldn't retire anybody, but he helped out, and because of that they all looked out for John."

Sometimes Johnny did favours to be kind. Sometimes he did them to earn respect. And sometimes he wanted the person in his debt to further some nefarious deal he had in mind. There are several examples of Johnny's largesse.

In the late 1980s, a Toronto lawyer came to Johnny with a problem. He was in debt to an impatient bookie and loan shark from New York state for $5,000 and could not pay. Johnny lent a helping hand; he told the loan shark to lay off the lawyer. Johnny had plans for this lawyer who was now in his debt, but it did not work out as Johnny had hoped. The lawyer lost his licence and fled the area before he could help in any schemes. Some time later, Johnny was in Niagara Falls with one of his key lieutenants, Carmen Barillaro, and they bumped into the New York loan shark. The loan shark said Johnny owed him $5,000. "What? I never lost nothing to you," Johnny replied. The loan shark reminded Johnny that he had lost what the lawyer owed him because he had done as Johnny asked. "Will you take $3,000?" Johnny asked. The loan shark nodded. Johnny reached into his pocket, pulled out a roll of cash, and handed it over. Johnny then shrugged and walked away.

Johnny's influence did not just extend to gamblers and loan sharks. He interacted with common businessmen and officials with some very large corporations. One such businessman was a hard-working immigrant who started a small haulage company near Hamilton's industrial waterfront. Because of cutthroat competition and sky-rocketing interest rates on loans in the early 1980s, the company couldn't tough it out any longer. Things got stretched just a little too thin, and in the summer of 1981, the haulage company declared bankruptcy. The events that happened next were investigated by Hamilton police, but no charges were ever laid.

It is said that the business owner turned to Johnny in an effort to ease his financial hardship. Since the two were from the same working-class neighbourhood as the Luppino family, the business owner likely made the acquaintance of The Enforcer through Natale Luppino, one of Giacomo Luppino's sons. Johnny is said to have been instrumental in helping convince a large and prominent Hamilton company to grant a lucrative hauling contract to the man's troubled firm. In return, Johnny was given a down payment and was to get a considerably larger remuneration sometime later. When the subsequent compensation did not meet with Johnny's approval, one of his better-known enforcers paid a visit to a member of the business owner's family and threatened to take him for a ride. Such an offer, if accepted, might have ended up being a one-way trip.

Until the day he died, Johnny was constantly looking for a swindle, a scam, a way to make a buck, big or small. Even the moment before he died, Johnny was talking to his killer about money. He had big dreams—plans not limited to the world of *Criminal Code* violations—but Johnny's background often made seeing them come to fruition rather difficult. Despite Johnny's influence, many people just could not stomach dealing with him.

He tried to get municipal zoning approval for a large hotel in Hamilton's downtown core in the mid-1980s, a deal scuppered largely because of nervousness over Johnny's role behind the paper-thin barrier he threw up to hide his participation. A decade later, when the city was constructing a large railway and commuter bus station, he bought up real estate near the station site. He figured people working in Toronto would flock to the lower real estate prices in Hamilton, and a tidy profit could be made by snapping up old houses, renovating them, and then putting them on the market for wealthy couples fleeing the big city. The inter-city migration never took off.

Johnny even asked John MacMillan, a former money launderer of Johnny's, for a copy of the North American Free Trade Agreement because "He wanted to know how we could use it; what doors it would open," MacMillan said.

Johnny's love of gambling was piqued to a fever pitch when the Ontario government was considering legalized gambling and casinos. He was intent on owning a piece of the envisioned large-scale casino action. It was a job he knew he would excel at. Johnny's vision was to buy up all the old music halls and movie houses across the province, and, once legislation was passed allowing casinos, to turn all the theatres into casinos, a massive chain of small, legalized gambling dens in cities and towns clear across Ontario. It was an impressive idea that could have made him millions—if it had worked out. Unfortunately for Johnny, it was completely out of sync with what the province was planning, which was to create a very few, tightly controlled, large, destination casinos.

Johnny also initiated talks with an American casino pit boss about setting up a casino in Nevada, with the pit boss acting as the apparent owner. With a St. Catharines lawyer and a few key advisors, Johnny met with the pit boss in a hotel in a small Ontario town to discuss the possibility. It was a discussion that almost landed them all in hot water. Nevada has very strict ownership laws on its casinos, and hidden ownership is punishable by up to 20 years in prison. Police in Canada were privy to the discussions, and officers considered charging Johnny and his cohorts with conspiracy to commit an indictable offence. Crown lawyers told the officers it would not wash; the conspiracy was in Canada, where it was not against the law to hide ownership of American enterprises, and this was certainly not considered an extraditable offence. Johnny's dreams of legally becoming a gambling impresario were again dashed, once American authorities were alerted.

Such a dream was terribly unrealistic. He would never have been able to shed his criminal record, his notorious name, or even his habit of never passing up a chance at a swindle. His fame might have attracted a number of thrill-seeking businessmen, his position might have made him a figure of grudging respect throughout his community, and a few politicians, lawyers, and businessmen might have flirted with hidden deals with Johnny, but in the end, that third type of person—the one who would never deal with a gangster—won the day.

It must have been a sad irony for Johnny, if he ever fully realized it: in the later years of his life, his name was intimidating enough that he could make money just by mentioning it—but the notoriety that came with that status prevented him from enjoying his profit as he wished. He was destined to spend the rest of his days hiding his name from ownership papers, and investing his money in secret or in underworld enterprises. The sad truth of Johnny's existence during his days as Ontario's reigning don was that wherever he went, whatever he did, whomever he spent time with became a matter of public concern, and any business he knowingly showed an interest in became the subject of police investigation.

Johnny Pops could never emerge from the shadows The Enforcer had created.

22

As an aging mobster, Johnny Papalia shed much of the explosive anger and bellicose behaviour he was famous for, and started mastering the more subtle sense of power and respect expected of an old don.

While Johnny would, for many, eternally remain The Enforcer, later in his life he needed little muscle to get his way. He needed only to ask and, if what he wanted was at all possible, his younger, dutiful associates would see it done. As Johnny matured, he put profit ahead of fisticuffs. He was, in crime lingo, an "earner," and in the modern world of the Mafia—where profit really mattered above all else—there was little better one could say about a crook than that. Money was the modern replacement for "respect," the commodity *mafiosi* of the generation before had valued the most.

In the late 1980s, police officers tracking organized crime were already counting the days until Johnny's death. He was pegged as ill, old, and having a tenuous grip on power. It was suggested he was growing senile, and even showing signs of Alzheimer's. Confidential police reports suggested Johnny might not survive more than a few years—predicting he would be assassinated as he became weak, or die quietly in his bed of natural causes—and intelligence officers were *umm*ing and *ahh*ing over what that might mean to the always complex and sometimes fragile underworld. To be sure, Johnny was ailing. He needed a pacemaker to keep his worn heart beating, and gallstone after gallstone kept making a painful journey from his gall bladder to his small intestine.

His age, his ailments, and his love for his family all contributed to Johnny's solemn vow never to go to prison again. If there was anything Johnny was afraid of late in his life, it was the prospect of again being put behind bars. Johnny admitted the thought petrified him.

"I've been to prison; I've spent too much time in prison," he said. "At my age, prison's just awful. I can't go in there. I can't stand the thought of going back." His fear drove him to become a most careful crook. He abandoned direct involvement in the drug trade for fear that a second dope conviction would send him away for life. He was also reluctant to risk breaking his parole condition not to leave Hamilton's city limits as he served out his sentence for the Stanley Bader extortion. Johnny's fondness for Chinese food almost got the better of him on one occasion, however, when he yearned for a plate of steaming *chow mein* and chicken balls from Lee's Garden, a Chinese restaurant in Burlington—just yards outside of Hamilton. Johnny would drive out towards Lee's and stop right at the city border, sitting and waiting, chain smoking, while someone ran to collect his dinner. It was a wise precaution. Police were watching and waiting, ready to charge Johnny with a parole violation if he stepped across that municipal line. Police officers, secretly watching him in unmarked cars, whispered to each other in frustration: "Come on, John, come on, go for Chinese food, go on."

Johnny was careful to the point of paranoia. His fear of prison did not mean a cessation of crime, however, any more than his doctor's warnings against smoking stopped him reaching for his cigarettes.

He developed a system to insulate himself from prosecution. He met with young, loyal henchmen, and, while walking along the street, quietly gave instructions. He chose his words carefully, so that on paper they looked vague, perhaps meaningless, and certainly open to interpretation; in person, through voice inflection, hand motions, and body gestures, his meaning was perfectly clear. Through thousands of these walk-and-talks, Johnny sent hundreds of lieutenants, family members, friends, allies, and those just sucking up to him, off to do his bidding, which one day might mean getting him a meat sandwich, and the next, stomping on a businessman who had promised a favour but never came through.

During these supposedly quiet years, when Johnny was trying to play it safe, he was perturbed—but not entirely surprised—to find himself a leading suspect for a string of slayings.

Sure, Johnny helped swindle $300,000 from Stanley Bader, but by testifying against him, Bader robbed Johnny of four years of freedom. It was an act that Johnny would never forgive.

Shortly after the 1976 trial, Bader wisely steered clear of Toronto, Hamilton and Montreal. Leaving behind his family, friends, and job as sales manager for a diamond dealership, he moved into a posh, two-bedroom townhouse in a well-appointed part of Miami with his third wife, a woman almost 20 years his junior. The leased property, at $1,500 a month, was part of a well-guarded development called the California Club. In Florida, Bader maintained his shady work habits, conducting legitimate as well as underworld transactions in diamonds, precious stones, and drugs. He had even come to the attention of state authorities, who were working to deport the businessman. Bader's biggest worries, however, did not stem from an unwelcoming government. In February 1982, he received an ominous phone call.

"Look over your shoulder—you won't live out the week," the caller said. Two or three other threatening calls followed, and Bader changed his phone number, but not before receiving one last message: "This is in revenge for five years ago." Bader had enough enemies to make the threats believable, but it did not prevent him from answering a knock at his front door at 2 a.m.—a knock interrupting a quiet evening he was sharing with his wife and a bottle of wine.

"Who is it?" Bader asked.

"Open up—it's Bobby."

Police suspect the wine lowered the guard of this normally cautious man. When Bader opened his door, he was greeted by a hail of bullets to his head and chest. He died on his doorstep, with his wife screaming: "Please help me—my husband has been shot!"

Did Johnny Papalia arrange to have the man who squealed on him hit? Police in two countries put him at the very top of their list of suspects. He certainly had a motive; revenge is a powerful part of a *mafioso*'s life.

Police suspicions mounted when they learned an associate of Johnny's, a businessman from Toronto, was one of the last people to see Bader alive. When police saw Johnny meeting with this businessman in a Toronto nightclub not long after the shooting, they slapped wiretaps on phone lines in Hamilton and Toronto—but no charges materialized.

An underworld source who knew Johnny well for many years does not believe Johnny had a hand in Bader's death.

"I was the type of guy that John would brag to, so I don't think he would lie to me on that. When Stanley Bader got hit, we were 99-percent certain it was going to happen, but not necessarily from John. We heard that Stanley was dealing with some drug people in Florida and he got some very bad people mad at him. I discussed it with John right afterwards and John just said: 'I just don't want to talk about it,' giving the image of just go and think whatever you want to think. To me, it was as if John didn't want to have to say 'no, I didn't do it.' We never had knowledge of John doing that."

Johnny certainly remained bitter about being jailed for the Bader extortion. But he always insisted he did not kill Bader—or anyone else, for that matter.

"It wasn't an extortion," Johnny said in 1986. "It was a swindle. That's not the same thing. A party owed some money and I helped out. That's all it was." He angrily rejected any suggestions he was involved in Bader's early demise.

"Bader was a treacherous snake. But whatever you write," he said to *Globe and Mail* reporter Peter Moon, "don't say I ever killed anyone. I've never murdered anyone."

It was an issue so important to the *mafioso* that he had his brother Rocco drive him out to the *Globe*'s newsroom hours after the interview.

"He turned up that afternoon at the paper," Moon said. "They called up to me from the lobby and said there was a guy to see me by the name of John Papalia. I thought they were putting me on. I go down and John is there and Rocco is in the car—it's a Cadillac, this big long Cadillac. And he gives me an affidavit. He said 'I want you to put this in the story. Everybody says I killed this guy. I never did.' "

The affidavit, signed by Bader in 1980 in Florida, said Bader had been pressured by the RCMP into testifying against Johnny, and Johnny was, in fact, not part of the extortion plot.

"At no time was I threatened by, or forced to give funds to, John Papalia," it read, "and it is my opinion that he was the victim of an overzealous law enforcement agency whose actions were misguided."

As evidence that Johnny did not kill Bader, it was remarkably thin. As evidence that it was important for Johnny not to be seen as a murderer, it spoke volumes.

Did Johnny kill Bader? Or anyone else in his violent life? Did he order others to kill on his behalf?

Johnny's protestations aside, it is not an easy question to answer. There was no shortage of blood in Johnny's long life—and death—in the Mafia. His name has been linked to well over a dozen slayings, starting with rumours that he had a hand in making bootlegging king Rocco Perri disappear in 1944—if, in fact, Perri did not vanish of his own accord. Johnny is also said to have been involved in some way in the deaths of Crown Cabs driver Tony Codispodi and local cardsharp Anthony (Tony DP) Kuternoga. Both men had connections to Johnny and were shot in the head, gangland-style.

In the book *Deadly Silence*, an exploration of Canadian Mafia murders by Antonio Nicaso and Peter Edwards, the pair of investigative journalists suggest Johnny was the trigger man in the 1983 killing of Toronto mob boss Paul Volpe. The scenario they present is Johnny shooting Volpe while another Hamilton mobster drove the getaway car, with a representative from Buffalo there to observe. Although Johnny had read the authoritative book, he never took issue with the theory, despite a brief conversation with Nicaso after its publication. Others do not agree that Johnny killed Volpe. In his book *Mob Rule*, James Dubro quotes an officer who investigated the slaying as saying: "Papalia is suspect number eleven on a list of the ten most likely suspects."

The list of those who may have fallen prey to Johnny is even longer.

When Niagara Falls businessman Louis Iannuzzelli, whose family owned the Hilltop Motor Hotel and the House of Frankenstein wax museum in Niagara Falls, started a successful loan shark operation on Johnny's turf, The Enforcer took offence and told him to cease and desist—or else.

Iannuzzelli had a very special friend, however, who had lived in Canada many years earlier and who was an old-time friend of Johnny's father, as well as of Tony Sylvestro, and even of Rocco Perri. Dominic Longo was interned along with the other *mafiosi* during the war and was a long-time racketeer and bootlegger. A very resourceful man, Longo left Canada virtually penniless and headed south, surfacing sometime later in California as the owner of the largest Toyota dealership in North America. His business success did not mean he loosened his old mob ties; he maintained influence in the area, despite the long distance, as an old don. Iannuzzelli reached out to Longo and told him of his predicament. Longo sent word back through underworld channels to Johnny: Leave Iannuzzelli alone. Johnny always respected his elders and bowed to higher authority. Iannuzzelli continued his business as he pleased. Dominic Longo, however, was an old man, and it was not long before he died a peaceful death in sunny California. In October 1985, within three days of the Toronto police first learning of Longo's death, Iannuzzelli went missing, was presumed dead, and his body was never found.[1]

"If you asked me who I suspect did it," said a policeman who investigated the case, "the suspicion is Carmen Barillaro and [another Papalia lieutenant active in the Niagara peninsula] at the behest of John."

Johnny staunchly denied involvement in Iannuzzelli's death, although he admitted he had known the man for 40 years. "I had nothing to do with it—and that's presuming he is dead," Johnny said.

[1] Officers looking for clues in Iannuzzelli's disappearance said that searching the Niagara Falls wax museum and horror house—where they would stumble upon closets full of artificial body parts—was one of the more surreal days of their careers.

Walter (Wally) Chomski had a wonderful sense of humour that ran to the black side of things, especially when poking fun at his own miserable luck. Unexpectedly seeing the familiar face of a veteran Toronto cop at a racetrack, he asked the officer if he had retired yet from the force. The officer had not. "Well," Chomski said, "when you are ready to go, let me know, 'cause I've got a job for you." The cop then asked Chomski what kind of job he had in mind. "I'll give you five hundred a week—I want you to start my car for me every morning."

The joke, of course, was not a subtle one. One day near the end of 1974, Chomski, a professional gambler and successful loan shark, started his Lincoln Continental and set off a fierce bomb blast that sent the transmission ripping through both the car's undercarriage and Chomski's leg. He had been close to Johnny for years, but had fallen heavily into the mobster's debt. Among the professional swindlers and cardsharps of the underworld, Chomski's tenuous situation with Johnny was well-known, and when word circulated of his near-fatal ignition, everyone quickly assumed it was Johnny's handiwork. The bombing was never officially solved.

"Walter told me that he believed John Papalia was the one who blew him up," said the veteran police officer who has known Chomski for years. "He blamed John for it. He wanted to confront John about it. When you look for a reason why John would do it, it might be because Walter was infringing on his territory as a bookmaker and as a loan shark."

There were other bombs found suspiciously near people with whom Johnny had a beef.

Maxie Bluestein found one under his Cadillac years after standing up to Johnny in the Town Tavern. It came at a time when Johnny was again making overtures to Maxie for his enterprises.

Myer Rush, the stock swindler who told police about Johnny's heroin ring in exchange for leniency for his hotel room capers, also had an ugly brush with the wrong side of a bomb. After speaking out against Johnny, Rush relocated to England but was called home to Toronto by court order—extradited to face charges in a $100-million stock fraud.

In November 1967, while he was staying at the Sutton Place, the city's newly opened and very posh hotel, a bomb placed under his bed tore the place apart. If not for the buffer of the new and sturdy bed and mattress, he surely would have died on the spot. Naked and bleeding, Rush crawled to the door of the burning room, where firefighters found him clinging to life. Things looked so grim when he was taken away that police told the press he was dead. At the emergency room operating table, however, doctors and nurses worked furiously to save his life.

"On entering the operating room, I beheld what must have been a robust body, literally torn to shreds," said Yvonne D'Souza, a young operating room nurse who helped repair the charred flesh. "At the back of my mind I figured that there was just no chance that the victim could survive this ordeal. Two-and-a-half tense hours later, our team having done our best, we wheeled him into the recovery room, hoping for the best." In the end, he made a remarkable recovery, portions of which were spent in the Don Jail's hospital ward.

Many eyed Johnny and his organization as being at the root of the attack. Johnny was about to be released from the U.S. prison where he had been sent, in part, because of Rush's rash words. When the timer used to detonate the bomb was found to have been bought at the Eaton's department store in Hamilton, the involvement of Johnny's gang became hard to dismiss.[2]

And more recently, in 1995, police believed Johnny ordered an explosive placed under the car of a man in Guelph. The man was the brother of a businessman who had crossed Johnny when an investment with him turned severely sour. The bomb was spotted before detonation. "He could have murdered this guy," said a police officer.

These bomb incidents could be taken as evidence Johnny had a willingness to kill. But, again, no charges were laid, no court case assessed

2 Myer Rush outlived Johnny by more than two years, dying in a nursing home in November 1999 at the age of 74.

the merits of the evidence, and, after more than four decades in the top echelons of the Mafia in Canada, Johnny was never convicted for anything more bloody than beating poor Bluestein almost to death back in 1961.

So, did Johnny kill?

"John told me no," a former Papalia associate said.

Ron Sandelli, a retired staff inspector with the Toronto police intelligence unit, said Johnny was "probably telling the truth—in a stretched way.

"He may never have pulled the trigger himself, but for him to say he never killed anybody when he directed other people to do it, I find hard to believe," said Sandelli. "That is basically how the mob works. It works on favours being done. A lot of people think it is money being paid out all the time, but it isn't necessarily money, I think in more instances it was favours."

A readiness to kill may instill deep fear in people, but it was not always an image Johnny was quick to project, even to those close to him in the underworld.

A Toronto hotel manager once introduced a friend to Johnny, and the friend then borrowed a large sum of money from him. When this friend disappeared without paying it back, the hotel manager was terrified Johnny would come after him for a pound of flesh. When Johnny heard of the hotel manager's fear through emissaries sent to him, the mob boss laughed.

"He sees too many movies," Johnny said to those around him. "I'm not interested in that; it would bring a lot of heat. Tell him just to stay away from me. I'm hot at him and I'm liable to give him a whack in the mouth if I see him. But I'm not interested in killing."

23

"The mob made a significant mistake," said Ken Robertson, the recently retired chief of police in Hamilton, thinking back 20 years to his toughest investigation. Of course, this was long before he became the city's top cop—back, in fact, when he was a bright, ambitious young detective.

Starting in the mid-1970s, while Johnny Papalia was in jail for his extortion conviction, the city of Hamilton and its suburbs were literally exploding with a string of bombings linked to organized crime.

"It was still being investigated in isolation by members of the police service—we maybe had eight bombings over five years, and we might have had three or four different detective teams working on them," Robertson said.

He was called in to the office of Hamilton's then deputy police chief Keith Farraway, who told him he had to do something to stop these bombings. The case came to Robertson because he was then a member of the Joint Forces Unit (JFU), an élite group of cops from Hamilton, Halton, the OPP, and the RCMP, trying to put Hamilton's Mafia bosses in jail. The bombings became a priority case, code-named Operation Boom. It was a tough assignment with few clues. The JFU, however, had a lucky break.

On June 3, 1980, a huge bomb set to blow up La Favorita Bakery on Concession Street failed to detonate. The bomb's design was simple: The minute hand of a wristwatch became a one-hour timer, and when it made a full rotation it bumped into a screw that had been drilled into the face of the watch; the screw was to send an electrical current through a short length of wire to detonate the dynamite. When the device was constructed, however, too much glue was used, and the excess glue dribbled down the length of the screw, insulating it, blocking the electrical current and preventing the bomb from detonating. This was the mob's significant mistake, and not only did it save a good chunk of Hamilton real estate from blowing skywards, but it gave police a whole bomb to examine, boosting their sagging investigation. After intensive work with street sources, thousands of hours of surveillance, and wiretap recordings, police pieced together the large extortion and bombing ring.

"It allowed us to track backwards to who was stealing the dynamite, who was selling it, who was buying it and linking the outlaw bikers to the Musitanos," said Robertson. Everything unraveled. It was a sad variation on the old Black Hand extortions. Victims were being threatened and attacked, and then approached for a payment to make it all end.

"The best work we did was that bombing case," said Robertson.

It was a case that highlighted modern Mafia activity in a city steeped in mob traditions. It showed how traditional *mafiosi* were in league with bikers. It showed how organized crime was not just an internecine affair, but one that had dangerous ramifications for a wider, peaceful population. It was indeed a successful case and an example of how police could put a dent in organized crime. Tony Musitano was sentenced to 15 years in prison for bombing and arson. But it did not come cheap. It is said to have cost police more than $1 million.

Despite a few notable successes, the record of jailing mobsters has not been impressive in Canada. Prohibition-era officers in the 1920s put an axe through many a barrel of bootleg booze, but left Rocco Perri largely untouched. The Mafia dons who replaced Perri did not face prosecution.

Police in Canada had little understanding of the Mafia, and few believed it truly existed outside Sicily.[1] In Hamilton, where organized crime had certainly made a mark, chasing mobsters in the late 1950s and 1960s largely fell to Albert Welsh and Mike Pauloski, a pair of staff sergeants who ran the Morality Squad and reported directly to the deputy chief. They tailed Johnny and his boys around town, closing down gambling joints and card games and earning nothing but animosity from The Enforcer.

"They were the most hated officers by organized crime figures because they were always on their tails, chasing them every day, never letting up," said Sally Pauloski, Mike's widow.

"And the gangsters fought back the only way they knew how: for three weeks solid they harassed us. They would call me while Mike was at work and pretend they were from the city morgue, saying, 'We have the body of Mike Pauloski lying here, could you pick out a suit of clothing for his body?' They would send wreaths to all of the funeral homes with Mike's and my names on them. They would have Chinese food for a party—that we weren't having—delivered at 3 a.m. There was a truckload of lumber dumped in our driveway. There were fire trucks showing up in the middle of the night with their sirens and lights going, because they were told our house was on fire. We had movers show up, saying they were there to collect the furniture. They told me on the phone, 'We know you have a son.' They called me every hour—on the hour—all through the night. One night, at 2 a.m., Mike was out doing a job and he came home early and I was ready to crack up. I was just devastated by all of the harassment and I told him I didn't know how much longer I could take it. And just then, the phone rang—and it was them—and Mike answered it and he said, 'I swear to God, I will not rest until I have you hanging from your balls.' And from that night on they never bothered me again," she said.

Johnny then tried a different tack. A Papalia family member asked to meet with Pauloski at the Chicken Roost, a downtown fixture that served chicken on a bun with gravy. "They offered him a lot of money

1 One notable exception was Frank Zaneth, an Italian-born RCMP officer who, throughout the 1920s and 1930s, tried to infiltrate the Italian gangs. Zaneth was later promoted to become the RCMP's deputy commissioner.

to leave them alone. They thought they could buy him off, bribe him. He said 'You know what you can do with that money? Go shove it you-know-where,'" she recalled her husband telling her.[2]

In Toronto, John Leybourne and his partner, Tom Stewart, along with a few other members of the Toronto force's anti-gambling section, were also crashing into illegal gambling dens. Maxie Bluestein and Johnny and his men were their biggest targets.

"We didn't carry out long-term intelligence operations, but on a daily basis we chased down and arrested operators of bookmaking operations and gambling clubs, large and small," said Leybourne. "Our theory was that if we didn't get the big guys all the time, if we cut off the arms and legs of the octopus and, in particular, cut the cash flow, they would eventually feel the pinch."

Long-term and intelligence-led operations—such as they were at the time—were the Mounties' job.

"We were just starting to understand a little bit about organized crime," said Robin Ward, a retired RCMP staff sergeant who worked early mob cases across Hamilton and Niagara.

Police across Ontario, however, were working in a political climate in which denial was the order of the day.

As attorney general for Ontario during the latter half of the 1950s and the early 1960s, the Honourable A. Kelso Roberts was the point man in the provincial government's response to organized crime when the American influence on Canada's Mafia was in its infancy.

At the age of 19, Roberts, then an officer fighting in France during the First World War, was captured by the German army. After a daring but brief escape, he spent the remainder of the conflict in a prisoner of war camp. Returning home, Roberts completed law school and moved to Toronto as a partner in a respectable firm. With his decidedly blue-blood looks—a deeply dimpled chin and gravelly moustache—he made the easy leap from law to politics in 1943. During the

2 Mike Pauloski died in a car crash in 1972 at the age of 46. "At his funeral, all of the gangsters were lining up to get into the funeral home," said Sally Pauloski. "They said they were there to pay their respects, but I think they wanted to make sure that he was dead. Albert Welsh went up to them and told them, 'You're not welcome here.'"

heyday of illegal gambling, the invasion of Canadian rackets by an organized American cartel, and the development of sophisticated narcotics smuggling rings, Ontario's newly minted attorney general announced his major goal for his tenure in office: traffic accident prevention. Roberts publicly scoffed at reports that the Mafia was the "cement that binds the crime structure."

Inaction by the government at that crucial, formative time helped Johnny spin his dangerous web. And in 1961, Johnny's outrageous actions—the Bluestein attack, the French Connection—exposed the government's ludicrous denial. That year the Conservative government took a beating from opposition parties over its stand on crime. New Democratic Party chief Donald MacDonald, with great foresight, told the legislature: "The dangers of the leaders of organized crime digging themselves in through legitimate businesses is an extremely important phase of this whole problem." Roberts tried to soothe his ruffled critics. But when he took action, it was limited to organized gambling, and even then it was not to curtail the Mafia, he said, but as a preventive measure: "Some of the lawlessness and crime syndicates which were rampant even recently in parts of the United States could develop rapidly here too if we were not prepared to meet them and to show them it does not pay to operate here." By the end of 1961, Roberts was pressured to establish a Royal Commission on Crime, and appointed Justice Wilfred D. Roach to head the probe.

Justice Roach heard a lot about gambling, "sin dens," the Three Thieves, and The Enforcer. He also heard some unsettling news about the attorney general's office. The commission was told that two years after Roberts took the post, he told the commissioner of the OPP to cease the non-stop police checks on those frequenting gambling clubs and then ordered police not to raid the establishments unless they received complaints. William Common, deputy attorney general, testified that in 1957 he suspected information leaks from the OPP to criminals, and W.B. Bowman, director of public prosecution, told of an MPP intervening to stop public prosecution of some 30 pinball machine operators. Despite serious suggestions of political corruption, the commission zeroed right in on Johnny's partners, professional gambling bosses James McDermott and Vincent Feeley, largely ignoring the other players. Somehow, these two men became the fall guys for the entire crime industry, and the full weight of the government came down upon them.

In his final report, Justice Roach described McDermott as "shrewd, evil and cunning . . . [and an] audacious liar who will stop at nothing to advance his own cause," and Feeley as "a public menace." The Roberts-appointed commissioner backed Roberts's view of crime and—like Maxie Bluestein—completely missed Johnny's emerging leadership role in Ontario's underworld.

"As a result of my investigation—and it was as complete as I am able to make it—I now report to you that there has never been, as far as I was able to ascertain, any syndicated crime in this province," Justice Roach concluded. "The words 'The Mafia' are frightening words, but the fear that The Mafia could be a continuing organization and operating even in Canada should not lead us to think that it is in fact still subsisting, and there was no evidence before me that it does subsist or that any of the activities of those engaged in organized crime were in any way associated with The Mafia."

If the Town Tavern melee and Johnny's French Connection arrest did not awaken the government, another alarm went off in 1963 when Joseph Valachi, one of the co-conspirators in Johnny's heroin ring, stood before a United States Senate committee and made history as La Cosa Nostra's first public informer. Valachi outlined an organized crime syndicate across the U.S. and into Canada, and revealed Johnny's connections to Magaddino's mob.

"Buffalo and Canada is all one," Valachi said. Johnny, Paul Volpe, Volpe's brother Albert, Danny Gasbarrini, Alberto and Vito Agueci, and two brothers from Guelph, Ontario, Frank and Charles Cipolla, were named by various witnesses as eight members of Buffalo's La Cosa Nostra family.

The testimony from Valachi, and the very public activities of Johnny, prompted the Ontario Police Commission to recognize the threat of organized crime and to first admit its existence in a report in 1964. That report led to the creation of a special criminal intelligence division the following year, and in 1966 to the formation of the Criminal Intelligence Service Ontario (CISO), an association of intelligence officers from Ontario's major municipal police forces, RCMP, OPP, Montreal city police, and the Quebec provincial police. By the late 1960s and early 1970s, police forces across Canada were finally aware of the existence and power of La Cosa Nostra in the United States and of the fact that members of the organization lived and operated in Ontario and Quebec. Police had identified about 30 actual Mafia members in Canada by the summer of 1971, as well as a growing list of criminal associates who outnumbered the *mafiosi* by 10- or perhaps 20-to-1. By then, however, the syndicate the government had for so long denied even existed had grown too many tentacles to count.

The recognition of and increased enforcement against organized crime, surprisingly, had very little impact in Hamilton.

"As a young constable I can remember walking a beat in the city of Hamilton and hearing rumblings about organized crime people—particularly people like the Papalias—and what a significant role they played in the criminal underworld," said Robertson. "One of the things that always amazed me was, how did they get to be the figures they were in a community where they were so known to the public and known to police?"

He probably had a few ideas. He will not talk about why he went directly to top police brass about setting up a special, separate unit to tackle organized crime. Some of it may have had to do with things cops rarely speak of. The fact of the matter was, while organized crime was solidifying a base in Hamilton, some of the cops—just a very, very few—did not seem to mind. There is no doubt some officers had slipped in their duty. When some Hamilton gamblers went to one well-known bookmaker near the racetrack in the city's far east end, they often stopped for a drink at the Jockey Club across the road. It was sometimes a sound investment. At the end of the bar, a simple sign was slung over a peg advertising the daily special. Occasionally, the sign would hang upside down, likely frustrating casual drinkers and diners, but suggesting to those in the know to stay where they were. With a drink in hand, they could then watch as police arrived in force to raid the bookmaking joint across the street and arrest the unfortunate few inside.

There were a number of rumours of police complicity—and one shocking case a few years earlier that was kept scrupulously quiet.

Hamilton Morality Squad officer Albert Welsh had been steadily promoted for his solid service within Hamilton's police department to the rank of deputy chief. It was a blow to everyone when he was over-heard by the OPP, tipping off one of Johnny's bookmakers to an impending police raid. The case was kept quiet, and Welsh resigned without the public ever knowing. What did it all mean? No one knew for sure. Welsh maintained the bookie was a good informant and that his arrest would have set back law enforcement efforts. But two things are certain: the mob seemed immune to serious prosecution in Hamilton, and some cops from other forces did not trust the city's police.

"When you came into Hamilton to do some work, you really didn't want to let Hamilton [cops] know," a police officer from a neighbouring force said of Hamilton's reputation in decades past. The JFU initiative erased much, but not all, of that misgiving.

While Robertson was first poking his nose into organized crime in Hamilton, things were heating up substantially between cops and mobsters elsewhere in the province.

In April 1977, the RCMP, OPP and Toronto police unleashed the Combined Forces Special Enforcement Unit (CFSEU) as a perma-nent operation targeting organized crime. It was a smart move, one accessing the past and anticipating the future. History showed the best attacks on the mob came from police forces working closely together. The charges in 1975, for example, against Johnny, Vic Cotroni, and Paolo Violi in the extortion scheme showed how cooperation between cities was just as important for police as it was for the mob. The need for decoding the often complicated communications and daily activities of a Mafia boss had been met by expanded police intelligence units. But watching gangsters was not doing much to stem the tide of crime. What police really needed were convictions. This led to a shift in philosophy towards a more proactive approach, and the formation of an élite organized crime unit.

The CFSEU was wrapping up Project Oblong, a probe into Toronto Mafia boss Paul Volpe's loan sharking operations, and had achieved in its short life a number of successes, when Robertson looked into its activities. He felt Hamilton could also do with a joint forces unit, and in 1977, he went straight to Deputy Police Chief Farraway to suggest an ongoing unit based in Hamilton to go after the city's prodigious *mafiosi* full-time.

Robertson had stumbled upon what appeared to be an elaborate furniture and appliance fraud involving organized crime members—albeit a different group from Johnny's—and suggested it would make an excellent test case for a new team to tackle. Prior to the JFU's existence, the message he got from some in the police department in response to his interest in the case was "Don't get too involved," Robertson said.

"I learned it is a very tangled web they weave and it is very difficult to investigate. They are very insulated from prosecution, not by a corrupt justice system but by a system of operation that keeps them away from doing the dirty work themselves. They are very, very difficult to get at, and no one had taken the time or the money to do anything about it—it was just too high of a mountain to climb with the resources and expertise we had."

The Hamilton JFU started in July 1977 with nine hand-picked officers: two from the RCMP, three from the OPP, two from Hamilton police, one from police in Halton (a region bordering Hamilton, encompassing Oakville and Burlington), and one from Toronto who had worked with the CFSEU. Over the course of several years they had offices at Hamilton's old, cramped Sherman Avenue police station, an abandoned OPP detachment in Waterdown, an office block in downtown Hamilton, and an industrial plaza in Burlington. While in their anonymous office tower on James Street South in Hamilton, officers thought nobody knew who or what they were.

"We thought we were so undercover, but I took a tire in to be fixed [at the local gas station] and when I went to collect it they had written

'RCMP' on it in chalk to identify it as being mine," said former OPP constable and founding JFU member Jack McCombs.

The old JFU officers are proud of their accomplishments.

"We were able to get into the inner workings of organized crime," said Robertson. "I don't think it was any secret that the joint forces existed and were targeting sophisticated organized crime, but I don't think they realized we would be as successful as I think we were."

Their first effort, however, floundered. The investigation stage of the Garfunkel's Furniture case went well, and several people were arrested in well-planned raids. When Robertson moved to arrest Mike McGale—a powerful enforcer for the group and later an important enforcer for Johnny—outside the Royal Connaught Hotel, McGale took a swing at him. Leaving nothing to chance, Robertson decked him with a left hook. The enforcer went down like a ton of bricks. He had been bested. However, theft charges against Rocco Luppino, a son of Giacomo Luppino; Art Tartaglia, one of Johnny's early associates; store owner and former city mayoral candidate Jean-Claude Garofoli, and others were thrown out of court because of lengthy delays.

"It wasn't one of our success stories," Robertson admitted.

The JFU did have several successes. A probe into the illegal takeover of a Hamilton meat company lead to fraud convictions against Antonio and John Luppino and Gerry Fumo. The trio's trial led to a landmark court ruling in 1982 that acknowledged the Mafia officially existed in Hamilton, Toronto, and Montreal.

Over the years, the JFU faced a number of critics. The unit was branded by some defence lawyers as a bunch of dangerous super-cops who trampled on civil rights by singling out people for special scrutiny. One lawyer said having "special" police made them think they had "special rules." And Johnny Papalia himself once took a run at the JFU. Johnny said he got unduly harassed by "ambitious police."

"For a guy who's been doing so much in this country, [the police] haven't been able to come up with anything on me. Something stinks," Johnny said. "They've got nothing better to do than run around following me all the time at the taxpayer's expense."

Johnny was right about one thing. For the amount of time, effort, and money police spent watching and investigating him, he fared remarkably well. It was a frustrating experience for officers.

"As far as successful prosecutions of John Papalia by our unit, it never really happened," said Ron Sandelli, retired staff inspector with Toronto police. "We probably gleaned more intelligence on him than anything else. We knew who his associates were, what type of crimes John was involved in. But whenever we had something we felt was tangible, that we could go to court with, either witnesses were reluctant or we didn't have enough evidence."

"How do you get to him?" asked former JFU member Ian Knox. "We always wanted to target Papalia, to bring in Papalia, but the problem was, how do you do it? It seemed an almost impossible task."

Law enforcement as a whole had something of a renaissance in mob busting during the 1980s. In the United States in particular, Mafia bosses tumbled. The top ranks of more than 20 Mafia families were indicted during that decade. Closer to Johnny's home, police fought on many fronts to replicate that success.

In the mid-1980s, in an unusually concentrated attack, Johnny became the primary focus of a joint police operation code-named Project Outhouse, an attempt to thwart Johnny's renewed move to control loan sharking and illegal gambling rackets in the province, as well as two other targeted police operations. Police tried to hit him directly, and at the same time work on his underlings to rat out their boss.

Undercover officers tried to infiltrate his organization. Dressed and acting like hoodlums, officers spent night after night hanging around bars and strip joints with known Papalia hangers-on and career criminals who had agreed to introduce each officer as a criminal friend. Whenever an introduction was made, however, the infiltration went nowhere. Unlike those who fell for FBI Special Agent Joseph Pistone in the guise of "Donnie Brasco," Johnny did not bite.

"You can't infiltrate Johnny Papalia," said Sandelli. "It would take you forever to infiltrate somebody like that to the extent that you would be a personal trust to him, that he would take you as one of his boys to tell you to do things for him. It wasn't for lack of trying, he was just too smart. I tell you, this guy was like a fox."

Whenever police nabbed an underling or known associate, they tried to convince him to turn on Johnny. Reduced sentences, dropped charges, protection—all were offered to get criminals to testify against Johnny or his top associates. All seemed more interested in serving time than betraying Johnny.

"Some of them would have died for him," McCombs said of Johnny's lieutenants. Johnny also had a keen ability to sniff out loyalty, and he identified potentially weak links in his own organization and gave these people special attention, monitoring them closely, steering them from unwanted associations outside his organization, and using appropriate discretion when dealing with them.

Johnny knew he was under constant surveillance. There were secret police microphones in his business offices and on his phone lines. Johnny rarely discussed crime in places where he thought there might be bugs.

"If he had something to talk about, he would never sit in his office and talk about it. Everything was a 'walk and talk,'" said Sandelli.

Johnny got plenty of exercise walking up and down the street, around the parking lot, and into the park at the end of the street. In an effort to listen in, police officers placed a series of microphones hidden in parking meters all along some of Johnny's preferred walking routes. Police even tried, unsuccessfully, to convince the Canadian Armed Forces to place bugs in every tree dotting Central Park, which was at the bottom of Railway Street. Both Johnny and his brother Frank felt persecuted. Frank once accused officers of killing a yucca plant inside his house by trying to use it to hide a microphone.

Johnny would often pull someone over to one part of a room to talk, saying, "Come over here, we'll talk over here, that might be wired." But when he got to the new spot, he would change his mind, saying, "Nah, it might be wired over here, let's go over there." He often ended up in the spot where he had started. And sometimes, ironically, he even moved the microphone with him wherever he went, because the person he was trying to talk with in private had been wired by the police.

Police managed to convince some criminals to wear a wire into Railway Street and at other meetings with Johnny. It took a tremendous amount of courage for informers to enter the lion's den, especially given the poor state of technological miniaturization at the time. One microphone was built into a belt so thick with batteries that the person carrying it was forced to wear heavy, loose-fitting clothing—even in the middle of summer. One person who wore a wire when meeting with Johnny and his associates said it was always a nerve-wracking experience, fearing the wire would be found. He said he would probably have gotten out of the room okay, because Johnny never carried a gun, but he would never have been able to walk safely around Hamilton again.

"It would have been a horrendous situation if he had found the wire," the informant said. "To John, it would have been the fact that he was taken for a fool, which he couldn't handle; that he had trusted somebody that he couldn't. No question, I would have had to move. John would have had me hit. Killed. It would be such an insult to him that he put me in his confidence, that he let me know what he was trying to do. He would have looked like a complete fool. To save face he would have had to order a hit on me, he would have had no choice."

Video cameras were also set up by police to keep a watchful eye on Johnny's popular haunts. Police sometimes used the top floor of the Bell Canada building near Railway Street and the roof of Sir John A. MacDonald High School, which overlooked Johnny's office. There had once been a video camera hidden in the street lamp at the end of Railway Street overlooking the parking lot where Johnny was shot. If it had still been operating at the time of Johnny's shooting, an officer said, the whole messy ordeal would have been caught on tape.

Officers also spent a lot of time just watching Johnny in person.

They followed discreetly when he went out, watched him as he came home, watched whom he was meeting with, whom he talked to, where he ate, and whom he ignored. It was often a concerted effort, with Hamilton police starting the tail and then passing off to Toronto police halfway between the cities, usually somewhere in Oakville. On his return trip, the pass-off went in reverse.

Johnny was a man of certain sensibilities and he once took offence that there was a "lady Mountie" following him.

"What's the world coming to?" he asked. "I don't mind these cops following me, but when I have bits and pieces of me out and there are girls following me, there is no honour in that."

Said Sandelli: "He felt policemen today were too sneaky. They weren't like policemen in the old days, when if they had a problem with you they would sit down and talk to you; that today they were just out there lurking everywhere and didn't have the balls to sit down and talk to you."

When McCombs and Knox heard what Johnny was saying about them, they decided to call his bluff—*if* he was bluffing. The partners headed over to Frank's house. They wanted the younger brother to phone Johnny and arrange a meeting.

"He wouldn't call him," McCombs said. "He was terrified at the notion." The officers next stopped at Steve Koaches's apartment. Koaches lived in the same building as Johnny did—four floors down from his boss.

"He invited us in," said McCombs. "He had a big cut on his forehead and a tire iron lying out on the couch. He was frantically chasing a bird around his apartment. His pet bird had chewed through the wires of his stereo and he was chasing it, saying, 'That fucking bird, if I could catch it I'd kill it.' He had smashed his head on a kitchen cupboard while running to catch the thing."

Despite their bizarre visit with Koaches, the officers were still not able to arrange a meeting with Johnny. Like Frank, Koaches refused to disturb the boss with such a matter. With few options left, the officers just walked up the four flights of stairs to the penthouse floor and banged on Johnny's door. It was about noon on a Sunday. Johnny was reluctant to let them in. It might have been out of fear that the officers were really there to place a bug, but the officers think it had more to do with the state of Johnny's apartment.

Johnny opened his door a crack with the security chain still on it. The officers said why they were there, and Johnny was quite receptive to the idea and said he appreciated the visit, but he could not let them in.

"My place is a mess," he told them. But like his underling with the bird, Johnny had a little pet trouble of his own. Johnny's yappy little chihuahua, which Knox and McCombs called his "little attack dog," squeezed through the crack Johnny had opened in his apartment door. Johnny now had no choice but to unchain the door in order to retrieve his dog, which was running around the hall by the elevators. The officers saw what the mobster meant when he said his place wasn't tidy.

"It was a mess; an absolute pigsty," said McCombs.

In the late 1970s, when Johnny was again in jail, an associate of his, Vic Mancini, was planning a wedding, and Danny Gasbarrini took it upon himself to organize a stag. Police anticipated a number of interesting people would attend the festivity in a rented church hall. Red LeBarre, one of Johnny's lieutenants, was just returning from visiting the boss in prison, and police were interested in knowing whom he might carry messages to and whom he had business to talk over with. Police surveillance officers set up in a hidden vantage point inside the church, overlooking the hall, surrounded by curtains. They brought in video and camera equipment to record the activities. (They also brought with them several plastic bottles to urinate in because they would not be able to leave their stake-out for the next 12 hours.) Along with the host and the guest of honour, police watched Red LeBarre, Rocco Papalia, Bruno Monaco, Hamilton city councillor Ed Fisher, and others party into the night. They watched as a vacation trip courtesy of Trade Wind Travel, Harry Apigian's agency, was raffled off—with Gasbarrini saying to not let guests know the trip was only for one person. Later, after the party had died down and the guests had left, the cramped and stiff officers tumbled out of hiding. They later showed the video to an expert in lip reading to see if he could make out any of the conversations. Little of value was discovered.

On a few other occasions, police felt charging Johnny was not possible based on their evidence, and were forced to content themselves with foiling some of his schemes. Sometimes it involved unofficially "threatening" the mobsters, pointing out to them that police knew all about what they were planning to do and that if anything happened to a specific victim, police would come down hard on them.

Other times they just stopped the money from getting to the mob.

In about 1985—although they could not arrest him for it—police managed to stop Johnny getting his hands on what he had dubbed his "retirement fund." The scheme would have netted Johnny and his associates about $10 million in the course of one month—to be split very unequally. Johnny was to be taking half and his several partners were taking varying proportions of the remainder. It was an elaborate and rather ingenious scheme involving lots of paperwork to establish dummy companies that were applying for hefty mortgages to develop property. The scheme was that when the mortgage company issued a substantial sum, the companies would just disappear. The companies were arranged to prevent their being traced back to Johnny. Police managed to intervene after catching wind of the scheme, and no money was issued. But neither were arrests made.

Officers sometimes tired of the cat-and-mouse game of just watching and waiting, and resorted to having a little fun. If you could not arrest the mobsters, spooking them was an option.

When police were wrapping up their investigation into the Papalias' alleged home insulation fraud, they sent tow trucks in at night to seize the company's large blower trucks, used to install the foam insulation, right from the parking lot outside 20 Railway Street. The next morning, those coming into the office were aghast to find the trucks missing, although they seemed to immediately assume it was a police seizure and not a criminal theft. Police were secretly listening to the conversation taking place in the Railway Street office and said they heard Frank Papalia complain that the cops took the trucks without even letting them know.

"That's just theft," Frank complained. One officer was unable to resist the opportunity. He immediately picked up the telephone and called Frank at the office.

"Frank, it's me. I just want to let you know that we took your trucks."

Frank turned to his associates and hissed: "They're listening to us!"

What makes organized crime investigations successful? "You need to be focused," said Robertson. "It takes a lot of energy, a lot of patience, creativity and teamwork. Sometimes these investigations take months and sometimes years."

The police expended significant effort and literally millions of dollars chasing Johnny. Despite successful prosecutions against members of the Luppino family, the Musitano family, Johnny's brother Frank, and other mobsters and associates around Ontario, the Moby Dick of crime largely eluded them.

If the beginning of Johnny's Mafia leadership was marred by plenty of prison bars, it has to be said that in the last quarter of his life, in the battle of Johnny versus the police, Johnny won.

In the end, it was not police, but a fellow crook, who ended Johnny's reign as one of the longest-ruling crime lords in Canadian history.

24

"If God is for us, who can be against us?"

That Bible reading at the June 5, 1997, funeral of Johnny Papalia, taken from the Book of Romans, was seen in a whole new light, given the perplexing murder mystery confronting police. From the moment Johnny's body slumped to the pavement, no one thought his shooting would be an easy case to crack or a mundane investigation to pursue. After a lifetime in crime, there was almost no end to the list of people who might have a motive to take a shot at The Enforcer.

Young, ambitious members of his own organization, frustrated by Johnny's longevity and unwillingness to step aside, might have grown impatient. After all, late in his life Johnny became known by many young mobsters—behind his back—as "The Old Bastard." Someone who owed Johnny money but had no means to pay might have struck before being struck. A relative of a victim, or suspected victim, of Johnny's underworld handiwork might have raised the nerve to seek revenge. A younger, more aggressive Mafia faction from Toronto might have wanted to end the special place Hamilton had as the heart of the underworld. Johnny's masters in Buffalo might have wanted to remove him because he was a threat to their leadership, since it is said that Johnny, as one of the oldest active members of Magaddino's La Cosa Nostra family, was exerting more and more influence south of the border. A motorcycle gang might have wanted to consolidate its power within the underworld and no longer have to deal with Johnny

Pops, who was notoriously distrustful of bikers. Some even speculated he was shot by a small-time hood who wanted to make a name for himself by striking out at someone who was truly larger than life.

One particularly powerful and persuasive theory emerging after Johnny's death was that a rival Sicilian Mafia faction from Montreal, the Rizzuto clan, along with its fellow Sicilians, the Cuntrera-Caruana family, might finally have decided to forcibly take Ontario's crime franchise from La Cosa Nostra by forging some form of alliance with Johnny's Ontario rivals. This theory pointed to a far-reaching and fundamental change in Canada's criminal orientation. It at once suggested a shot at the Calabrian boss by Sicilian *mafiosi*, and a blow against the American La Cosa Nostra by a group closely aligned with the Mafia of Sicily. In a perverted sense, it was seen as a war of independence, ending the practice of Canada-based Mafia bosses acting as branch-plant operations for American crime lords, and as a continuation of the secession started in Montreal when the Rizzutos led a Sicilian coup that toppled Paolo Violi and his Calabrian colleagues who answered to New York. The theory became more credible and exciting when it was learned that Alfonso Caruana, the reputed head of the Cuntrera-Caruana family—a wealthy, global organization and perhaps the most powerful Mafia family in history—had relocated to Ontario and was living quietly in a rental home in Woodbridge, just north of Toronto.[1] And when stories emerged of two secretive dinner meetings taking place shortly after Barillaro's slaying—one in a restaurant on Toronto's Spadina Avenue and the other in Woodbridge— during which well-known criminals from Hamilton spoke at length with a ranking mobster from the Rizzuto family of Montreal, the theory of high-level Mafia involvement became very seductive.

All of these theories were plausible. All were probed by police and the media. On Railway Street, however, the case was not open to such

---

1 Caruana's presence in Ontario was first publicly revealed on June 5, 1998, in a large exposé by this author in the *Hamilton Spectator*. See "Canadian haven: Alleged Mafia boss living quietly near T.O." on page 1, and "Mr. Big," on page 8. Caruana and two of his brothers were arrested six weeks later, and at the end of February 2000, pleaded guilty of conspiracy to import and sell narcotics. Alfonso was handed an 18-year sentence.

speculation. It was not lack of imagination that eliminated the guess-work, but rather, better information; someone had recognized Ken Murdock, the man who sent Johnny to the grave.

Murdock was not unknown on Hamilton's streets, where he grew up in tough neighbourhoods surrounded by tough men. His biological father was a truck driver who took no part in raising him, and his mother was not exactly the mothering type.

"Mother was never home hardly, and as far as I'd say a stable family upbringing, I didn't have that," Murdock said. "I love my mother, but back then, it's a parent that refuses to grow up, you know. She felt, maybe, that having kids at an early age that she still desired to go out and party and everything else . . . She didn't focus too much on the family aspect of things." Murdock grew up in one of Hamilton's rougher areas, the North End, a neighbourhood bordered by water-front piers to the north and west, heavy industry to the east, and rail-way tracks and the local jail to the south.

"The North End of Hamilton opens your eyes to a lot of things," said Murdock. "Number one is, for a kid—for a boy—you've got to be tough . . . Moving down to the North End is just different; just different personalities, harder individuals. You know, aggressive. Going to school when I was younger, I was always the biggest kid in school so I'd always get the shit kicked out of me because I didn't know how to fight," he said. It was a shortcoming he would soon remedy. One sunny day, in his mid-teens, Murdock was walking out of a variety store with an ice cream cone, when another teenager sucker punched him. The boy's fist caught Murdock sharply in the head, knocking him to the ground.

"By the time I woke up, my ice cream was melted on my chest . . . . I finally said 'Enough's enough, it ain't happening no more.'" Murdock finally started fighting back. In this case, it meant going home and grabbing a large sword before chasing after his assailant. He then joined a karate club and, over years, mastered the art of self-defence. Once turned on, his aggressive new attitude was difficult to turn off.

"I'll fight at the drop of a dime," he admitted.

Murdock was impetuous, violent, and strong. Once, when emerging from another stint in jail and looking for a job, he walked into Bannister's, a large and sometimes rough strip club in the heart of Hamilton's downtown, and asked the head of security for a job as a bouncer.

"We already have somebody," the man said, pointing upstairs to the large man standing outside the DJ's booth. Murdock simply walked through the club, trotted up the stairs, approached the bouncer, and— without a word—started beating him.

"[I] gave him a couple of shots to the head, kicked him while he was down. He got up and I told him to fuck off, he didn't work here anymore." When the man in charge of security tried to break the fight up, he too was thrown down. "I got my job," Murdock said.

It was a lifestyle that naturally led to crime, jail and links to some of the more established criminals in town. In the 1970s, a young Kenny Murdock had been introduced to Dominic Musitano, the Mafia don, by Murdock's stepfather, Big John Akister. In 1984, Murdock once again found himself in the presence of a Musitano, this time while behind bars. During a stay in Hamilton's jail for armed robbery, Murdock's cell was on the same floor as that of Dominic Musitano's brother, Tony. Tony had been in prison for a string of bombings but had been transferred to the Hamilton jail while he answered to fresh charges stemming from his involvement in the murder of Toronto mobster Domenic Racco.

"Tony and myself were up there shooting the shit and stuff like that, playing cards. He knew my father and he asked me . . . 'When you getting out?' and I told him," Murdock recalled. "He said, 'Listen, when you get out, go back down to the shop and watch the kids.' Pat was running the business. It was, I believe, a scrap yard then. Pat was a little bit younger back then, and I guess Tony just felt having more guys just to watch out for Pat [would be a good idea]."

Murdock also kept in touch with Dominic, who was staying in the jail's hospital unit. Whenever Murdock saw the doctor he would visit with Dominic, and a strong bond was built. He made a promise to

Dominic that he would do everything he could to look out for his children.

"If you make a promise, you keep your promise," he said. "I made a promise to the old man before he passed away, and I kept my promise. Dominic was a beautiful man. I guess they anticipated me running the old man down when I was testifying. How can you run a guy down when he has done nothing but help you? You call it like you see it—he was a wonderful man. He was many things, but he was honourable." Murdock said it was his attempt to keep that promise that pulled him down the deadly path to where he is today.

When Murdock was paroled on October 29, 1984, he headed to the Musitanos' scrap yard. Pat was 16, and Ang, just seven. That was his entrée into the higher echelons of organized crime and he proceeded to earn the family's trust through loyalty and ferociousness.

"Since knowing Musitanos, I have never talked to another member of another family. I may have talked to—'Hi' and 'goodbye' and stuff—but I don't involve myself with nobody else. I really don't give a shit for anybody else other than who I'm with," Murdock said. "I feel very much for these people. I'm not in and I'm not out, I'm sort of in the middle. I do my own thing, although I'm there for them when they need me." As an Irish-Scots mix, he stood no chance of being initiated into a Mafia family, but the Musitanos rewarded his loyalty by giving him a gold signet ring, engraved with his initials. And when Dominic died, Murdock was asked to be in the old don's honour guard, a cluster of men who respectfully snapped to attention when Dominic's wide coffin was carried out of the cathedral and pushed into a hearse.

Murdock was willing to do almost anything for the family. When asked if he would have killed someone for $1,000, he quickly replied: "If it was for the family, I would have done it for nothing." Murdock racked up a significant criminal record: possession of narcotics, assault causing bodily harm, breaking and entering, armed robbery, possession of a prohibited weapon, assault with intent to wound, use of a firearm during the commission of an indictable offence, mischief, failing to remain at the scene of an accident, possession of stolen property, extortion, and conspiracy to commit extortion.

Murdock came to true prominence within the underworld, however, around dinnertime on November 21, 1985, when, at the age of 22 and on parole, he added "contract killer" to his dark résumé. His descent from street hood to hit man came less than one year after he started hanging around with the Musitanos. Murdock said two men associated with the crime family approached him through "a series of conversations" that gauged his willingness to kill for the family.

He must have passed the test, because he was soon asked to kill Salvatore (Sam) Alaimo, 53, a janitor at Stelco, Inc., Murdock said. The motive? "From what they told me, it had something to do with money and family. I didn't ask them questions."

Sitting in the front passenger seat of a car and clutching a submachine gun, Murdock rolled down the side window as the car quietly pulled to a stop at the end of Alaimo's driveway on Florence Street. His target, a father of five, was inside the garage, working on a car.

"We drove by, the garage door was up. I just pointed and let go," Murdock said. It was not until the next day, when he read about the murder in the newspaper, that he knew Alaimo had died on the garage floor with a bullet in his head and another in his leg. Although Murdock had been promised $10,000 for the deed, he said he received only $3,000 in dribs and drabs.

All of Murdock's crimes brought him some prominence within the underworld, so it is not surprising that when he went calling on Railway Street, he was recognized. The stranger chatting with Johnny when he was interrupted by Murdock was a designated enforcer watching over The Enforcer, and he easily remembered Murdock. How could he not, since Murdock boldly introduced himself by name just minutes before pulling out his gun—"He's dying. Why lie?" is his explanation. Johnny's enforcer knew well the underworld code, and while he told some people who Johnny's killer was, he certainly did not pass Murdock's name on to police. Instead, he merely gave a description: approximately 35 years old, 5-foot-9, 160 pounds, with a dark moustache.

Word soon got out—onto the street if not immediately into the hands of police—and those who followed the underworld closely were buzzing about Murdock's suspected involvement for months.[2] Word

THEN AND NOW

Although Ken Murdock looks healthier and happier in prison (as seen recently, below) than he did when arrested in 1998 (right) for killing Johnny, he says his prison stay has not been peaceful. He simply wants to complete his sentence and then live quietly back in Hamilton.

Railway Street: Where Johnny was born, worked, and died. The dead-end street backs onto an inner-city park along Hamilton's industrialized waterfront. The Papalias' office is halfway down and set back from the street, largely out of sight, on the right.

Headquarters: Erected on Railway Street in 1961, on the same plot of land where the Papalias' family home once stood, this office is where Johnny took care of business; the parking lot to the left is where he died.

THE MUSITANO FAMILY

Dominic Musitano: Pat and Angelo's father

Pat Musitano: Charged in Johnny's slaying

Angelo Musitano: Also charged in the slaying

Angelo Musitano Sr.: "The Beast of Dellanova"

Tony Musitano: From bombings to dry cleaning

Watched: When Pat came to the funeral home to say good-bye to Johnny, he walked in tight formation with (left to right) Ivan Gallo, Percy Regimbal (face mostly hidden, the man Murdock says helped him find Barillaro), George Silvestro, John Clary (a long-time partner of Barillaro's), and Mimi Mercuri.

FILLING JOHNNY'S VOID

The takeover: After Johnny's death, police say gangsters from Montreal made deep inroads into Ontario's underworld. The remnants of a large, sophisticated gambling ring, dismantled by police in 2001, shows that guns, drugs, masks—and a police-issue bullet-proof vest—mixed easily with the hefty proceeds of illicit sports betting.

"Joe Bravo"

Pre-Arranged Funeral Plans

5 10:56A

Guy Panepinto

Stumbles: Alfonso Caruana, one of the world's most significant *mafioso*, moved from Montreal to Ontario but was arrested in 1998. Juan "Joe Bravo" Fernandez went to prison in 2004 after passing a handgun in a dirty sock (top) to a police informant with orders to kill a rival. Bravo had replaced Gaetano Panepinto as Montreal's man in Ontario after the hulking mobster was killed in an ambush in 2000. Panepinto's funeral attracted bikers who later became Hells Angels (bottom).

Alfonso Caruana

Gerlando Sciascia:
Gave the signal to shoot

Vito Rizzuto: Wanted for
slayings; says not guilty

Joe Massino: Powerful
boss of New York family

Leaving New York: U.S. authorities hope this surveillance photo will help bring Vito Rizzuto to trial in New York City. Police say it was taken May 6, 1981, and shows Rizzuto (middle, carrying garment bag) leaving a Bronx motel the day after three captains were killed. Joseph "Big Joey" Massino, who became the New York family's boss and was convicted in 2004 of seven counts of murder, waits to get into the car (right), while Gerlando "George from Canada" Sciascia, who was later killed, looks for the car keys (left).

Relaxing: Vito Rizzuto (seated, left) with his associate, Juan "Joe Bravo" Fernandez (seated, right). Bravo, a Spaniard, was twice ordered deported from Canada but still managed to muscle his way to a senior position in Ontario's underworld, representing Montreal's interests after Johnny's death. Standing (centre right) is Frank Campoli, who was named in court as a director of a recycling firm with several government contracts.

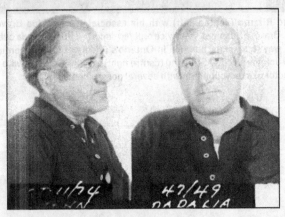

Jailbird: If he had not spent so much of his life in prison, Johnny likely would have grabbed a much larger share of the nation's underworld. In the late 1950s (top); showing signs of prison rot in the mid-1960s; and his final arrest in 1974 (bottom).

also got back to Murdock. After shooting Johnny in the head, he said, he went to a Hamilton restaurant to meet with the men who had arranged the slaying. There he was told the Papalias knew who he was and what he had done. Perhaps as part of his payment, or perhaps to buck the hit man up, he was given 40 grams of cocaine.

The day after Johnny's murder, Hamilton police successfully applied for court authorization to secretly record the phone calls of several people as part of their investigation; Pat and Ang Musitano were among them. Police, however, told the judge that the pair were not considered suspects in the death but that they might be in a position to know something about it.

Shortly afterwards, police investigating the shooting interviewed one of Johnny's key lieutenants, Carmen Barillaro, a restaurateur and Niagara Falls' crime lord with a criminal record dating back to 1970. Police would not say whether their interest in Barillaro stemmed from his being a witness, a suspect, or just a man carrying some of the missing pieces of the puzzle. Whatever secrets he carried, however, became hopelessly inaccessible after Murdock knocked on the front door of Barillaro's home.

When Johnny was no longer at the helm, Barillaro started asserting himself within Ontario's underworld; he was suggesting he was Johnny's heir, the man best able to take the top leadership position within the Papalia organization. It was not an absurd assumption for Barillaro to make. He certainly was a trusted and experienced *mafioso*, one loyal to Johnny and to Johnny's Buffalo masters. He was a made member of Magaddino's La Cosa Nostra family, and, being so close to the remnants of the rapidly declining Buffalo organization just a short hop across a porous border, he was tighter with the Buffalo mob than any other gangster in Canada, apart from Johnny and Frank Papalia. Barillaro headed a crime group of his own in Niagara Falls, and was one of more than a dozen lieutenants that answered directly to Johnny.

---

2 The news that Johnny's killer was known to both police and Johnny's family, and was, in fact, already in jail on an unrelated matter, first appeared in the *Hamilton Spectator* as part of this author's Gangland series on June 4, 1998, six months before police went public with Murdock's arrest.

In 1988, Reginald King, an RCMP officer and expert on organized crime, testified in court that Johnny and Barillaro were close. He presented police surveillance photographs of the two meeting, and said that while Johnny was the top mob boss in Ontario, Barillaro was pegged at "about seventh or eighth." In the decade that followed, Barillaro steadily climbed in that ranking through continued criminal activity and vocal devotion to Johnny. His criminal acts were not always successful; over the years he was convicted of possessing and passing counterfeit money, conspiracy to traffic in a narcotic, conspiracy to import a narcotic, and conspiracy to commit murder.

With true Mafia panache, Barillaro juggled legitimate business with his criminal activity. He ran a variety of companies from hair salons to a crafts store. He also seemed a generous man. While claiming severe financial difficulty—he filed for bankruptcy on Christmas Eve, 1986— he let a friend have and use his credit card at will. His bankruptcy papers claimed he had no assets and netted $245 a week as the manager of Murphy's Restaurant in Niagara Falls. A year after his bankruptcy, an irate Barillaro found the money to hire a supposed contract killer willing to execute a drug dealer who owed him money, and, in a shocking display of equal opportunity employment for the mob, he hired a woman to do the job. Barillaro probably wished he had stuck to the Mafia's sexist traditions; the woman became a police informant and secretly recorded conversations with Barillaro as they arranged the hit. He demanded the killing be done at the busiest street corner in the city, as a public statement about the consequences of not paying debts to the mob. (His brazenness was not surprising; Barillaro really felt he owned the town, going so far as to have his henchmen stop people from parking in his favourite public parking spots just in case he wanted to use them.) With the tape of him ordering the murder in police hands, Barillaro was charged with conspiracy to commit murder. He pleaded guilty and was sentenced to three years in prison. A year-and-a-half later, thanks to Canada's parole allowances, he was out of prison and arranging large, cross-border drug shipments. Two months after his release, Barillaro was one of eight men caught by police holding $2.2-million worth of cocaine and marijuana. Barillaro just couldn't keep clean.

Barillaro was loyal and ambitious at the same time. He had plans to take a larger piece of the Papalia pie when Johnny was ready to pass it on. It spoke to Johnny's feeling of invincibility that he had not anointed anyone as his direct successor. It was perhaps his biggest strategic mistake—one that left him, and his organization, vulnerable to attack. Johnny's talent for choosing the right people for the right job failed him just when his organization needed it most. Barillaro, however, was clearly grooming himself for a leadership role. He was willing to bide his time, to wait until Johnny left the underworld on his own terms. Barillaro's devotion to Johnny led him to speak hotly about revenge for the execution of his boss.

After Johnny's slaying, a meeting of the old Magaddino La Cosa Nostra family was called to order in Buffalo. At the table were the few remaining men of power from Buffalo, Rochester, Lewiston, and Niagara Falls, N.Y. Also there were Frank Papalia and Carmen Barillaro, said Murdock.

"There was a meeting over in Buffalo, the meeting of the so-called minds," Murdock said. The talk in Buffalo was about who had attacked the family, what it meant, and how they should respond. Murdock's close association with the Musitano family was well known, and the Papalias and their Buffalo colleagues immediately placed the blame squarely on the shoulders of Pat Musitano, Murdock said. Barillaro was incensed and vowed to look after the family's vengeance himself.

"Word came back to Pat, more or less, that he was next. The only details that I got was the meeting took place and supposedly through the leader over there, the right-hand man trickled the information back, and Carmen was stated [as] saying at the table, at the meeting: 'I'll take care of the fat piece of shit myself.'"

It is perhaps not surprising that with the credible threat of Barillaro's retribution, gangsters in Pat and Ang Musitano's position would be nervous. "I had phone calls from them at 3 in the morning saying, 'Quick, I think somebody is around my house,'" said Murdock. "Of course, you grab the gun, get in the z-28, and go 120 [kilometres per hour] all the way there. And nothing."

On June 2, two days after Johnny's murder, police were keeping an eye on The Gathering Spot, the Musitanos' restaurant on James Street North at Robert Street in Hamilton, a place that family associates usually called simply "The G-Spot." Officers watched in amazement as Barillaro arrived and met with Pat. Like Johnny, these two experienced gangsters did not talk about such serious stuff in locations likely to be bugged. Instead of taking a seat in The G-Spot, they walked up and down Robert Street as they engaged in a serious and intense discussion. Police tried to record the conversation—with limited success. Later in court, Pat admitted Barillaro had accused him of orchestrating Johnny's murder, a dangerous accusation that Pat denied. The meeting ended without resolution.

Everyone, it seemed, knew Murdock was the killer, and many pegged the Musitanos as being the masterminds behind it. The day before Johnny's funeral, many members of the Papalia family took a break from visitation duties and gathered for refreshments at another restaurant that the Musitanos were associated with, the Italian Oven on King William Street. By coincidence, Murdock pulled up for a visit.

"Apparently John's relatives were inside, and I think Pat and Ang seen me pull up. Ang came out on the street before I even got in there and said, you know, 'There's cousins and all that, and John's family's in there. It's not wise to stick around here, you'd better leave.' So I left," Murdock said. Another time, Murdock was having a coffee in one of the Italian social clubs on Barton Street when someone approached and said: "Everybody's talking and saying that it was you that shot John."

"Did everybody know that it happened? Yes. Did everybody know that it was me that did it within a few days? Yes," Murdock said. "It bothered me that people were talking about it. I wasn't really afraid for myself, but I was afraid for my family. I naturally kicked the wife out of the house, packed her up and out the door, and she didn't have a clue as to why I kicked her out of the house. I gave her all the furniture. I gave her everything—the only thing I kept was a computer. I made it seem like a break-up. It was a hard, hard thing. You've got you and your wife out on the front lawn in front of your mother-in-law, crying your eyes out. It was a bad scene. A bad, bad scene. It hurt big time. After that, were precautions taken? Yeah, there were precautions taken."

"You set up cameras so you see anything around the house and sensors inside the windows. You set up and expect the worse. You have guns everywhere and that's life. You're not scared but very cautious," he said.

"Everybody was uptight, concerned about Pat's safety and everything else," Murdock said. Pat and Ang admitted in court that they invoked tight personal security while the unrest whirled around them. They ordered Murdock, the family enforcer, to keep a gun handy and remain in a constant state of readiness. Murdock grew uneasy with the situation.

"If something is going to happen, why are you waiting for it?" he asked the Musitanos. Murdock said there were wide-ranging discussions on where an attack might come from and who might pose a threat.

"There was discussions in and around that time and more or less everybody is sort of thinking out loud where would anyone come back to attack . . . Apparently things had been looked at from different angles, such as Luppinos—and when you're looking at Luppinos you're looking at Mike Moore and K-9; like anybody that would help out Papalias more or less," Murdock said, referring to members of the Luppino organization, a family enforcer, and Ion William Croitoru, known to everyone as Johnny K-9, a former president of the Hamilton chapter of the Satan's Choice Motorcycle Club.[3] "They were looked at and the concern was that something may happen to Pat through that way, possibly. And K-9 was basically to be shot and killed as well," Murdock said of an alleged "hit list" against potential retaliation. Some sources say the list extended to include six people, including older and young members of a rival family and another member of the Papalia clan, and, if successfully acted upon, would have left the

3 K-9, a former professional wrestler, is a man to be reckoned with; he pleaded guilty in 1999 to conspiring to bomb a strip club in Sudbury where he had been asked to remove his bike gang jacket. The bomb was instead used to blow up Sudbury's police headquarters in December 1996.

Musitano family as the last remaining centralized Mafia family of power and tradition in the city.

Pat and Ang never acknowledged the existence of an extended hit list. They did admit they discussed the matter of Barillaro's threats and agreed killing Barillaro first was the best option. Ang went to Murdock's home and told him that Pat had approved the hit, and on July 23, 1997, armed with a 9-mm handgun and with Ang sitting in the passenger seat, Murdock drove to Niagara Falls, speeding along the highway to ensure no one was following.

The pair went to Barillaro's Corwin Avenue home, but the mobster's car, a red Corvette with a white convertible top, was not there. They sat in their car at the end of the street watching his home through binoculars, Murdock said. Barillaro did not arrive. They pushed on, driving around the Honeymoon Capital in search of the marked man. They visited a hotel near Clifton Hill and a coffee bar near Queen Street. Like his boss Johnny, Barillaro was a creature of habit. As the pair drove past a motel where Barillaro often held court, Ang pointed out an empty parking spot where Barillaro usually parked his car, Murdock said. In a parking lot near the café, they spied the Corvette. Murdock went inside, carrying the gun in a pouch around his waist, and spoke with a man behind the coffee shop counter. Murdock had never seen Barillaro, and, as he had with Johnny, quickly came up with an excuse to be asking for someone he did not know. He told the counter clerk he was interested in buying the red convertible in the parking lot, and asked if its owner was in the restaurant. He was not, he was told, so Murdock bought two cappuccinos—or "cup of chinos," as Murdock says—and left. They did not know it, but Barillaro had earlier parked his Corvette in the café's parking lot for a rendezvous with two associates from Toronto, and the three had walked to a nearby restaurant for dinner.

Around 7:30 p.m., outside a doughnut shop, Murdock said, he and Ang met Percy Regimbal, 36, a Welland man who got his start in the vending business by buying machines from Johnny. Regimbal told them Barillaro had just returned home, Murdock said—although, when Regimbal was called to the stand at the Musitano's preliminary hearing, he flatly denied the allegation. Murdock and Ang then headed straight back to the mobster's house and, from a parking spot at the side of the road, watched through the car's rearview mirror as a woman, thought to be Barillaro's wife, left the house shortly before 8 p.m., followed a few minutes later by one of Barillaro's two teenage daughters. Believing Barillaro was now alone, they pulled into his driveway. Ang wanted to get out and do the job himself, but Murdock insisted he wait in the car. Ang reluctantly agreed, but said Murdock had to give Barillaro a message before he was killed.

"Let him know it's from us," he said to Murdock.

With the gun tucked in the front of his jeans and wearing the same baseball cap he wore when he had shot Johnny just two months before, the hit man opened the glass storm door of Barillaro's house—using his shirt tail as a glove to keep his fingerprints off the handle—and knocked.

It was about 8:10 p.m., and inside the house, Barillaro was on the phone to a friend, a local lawyer. When he heard the knock at the door, he put the handset down, with his friend still on the line, and answered the door; he would never complete that conversation.

Barillaro came to the door wearing shorts and a loose-fitting, short-sleeved, Hawaiian shirt.

"What do you want?" Barillaro snapped at the stranger, and Murdock asked him if he owned the Corvette in the driveway.

"Yes," Barillaro said. Murdock then asked if he would sell it.

"No," came the curt reply, quickly followed by a suggestion that the visitor should now leave.

"He wasn't very pleasant about it, but he told me to leave . . . He was pretty arrogant," Murdock recalled. While Barillaro was being his arrogant best, the fingers of Murdock's right hand were wrapping themselves around the butt of his gun. Murdock then pulled out the weapon and said: "This is a message from Pat."

"He stopped talking," recalled Murdock. "It all clicked in to him, it seemed to me. He shut the door . . . He's pushing on the door from the inside and I'm pushing it with one hand from the outside. And eventually I got it open. He ran from the door, once he knew I was getting in."

Barillaro retreated into the house as Murdock stormed in, but suddenly had a change of heart. Perhaps realizing he could never reach the loaded handgun he kept hidden in his golf bag, he turned and rushed at the intruder.

"He tried to run, tried to tackle me," Murdock said. The hit man fired twice. "Two shots went off in a split second, as fast as it would go."

The first bullet struck Barillaro in the torso, the second in the head. The bullets entered the mobster's body as he ran full force towards Murdock; although the bullets killed Barillaro, they did not stop his body's onslaught, and he continued forward, collapsing against the front door, pinning it closed from the inside.

"I was just wanting to get out of the house after he fell," Murdock said. "I pulled the door open but it ended up pulling the weight of his body and I pulled the door handle off . . . it just came off in my hands."

He then smashed a pane of glass in the door with his gun and reached through to the handle on the other side, and managed to slide Barillaro's body along enough to squeeze outside, all without ever really looking at the body. Murdock walked quickly to the car—still carrying the broken door handle—gave it and the gun to Ang, and drove away. Murdock's panic subsided and more rational thoughts surfaced. With what was probably a sudden, icy realization, he thought of his fingerprints liberally sprinkled about the inside of Barillaro's broken door. He decided to return to the house to remove the damning evidence. Turning sharply around the block, Murdock and Ang again pulled into Barillaro's driveway. Slipping back into the hallway, Murdock used his shirt to wipe down the inside and outside of Barillaro's front door. Murdock finally looked down at the mobster, and saw a lot of blood pooling on the floor.

As they drove away from St. Catharines toward Hamilton, Ang wiped fingerprints from the door handle and tossed it out the window into a grassy patch at the side of the highway, Murdock said. While Murdock drove, Ang removed the remaining bullets from the gun, wiped them down, wrapped them in a tissue, and stuffed them into a bottle. This, too, was thrown from the car. Once in Hamilton, they had one more piece of evidence to discard. Murdock drove to Cootes Paradise, a swampy area west of Hamilton with a small, man-made canal running through it. The gun used to murder Murdock's third victim was wiped of fingerprints and tossed into waist-deep water. Ang went to report to Pat on Barillaro's end. Later, when Pat saw Murdock, he thanked him for the service he had provided for the family.

Meanwhile, the man at the other end of Barillaro's telephone line had heard the gunshots and scurried over to his friend's house. At 8:19 p.m., he found Barillaro lying in the front hallway, dead on the eve of his 53rd birthday.

Murdock was now a serial killer.

25

Few thought the slayings of Johnny Papalia and Carmen Barillaro would ever be punished through the courts. Mafia murders rarely are. According to organized crime specialist Antonio Nicaso, there have been at least 26 Mafia murders in Canada since 1967 and not one has been definitively solved in the courts—although a few have ended in related charges, usually against a hired trigger man or an accomplice as opposed to the boss who directly ordered the hit.[1]

For 541 days, the mystery of Johnny's slaying remained unsolved by police, and for 488 days, Barillaro's shooting officially remained a puzzle. Police working on the murders played a very careful game with the media. Two months *before* Johnny was shot, police had secretly formed a task force, called Project Expiate, to probe three unsolved murders: Salvatore Alaimo's machine-gun death in 1985 and the murders of Ronald MacNeil and Steven Roy, two Hamilton cocaine dealers killed days apart in 1987. Police suspected all three were somehow linked to the Musitano family. Two months after Barillaro was killed, police wrapped the two Mafia murders into Expiate's mandate, again suspecting a Musitano link—but when reporters were first told of Expiate's existence, it was presented as a new task force established to probe only Johnny's and Barillaro's deaths. Sometime later, reporters

1 *Deadly Silence* documents 13 of the most colourful and important Canadian Mafia murders.

were told Alaimo's shooting was being "added" to the project. It was obviously a ploy to put pressure on those whom police believed were involved.

In the early hours of November 24, 1998, police detectives quietly started presenting their version of events by simultaneously banging on the doors of two homes in Hamilton. On St. Clair Boulevard, they came for 31-year-old Pasquale (Pat) Musitano. On Colbourne Street, it was Pat's brother, Angelo (Ang) Musitano, 21, whom they hand-cuffed and took away. Pat was charged with first-degree murder for Johnny's slaying. Ang was charged with first-degree murder in both Johnny's and Barillaro's killing. The brothers retained two of the brightest criminal lawyers in the province: John Rosen of Toronto, who had defended serial sex-slayer Paul Bernardo, and Dean Paquette, a leading lawyer in Hamilton, who, as a Crown attorney, led many of the prosecutions against the mob, including the 1983 case against Dominic Musitano for the Racco murder.

It was a shocking turn of events. At a carefully orchestrated press conference, senior officials from five police services announced the arrests and the incredible news that Ken Murdock, the trigger man in both of the murders, had struck a deal with authorities. While police were breaking the news, Murdock was breaking records for swift justice. Under heavy guard, he was led through a Hamilton court and pleaded guilty to three counts of second-degree murder. For killing Johnny Papalia, Carmen Barillaro, and Sam Alaimo, Murdock was handed a life sentence with no chance of parole for 13 years. Murdock's journey through the courts came after months of secret negotiations between the gunman's lawyer, Tom Ireson, and the authorities.

As it turned out, police had some pretty good ideas on the case, right from the start.

Murdock's downfall had really started back in late 1989—long before he had even met Johnny Papalia—when he impulsively robbed a Burlington jewelry store. It was a caper of vintage Murdock simplicity: "I walked in and I gave the fellow a shot in the side of the head, knocked him out . . . jumped over the counter, dragged him to the back and that was it," Murdock said. While he guarded the injured jeweler, his two colleagues cleaned out the store. It did not take long for police to nab Murdock in that case—he made no attempt to hide his face. And in 1991, when facing the prospect of years in jail for the heist, he approached police, offering information on the 1985 Alaimo homicide in return for leniency. When a satisfactory deal was not offered, he clammed up and took a six-year sentence. The information linking Murdock to the unsolved Alaimo murder, however, was quietly filed away by police, along with his known association with the Musitano family—and when the case was reopened shortly before Johnny's murder, the new detective handling it, Vic Rees, approached Murdock. Rees found him uncooperative.

"I don't know what you're talking about," Murdock told the detective. "Forget about the whole thing." Police didn't, and when Hamilton detectives were called to the scene of Johnny's murder, Murdock's name almost immediately came to mind.

"Ken Murdock was the only man in town who had what it took to kill Papalia," a veteran police detective said the day after Johnny's shooting. Another detective, Vic Rees, even went so far as to phone Murdock's pager, and, when the killer returned the call, ask him if he knew anything about Johnny's shooting. Murdock said he knew nothing.

In the middle of January 1998, Murdock was charged with possession of stolen property after police found him with someone else's computers. A month later, on February 18, he was arrested for assault causing bodily harm and extortion. He was denied bail, and police went to work on him. He was in jail awaiting trial when police played him a tape that suggested he was in danger from former criminal associates.

"Information came in off the street that there was a contract out to kill . . . Ken Murdock," said Ontario Provincial Police Detective Inspector Don Birrel, the head of Project Expiate.

Murdock said his own street sources confirmed the police's information. He was devastated by the betrayal. "I did a favour, I kept my promise, and here is what they were willing to do to me in return—make me part of the compost," he said. "They broke the rules, not me."

On April Fool's Day 1998, Murdock called Tom Ireson, a soft-spoken Hamilton lawyer who was once a police constable and had a brother who had recently retired as a high-ranking officer with the Hamilton force. Murdock authorized Ireson to approach the authorities about cutting a deal.

"Tom's a guy that is a very honest person and as a lawyer in Hamilton you don't really see too much of that," Murdock said, explaining why he chose Ireson, who had maintained a very low profile until this case.

On April 14, 1998, Ireson drafted a letter to police:

I have been retained by a client who can provide information to solve a number of cases currently under investigation including several murder investigations, i.e. Papalia investigation. My client also indicates that he can provide information that will result in a number of narcotics and Criminal Code charges against 20 or more people.

My client is willing to give oral testimony as well as other assistance and is aware that these investigations will involve some incarceration of his person. My client is willing to assist the various departments on an ongoing basis, but is unwilling to have on his person a recording device of a traditional nature because of the ease same can be discovered. My client is, however, willing to discuss use of a device of a subminiature variety.

"I sat and thought about everything I've done. I've thought about what could happen. A lot of it is self-serving, I'll be the first to admit it," Murdock said of why he contemplated cooperation. "I protect my own interests, I saved my own ass, you would say. Self-serving, yes. I didn't want to go to jail for the rest of my life. I want some time with my daughter. I wanted to . . . make the deal, do my time, come back out and maybe have 15 or whatever years I live, you know, before I die, but at least I die out here." After a series of discussions with police and Crown Attorney David Carr, Ireson arranged for his client to sit down for a face-to-face meeting with Birrel of the OPP.

"We sat down, we looked at each other, I looked him in the eyes, he seemed to be a straight-up guy. And he told me, more or less, here's where it's at," Murdock said. The main sticking point was how long

Murdock would spend in prison for his significant role in gunning down three people.

"You take three lives, normally you are given 25 years to life. You know that. So why not assume half the responsibility? That's the way I'm thinking. I'm trying to cut this thing down the middle. I had a figure in my mind, 12 to life," Murdock said.

Figures were thrown back and forth as Birrel and Ireson haggled. Ireson suggested 8, and Birrel, 18, as their opening positions.

"I turned around and I looked at Tom and I says, 'Tom, I don't want 8 or 10 years.' I said, 'I fucked up, I want to do my time.' Don said something about, 'How much time do you want to do?'" Murdock said. "I said, 'I'll do the time, I'll pay the price. Give me 12 to life, I'm happy.' And he said, '13?' and I said, 'Sold. 13.'"

"I had the GST added to it," Murdock later quipped.

After making the leap from contract killer to police informant—certainly a difficult choice for such a man as Murdock—he was moved out of the regular jail population, where he was awaiting trial for his role in the extortion scheme, and moved to the safer environment of an army brig Canadian Forces Base Borden. Starting in September 1998, he was grilled by police during eight recorded interrogations on the three murders.

On October 22, 1998, Murdock was handed a seven-page document outlining the agreement. He was to provide sworn testimony in any and all proceedings to which he was subpoenaed by the Crown arising from his statements. In return, he was promised parole eligibility after 13 years, a letter of recommendation to the National Parole Board when that time came, a new identity, and protection once his prison term was completed, if he wanted it. Murdock initialed each page and signed at the bottom of the last sheet.

One month later, just hours after the arrest of the Musitanos, Murdock started serving his term in prison. It was, his lawyer insisted in court, great remorse that led Murdock to spill his guts to police. Murdock was motivated not by fear or self-preservation, but by a desire to turn his life around, said Ireson.

"This is the first step to rehabilitate himself and change the life that has led him to be before Your Honour today," he told Judge Eugene Fedak.

All eyes then turned to the young Musitano brothers, whose family name was well known in southern Ontario. Pat and Ang came with a family legacy that rivaled the Papalias' for violence, blood, criminal activity—and Mafia ties stretching back to the same Italian village.

The patriarch of the Musitano clan, the great-uncle of Pat and Ang, was a quiet, harshly built man named Angelo Musitano. Before illegally relocating to Canada, he earned the ominous sobriquet "The Beast of Delianova."

Born in 1909 in Delianova, Calabria, The Beast earned a lengthy criminal record by the time he was 20; weapons offences, threatening, home invasion, conspiracy to commit murder, attempted murder, and military desertion. After shooting and wounding a man, The Beast was jailed in an institution for the mentally unstable.

In the summer of 1937, shortly after his release, he was playing cards and chatting with friends when one of the men brought up the touchy subject of The Beast's sister, Rosa. While The Beast was imprisoned, Rosa's husband had died, but rather than continue in perpetual mourning, she decided to get on with her life and seek solace in the arms of another man. Those ribbing The Beast at the card table did not tell him anything he did not already know, but to hear it spoken of publicly made his blood boil. He raced to the house where she worked as a maid. There he shot and injured his sister, who was said to have been pregnant, and dragged her bleeding body by her hair through the streets of Delianova to the front steps of her lover's home, where he finished her off with a dagger. Then, unable to find her lover, he killed the man's brother instead. Knowing he could no longer stay in his village, The Beast settled his affairs; he found a young farmer who owed him money, and when the farmer was unable to immediately settle the debt, The Beast killed him on the spot. Fleeing Italy, he stowed away on a ship that docked at Saint John, New Brunswick, and from there made his way to Hamilton after spending some time in the United States. In

1940, an Italian court convicted him *in absentia* to 30 years in prison. For the next 25 years, he lived quietly under the name Jim D'Augustino on Ray Street North in Hamilton. Even his nephews, Dominic and Tony Musitano, called him "Uncle Jimmy" rather than by his true given name. In the 1960s, Italian authorities were tipped off that if they took a peek at the Italian community in Hamilton they might find their long-missing man. After contacting the RCMP, police found that the man known as D'Augustino strongly resembled old photographs of The Beast of Delianova, and in March 1965, Canadian police arrested Angelo Musitano, Sr., then 56 years old, and deported him to Italy to face his sentence. He was imprisoned in Sicily, where members of his Canadian family would travel to see him, taking spicy sausage, olive oil, new clothes and other goodies to make his prison time as comfortable as possible. Despite their efforts, age and confinement took their toll, and shortly before his scheduled release he collapsed in the prison courtyard and died of a heart attack. His grieving family brought his body back to Canada and buried him in Hamilton.

The Beast had two nephews in Hamilton: Dominic, born in 1937, and his brother Anthony, born a decade later. These two men led the Musitano crime family after The Beast's unceremonious departure. The Musitanos, staying true to their Calabrian roots, formed a tight 'Ndrangheta cell rather than following Johnny's lead into the American La Cosa Nostra.

Pat and Ang are, respectively, the oldest and youngest of four children born to Dominic Musitano, a man who divided his time between tending fig trees and tomato plants in the backyard of his Colbourne Street home and running an impressive array of criminal ventures. He often worked with, but was always overshadowed by, Johnny. As a young man, Dominic was sentenced to seven years for an early display of road rage; he shot and seriously wounded a motorist whose honking irritated him. The driver likely felt his critique of Dominic's driving skills—"move it or park it"—was a good line until Dominic fired his loud rejoinder. Dominic was imprisoned again in 1985 for being an accessory after the fact in the slaying of Toronto mobster Domenic Racco. The involvement of the Musitanos in the murder of a man

Johnny promised to protect was seriously upsetting to The Enforcer, some say. The involvement of a powerful Calabrian *mafioso* from Toronto, however, who is said to have given the Musitanos his blessing in the hit, made retaliation an unpalatable option.

"There is nothing I can do," Johnny said a few years after the young Racco's slaying.

Dominic Musitano died on August 13, 1995, when the obese man's heart finally gave out. When the sad news reached his waiting family, the grieving entourage tore apart the hospital's emergency room, ramming a metal bed through a wall and smashing equipment onto the floor. Suspecting a cruel conspiracy, they were suspicious of how long it took an ambulance to reach their don after 9-1-1 was called.

Johnny did not attend Dominic's large and elaborate funeral service, held inside Hamilton's towering Cathedral of Christ the King. It was not a sign of disrespect towards his old colleague and sometimes rival; rather, he was keenly aware of the attention it would draw from both the police and the media. Johnny instead paid his quiet and private respects to the man and his family, telling them in advance not to expect him at the service. Afterwards, he demanded a full briefing on the funeral from several attendees.

Anthony (Tony) Musitano, an uncle to Pat and Ang, was sentenced to 15 years in prison in 1983 for the string of bombings that rocked Hamilton in the 1970s and were eventually solved by police in Operation Boom. While serving the first year of that sentence, Tony plotted Racco's slaying from his prison cell. Tony so upset authorities in Hamilton that in 1988, the police chief—backed by a unanimous vote from city council—asked the National Parole Board to deny him early release. He eventually was granted full parole in 1990. He returned to Hamilton, where he lives simply, running a large dry cleaning operation with his friendly wife. He remains witty, affable, and makes easy jokes about his past. "We launder shirts, not money," he quipped recently.

Pat and Ang Musitano did not flee the legacy of crime that their close-knit family has left them.

Pat is a large, gregarious man, well known around Hamilton. Growing up in a modest, working-class house on Colbourne Street, he quit school at the age of 16 to take over some of the family's scrap dealerships. In his round physique and facial features, he bears a striking resemblance to his father. His weight brings health problems, including diabetes and angina. In June 1994, at a fancy wedding with 1,000 guests in a Mountain banquet hall, Pat married Linda, a woman from a respected Italian family that runs an east-end bakery. It became one of the many restaurants and eateries in the family's care. In The Gathering Spot, Pat's restaurant on James Street North—the recipient of rave reviews for its culinary fare and inexpensive wine list—Pat was a friendly host. He moved from table to table, talking with diners; he sure knew about food, he would say, as he laughed and pointed to his large belly. Those who know his reputation as a mobster were taken aback, but his outgoing nature won many over. Pat came to public attention, however, for reasons other than his remarkable salads and big veal cutlets.

He was convicted of possessing stolen property in 1991 when he took the fall for the misdeeds of his father, who was on parole.

Pat Musitano was also president of P&L Tire Recycling Inc. in 1992, when he was found guilty of failing to make his Mount Hope tire dump conform to the Ontario fire code. Many observers laughed at the preposterous notion of buying a tire dump just as the environmental disaster of the Hagarsville tire fire was making tire handling one of the most carefully scrutinized businesses in the province. Pat and his father were handed a $1.8-million bill from the Ministry of Environment and Energy for the clean-up of their Mount Hope site, a bill Pat dodged with a 1993 bankruptcy claim.

In 1996, Pat and his brother-in-law, John Trigiani, were acquitted of conspiracy to commit arson and arson for the purpose of insurance fraud after someone tried to burn down the historic Collins Hotel in Dundas. Paper placemats were soaked in gasoline and stuffed into toasters set on timers; the hotel's carpets and floors had also been doused with gas. If one of the eight tenants living upstairs had not smelled gasoline and phoned the fire department, it might have been a deadly blaze. Noting that "suspicion heaped upon suspicion" does not add up to guilt, the judge freed the former proprietors of the hotel. The verdict perhaps did not come as a great surprise to Pat. The young mobster raised the ire of Justice Walter Stayshyn when, after the presiding judge announced he was delaying his verdict, Pat quipped: "Doesn't he realize I have champagne waiting on ice?" At the time of that attempted arson, Hamilton police were investigating Pat's father for several other suspicious fires. The wide-ranging fraud and arson investigation, called Project Toast, was an effort to figure out why well-insured Musitano properties kept bursting into flames.

In December 1997, Pat headed a list of almost two dozen people charged after a three-month investigation by the OPP's Illegal Gaming Enforcement Unit into a multimillion-dollar bookmaking organization that used pagers and cellular phones to take wagers on pro sports, particularly National Hockey League and National Basketball Association games. Police said this old-style bookie operation with a modern twist was taking in as much as $100,000 in bets per week and had a network for distributing illegal gambling machines to bars. At the time of the arrests, police alleged Pat was the leader of the betting ring and that his cousin, Guiseppe Avignone, 38, who had come to live with the Musitanos at the age of 13, headed the machine network. However, in September 1999, immediately after eight of the men pleaded guilty, the charge against Pat was withdrawn. Assistant Crown attorney John Nixon said it would not be in the "public's best interest to prosecute," adding Pat maintained "limited involvement" in the racket.

A close friend of Pat's said Pat is enamoured by the Mafia lore he was born into—both locally and globally. He loves Mafia movies, books, and the Hollywood image of how a mobster is supposed to look and act. In a strange twist of life imitating art, he seems to have blended his real-life experience of violence, money, and crime with the romanticized antihero from the movies. It is a persona he radiates, from his throaty voice, sunglasses, and careful facial expressions to the silk scarf he often drapes around his neck.

Ang is much younger, much thinner, and has had far less involvement with police and the courts than his brother Pat. He was still living with his mother when he was arrested, although he had a house on Ferrie Street available to him if he ever needed some down time. Since his father's death, Ang had frequently taken his mother to Holy Sepulchre Cemetery to visit Dominic's well-maintained tombstone, a large slab of red-and-brown marble set into the wall.

Ang was arrested in the same 1997 bookmaking sweep as was his brother, but charges against him were quickly dropped. He was charged with dangerous driving in November 1997, a penny ante charge in the scheme of things, for sure, but one that shed great light on police suspicions over the gangland shootings earlier that year. Fighting the driving charge in court, Ang's lawyer, Dean Paquette, contended police trumped up the offence so they could interrogate his client about Barillaro's murder. Paquette said the charge was laid so police could "exploit his incarceration."

According to court documents filed in the case, prosecutors admit Ang was under police surveillance on November 17, when officers followed his car from his home to Toronto's Pearson International Airport and back again. Only blocks from his home, it is alleged, he sped through two red lights. That night, he was approached at his home by police officers working on Project Expiate. Ang said in court that he refused to talk and closed the front door of his house. Through the closed door one officer asked: "Who killed Carm?" Three days later, he was arrested and charged with dangerous driving. While in police custody, Ang was again approached by the same officer, who asked him about Barillaro's shooting. Ang said one of the detectives said: "If I want to speak to you, I will speak to you, and this is my little way." The six-minute interrogation was videotaped by police. Ang allegedly put his head down on the table and refused to talk to the officers. Ang later pleaded guilty to the lesser offence of careless driving and was fined $500.

The driving charge against Ang is reminiscent of the police operation against Frank Papalia almost 20 years earlier, when he was stopped and charged with drunk driving so police could wire his car. Interestingly, the Crown lawyer then pressing that charge against Frank was Dean Paquette, Ang's lawyer.

Pat and Ang enjoy tremendous support from friends and family, and their pre-trial court appearances filled the courtroom with men and women nodding and smiling to the pair when they were brought out in shackles. Metal detectors were installed at the courthouse for their court appearances, and spectators were thoroughly searched—twice—by police. Evidence and documentation for the case amassed to staggering proportions: more than 50 banker's boxes stuffed full of audio logs, videotapes, transcripts of wiretap evidence, photographs, affidavits, transcripts of Murdock's evidence, police surveillance notes and other statements from the team of police officers probing the slayings. The Crown prepared an impressive list of witnesses whom it had subpoenaed, including retired police officers and at least one reporter. But the key to the case, and the star witness, was clearly going to be Ken Murdock, the man who admits to pulling the trigger on both Johnny and Barillaro. Murdock was put under heavy police guard. Officers wore armoured helmets and vests and carried machine guns whenever they moved him. Sharpshooters were placed on the rooftops around Hamilton's main courthouse when Murdock arrived to give testimony at the Musitanos' preliminary hearing. When Pat was first told that Murdock was to testify in court on behalf of Crown prosecutors for the case, said a source familiar with the police investigation, his face showed complete shock.

The dynamics were strange, even by Hamilton's unusual standards, when Murdock took the stand. For six days in June 1999, Murdock enthralled a courtroom with words, spoken bluntly and firmly, that are rarely heard—the admissions of a serial-killing Mafia hit man. News spread through the city of the no-holds-barred testimony, even though the contents of the hearings could not be reported in the media because of a publication ban, and people from very different walks of life came to watch and listen. Police officers who had investigated mobsters for decades uncomfortably vied with members of the Musitano family for seats; a former president of the Outlaws Motorcycle Club sat next to a curious lawyer; at least two men involved in separate gangland slayings were pushed shoulder to shoulder; and representatives of the victims' families were tucked in among supporters of those accused.

There were moments of black humour, such as when Murdock's bluntness bordered on the absurd. Murdock was telling the court how he had chatted with Johnny outside the Railway Street office the day he killed him. When asked by prosecutor John Nixon how the conversation ended, Murdock answered: "With a gunshot to the back of the head."

There were moments of touching melodrama, such as when Murdock implored Pat's defence lawyer not to ask him about the death of his stepfather. Big John Akister died in 1995. The large man had not felt well at Murdock's wedding reception, and the groom offered to forgo his honeymoon to see he got the attention he might need. Big John would not hear of it. The day after returning from his honeymoon, Murdock was eating steak and eggs at a local Golden Griddle when his mother called him on his cell phone; she could not reach Big John and his telephone seemed to be off the hook. Murdock sped to the man's apartment. When the door was locked and no one answered, he used his infamous flying kick to knock the door off its hinges. Inside Big John lay dead, half off the bed, with his telephone's handset knocked from its cradle at his side. In Big John's lifeless left hand, a police officer found a white card with a phone number that Big John apparently had been trying to call—it was Murdock's business card. When Paquette was cross-examining Murdock, he asked the hit man several questions about the death of his stepfather.

"Do we need to go along that line of questioning?" Murdock asked. "I'll be bawling my eyes out if we do."

There were curious moments when Murdock's personal relationship with the men charged reached beyond the witness box. Ignoring the tradition of witnesses speaking only to the judge or the lawyers, Murdock several times looked directly at Pat and Ang in the prisoner's box and directed his remarks to them.

"I've known Ang since he was 'yea' high. You know, like this is the hardest thing for me to do right here. It's tearing me apart inside because I do love these guys in a sense," he said in court before turning toward Pat and Ang. "Do you understand? Even though you don't believe it—I know you're hurt—I'm fucking hurt."

The testimony took on the quality of a *Who's Who* of the city's underworld, with names of so many of the major players—the Magnini brothers, Luch Pietrorazio, Joe Altamore, Mario Parente, Johnny K-9, Joey Avignone, Billy Rankin, and others—rolling easily off Murdock's tongue. At one point, Justice Timothy Culver, a judge brought in from out of town to hear the difficult case, stopped the proceedings when Murdock and the lawyers all started talking about Johnny K-9.

"Am I the only one in the courtroom that doesn't know what he means by 'canine'?" he asked. Police, lawyers, reporters, courtroom observers, even Murdock, all looked up at him, stunned. Yes, Judge Culver was, in fact, the only one who didn't know.

And there were a few tense moments as well, such as when Ang's lawyer stood behind Murdock rather than in front of him during his cross-examination. "I would appreciate it if you stood in front of the box instead of beside me," Murdock said to Rosen, ignoring the question the lawyer had just put to him. "Or else something might fucking happen, okay? Just get away from me, you fucking piece of shit." Murdock wasn't spitting venom just because Rosen was trying to poke as many holes as possible in his testimony. It stemmed from Murdock being steeped in jail house culture: Rosen's name was on some cons' black list for having defended Paul Bernardo.

After a lengthy preliminary hearing, Judge Culver ordered Pat Musitano to stand trial for the murder of Johnny Papalia, and Ang Musitano to stand trial in Johnny's, as well as Carmen Barillaro's, slaying. Murdock, however, never got his chance to testify at a trial. Behind the scenes, the lawyers had been busy.

On February 4, 2000, in a surprise move, Pat and Ang stood up in court and finally admitted that they ordered the slaying of a rival mobster. In a carefully arranged plea bargain, charges of first-degree murder against both brothers for the slaying of Johnny, and the charge of first-degree murder against Ang in the slaying of Barillaro, were all withdrawn. Instead, both brothers were charged with conspiracy to commit murder for ordering Murdock to shoot Barillaro, and both pleaded guilty. It was a deal that let the brothers escape facing trial for the murder of The Enforcer. Both men were handed 10-year prison sentences.

As Pat was led from the courtroom, he paused, pointed his meaty finger at Dominic Musitano, Jr., his younger brother, in the audience, and warned him to behave while he was in prison. "Don't be upsetting your mother," he said sternly. His concern for his family, in fact, was a large part of why he agreed to plead guilty to a crime he was not originally charged with, said Paquette.

"You can see this as Pat standing up and being counted for his brother," Paquette said of the deal. Rosen, too, said the arrangement was largely a family affair.

26

Two years after Johnny Papalia was killed, a small rock was set squarely into the earth in the picturesque grounds of the Holy Sepulchre Cemetery in Burlington to mark his grave. Beneath the black cross and the statue of St. Anthony of Padua—the patron saint of the poor—marking the Papalia family plot, the stone is simple and elegant, matching the tombstones of Antonio Papalia and Maria Rosa Italiano in both words and design.

Pray for the soul of a dear son, John Papalia, March 18, 1924–May 31, 1997, Beloved son of Antonio and Maria Rosa; Riposa in Pace.

The words are carved into the grey marble. A pot of fresh red and white tulips snuggled into the dirt beside it suggests someone has, indeed, been praying for Johnny.

A decade earlier, Johnny had said he was finally enjoying the life he wanted when he was a young boy—a life of substantial leisure. He took holidays away from Canada's harsh winters, traveled to high-profile boxing matches—always sitting well back in the stands to avoid the spotlight of the ringside seats—and spent time with his admiring family.

"Listen, I'm 62 and I'm tired and I have to crawl out of bed every morning," Johnny once said. "What's organized crime?"

Johnny may well have had to struggle to get out of bed in his twilight years, but he did not let that prevent him from maintaining a firm grip on crime. That apparent incongruency is fitting for Johnny, who was a man of tremendous complexity and irreconcilable contradictions.

He was a Mafia Godfather who was Canadian, cosmopolitan, spoke in English and struggled when relying on his Italian. He was thoroughly modern when compared to the old-world dons around him in his youth and yet lived with the discipline and self-control of the old ways until the end. He brought into his inner circle a multinational cast of criminals rather than sticking to the Mafia tradition of strictly Italian blood. His apartment was a ridiculous pigsty and yet he always dressed immaculately. He lived alone in a fading, rented apartment when he controlled an organization bringing in thousands of dollars each day. He spent lavishly on those around him and yet he was generally feared rather than loved. He denounced drugs as harmful and a terrible waste and yet had organized a multinational heroin smuggling ring. He lived a life of perpetual violence and swindles and then complained about holidays in Acapulco because the city had "too much crime."

Johnny was declared public enemy number one and yet made his fortune supplying the public with things they wanted: booze, gambling, drugs, loans without a credit history, prostitutes, and strippers. For some people, Johnny was a civil servant with cool sunglasses and most unorthodox methods; for others he was the source of addiction, financial ruin, fear, physical pain, and, likely, death. To his family, he was attentive, admiring, loving, protective and generous, but to some who called him a friend he was a conniving thief. He controlled an immense amount of wealth and yet died listed as bankrupt with no tangible assets in his name.

John Papalia was many things to many people, and he certainly left a legacy—perhaps even a lasting one—as one of the longest reigning crime lords in Canadian history. He spent more than 50 years steeped in crime across Canada and the United States—a decade of that establishing his power and four decades maintaining some semblance of control. An entire generation of gangsters, crooks and cops had lived every day with Johnny's looming presence until the day he died. His death marks the passing of the era when mobsters valued respect above money, and signals the end of Hamilton's domination over the province's organized crime.

In many ways, in death he retains what he possessed while alive—a reputation larger than life and a name more powerful than his physical might.

"It's been an interesting one," Johnny once said of his life. "But maybe I'd have liked it to be different."

Maybe.

EPILOGUE

KINGSTON, ONTARIO

Dressed in blue jeans and running shoes and with his hands thrust deep into the pockets of a green windbreaker, Angelo Musitano padded his way from the crowded inmate quarters of Joyceville Institution, a medium-security prison outside Kingston. A prison guard led the way down a wide corridor, past the staff lounge, where vending machines spit out candy bars and coffee, and into a well-lit boardroom. The cushioned chairs and matching carpet inside set a stark contrast to the view outside: twin 18-foot-high fences crowned with coils of razor wire, paint-chipped iron gates and a metal detector that greets all visitors to the "The Joyce," as the prison is known.

Ang's visitors that early morning of October 28, 2004, were two members of the National Parole Board and a lawyer he has hired.

Ang has not been seen in public since February 2000, when he and his older brother, Pat, were sentenced to 10 years imprisonment for ordering the death of Carmen Barillaro, the right-hand man to Johnny Papalia. The four years have not been particularly kind—nor overtly cruel—to the younger Musitano, now 27 years old. Flecks of premature grey splash through what was once jet black hair. He wears thin wire-framed glasses and, whether from the inactivity of his incarceration or the curse of his genetics, he is now stouter than when he stood, fit and defiant, in the prisoner's box of a fortified Hamilton courtroom to accept his sentence.

Appearing casual but uncomfortable, he moved towards the only empty chair at the prison's long conference table and nodded to each of the parole officials as they were introduced to him. He spoke softly when spoken to but initiated nothing. Parole hearings are always awkward forums, straddling as they do the world of punishment and envisioned rehabilitation; appropriately, Ang was referred to alternately as "169452-D"—his inmate number—and "Mr. Musitano."

Under Canada's generous judicial system, Pat and Ang became eligible to seek unescorted temporary absences on October 4, 2001, were able to apply for day parole on December 5, 2002, and became candidates for full parole on June 5, 2003. But it was not until late in 2004 that the brothers pressed ahead with serious parole applications. At hearings scheduled a day apart inside their respective prisons, both Ang and Pat made their case for parole. There was plenty to talk about.

Ang, through his lawyer, started with complaints. Prison officials unfairly targeted him because his file was stamped with the ominous words "organized crime," said Anik Morrow, hired by the brothers to help gain parole. That meant he had not been able to cascade down to a minimum-security institution, usually an important step before being trusted to rejoin the community. The special scrutiny Ang received from prison officials, police and the media, she said, also meant that he had been refused admission to halfway houses in Hamilton, Guelph and Ottawa. Still, Ang had high hopes. He wants to pursue an architectural drafting career and has a new girlfriend, he said, one he met during his imprisonment through a mutual friend; his letters seem to have won her heart and she has been visiting often.

The board had concerns of its own. There was a report in his file from police saying he was suspected of having a hand in a rash of restaurant bombings in Hamilton, which he said came as a surprise to him. Another document, an internal prison report, said he was allegedly running a bookmaking and gambling operation for inmates while in prison. That, said Ang, was an allegation "fabricated" by fellow inmates.

Then came talk of the murders. Ang pointed out that he was not even

276 • ADRIAN HUMPHREYS

in Canada when Johnny was murdered and did not return until after his funeral. He first heard about underworld unrest when he returned from Mexico and spoke to Murdock when handing him a bottle of tequila he had brought back as a gift, Ang said. "Kenny," as he calls Murdock, had "manipulated" him into fearing Barillaro, he said.

When he got into Murdock's car for their search for Barillaro, Murdock flashed a gun: "We were prepared to kill Mr. Barillaro at that point," he told the parole board. And although it was Murdock who went in to do the job, he reluctantly admitted he was prepared to have done it himself. "Maybe I would have got out and shot the man. Yes, I might have. I was terrified for my brother," he said. Ang said he heard a shot from the driveway, and, when Murdock returned to the car, the hit man passed him his weapon. "The gun was still hot," Ang said. "I knew the man was dead."

For Pat, his hearing inside Warkworth Institution, a medium-security prison on rolling farmland midway between Toronto and Kingston, the questions from the parole board seemed to make him even more uncomfortable. Although still a large man, Pat looked trimmer and healthier than he did when he was arrested. But when the two men on his parole panel started asking him about organized crime, he looked as if medical assistance might be required.

"I don't want to be difficult here," he said, shifting in his seat, squeezing a piece of paper towel, clutched in his fist, into pulp. "I'm trying to be truthful. You're asking me? I don't believe it exists."

Drawing incredulous looks from the board members, he was asked a second time, does he accept the existence of the mob? "No," he said. The belief that his family is connected to the mob has plagued him and his family for decades and continues to haunt his stay in prison, he told the parole board.

The day before the hearing, he won a grievance against a correctional officer who repeatedly called him "Tony Soprano," the lead character in *The Sopranos*, a fictional TV series about a U.S. Mafia family.

"My whole life I've had to deal with rumour and innuendo," he explained. "The police were always against us—me and my dad," he said. "I know they targeted my immediate family. I know what they did to me personally." He accused police in Hamilton of engaging in a campaign to disrupt his family's private lives and legitimate enterprises, including interfering with his bank applications for mortgage loans. "Police walk in and tell the manager not to lend me money," Pat said. That forced him to go to a private lender who charged a higher rate of interest. When he opened a restaurant, police targeted his patrons, threatening to issue infractions against them. And now, police are pressuring halfway houses not to accept him, he claimed.

Pat said he had no hand in the slaying of Johnny—"I didn't know why he thought I killed Papalia," he said of Barillaro, "I've known Papalia all my life." And he only struck out at Barillaro in self-defence, at the urging of Murdock who, he said, "played me like a yo-yo."

"How was I supposed to go to the police? We were brought up that the police was always against us. I could never go to the police," he said.

Set that aside, he told the parole board, and give him a chance. With plans to work in the catering business as a cook, he pleaded: "I want to go home to be a husband to my wife; go home to be a father to the children I may one day have. That is my goal. To get on with my life. It's been six years since I've been able to be a husband to my wife."

Most of the Musitano-owned restaurants in Hamilton have closed or changed hands, and Pat's $250,000 home on St. Clair Boulevard, with its remodeled cherry-wood kitchen, was put up for sale shortly after his incarceration.

The Musitano Mafia family's criminal interests are being kept afloat as best they can be, with three close associates taking charge of all day-to-day operations. "They're keeping their toe in the door jamb," said a man who spent years working with the Musitano clan.

When Pat and Ang finally emerge from their state-sponsored sojourn, they will be facing a world that is, from varying perspectives, both strikingly different and virtually unchanged from when they were taken from their homes by police.

ABBOTSFORD, BRITISH COLUMBIA

The irony of Ken Murdock's life behind bars is that, after agreeing to testify against his two former mob bosses, he will remain in prison long after Pat and Ang walk free. For his act of contrition, Murdock was branded a rat by the prison population, and the first four years of his 13-year minimum stay in prison have not been easy.

"I didn't ask for a name change, I didn't ask for witness protection. I just want to do my time and come home. Everybody just leave me alone," Murdock said recently from the British Columbia prison he calls home. Despite his plea for peace, some of his fellow inmates have refused to cooperate, and Murdock has repeatedly found himself facing angry convicts trying to prove a point or make a name by taking him on. Few fare well. His status as a cooperating witness entitles him to a measure of protection and separation from the general prison population, yet Murdock has declined these luxuries, a decision that has given him moral solace but near constant aggravation. During our most recent conversation, Murdock was in "the hole," a segregated area used for punishment, where he was placed after a brawl. He was nursing a broken right hand, caused, he said, by slamming it into another inmate who was intent on causing him grief. His opponent required hospitalization.

"It's not been peaches and cream. There has been a lot of turbulence," he said. "I've had one guy come at me with a blade. I took it off him, slapped him out. It's just continuous bullshit like this." Another challenger was a former kickboxing champion, another a member of an aboriginal prison gang.

The repercussions of his killings and unexpected cooperation with police have caused him more than physical aggravation; they have taken a psychological toll as well. "I have a lot of nightmares, still to this day," he said. "I think yesterday, last night I had one. It don't escape my memory. Little things will set it off. It's hard to live with, actually. But what can you do? It's had its effect. It would have been different if you were defending yourself, but you weren't. It's not a good thing to live with; you don't feel good about it, but you live with it."

Despite this, Murdock insisted he is not bitter, just relieved to finally be out of the game. "To me, the umbilical cord [to the Musitanos] has been cut; that's it, I'm happy, the games are over. Now I can just get on with my life. I don't have to be a tough guy, I don't have to be used, I don't have to be helping people, I don't have to be protecting people, I don't have to do any of that shit no more. I just worry about myself."

When asked if he resented that the sentencing tilted decidedly in favour of Pat and Ang, he paused, then said, "I don't have no ill feelings at all. You know what? You wipe your hands clean and stay clean and move on. They got 10, be happy. I got 13, I'm happy with it. I got 13 and I still kept a promise [to Dominic Musitano]. I just want to come home. I've got a program out here I've got to do, the violent offender program, and once it's finished I'm back home. I'll be back in Hamilton as soon as it's over. I'm not going anywhere. I'm not running. I have no hard feelings."

Does he think his laissez-fare attitude is shared by Pat and Ang? "Definitely not. You'd be a fool to think otherwise," he said. "But they know what I am capable of. They all know that. I also know that I am capable of not being that way. I don't want to be that way no more."

As he works through his sentence, he continues to work with a film-maker on a movie about his unusual life.

Murdock becomes eligible to apply for parole in 2011. He will be 48.

HAMILTON, ONTARIO

On Railway Street, the Papalia organization has been consumed by the banalities of life since the fresh sting of Johnny's murder began to fade.

Frank Papalia's health has been in slow decline. Like his brother Johnny, he, too, needed intervention for a faulty ticker. A successful triple heart-valve bypass operation slowed him down but did not prevent him from maintaining control over the day-to-day affairs of the business. It might be his advancing age or the grim reminder that comes with burying yet another brother, but Frank and his senior management team seem to be trying their dogged best to disappear as landmarks in the city's rough landscape.

"Frank—and Bruno, too—just want to get on with their lives, spend time with their grandkids and avoid hoopla of any kind," a friend of the family said recently.

"You think Frank is still out there busting chops?" asked another, rhetorically. Frank still spends his time at the Railway Street office and can often be seen coming or going or unloading a box from the trunk of the car he parks out front.

Business, however, is not what it used to be. With sales of home gaming consoles—PlayStation, Nintendo and Xbox—at a record high, the coin-operated arcades are being decimated. On the legitimate side, the Papalias have tried to offset the decline by adding CD juke-boxes to their repertoire and pushing Valley National Eightball Association pay-to-play pool.

Johnny's criminal crew has not been standing still either. When a reasonably young but deeply experienced career criminal from the east end of Hamilton was finally freed after spending more than a decade in a U.S prison on drug charges, he was not back in the city long before he was seen meeting with one of Johnny's top bosses. The subject of their friendly chat is unknown. But even as new blood appears to be flowing into the Papalia organization, the tide is decidedly ebbing away from Hamilton as a crown jewel of Canadian crime. It was Johnny, and Johnny alone, who seemed capable of keeping the province's underworld orbiting his city.

Hamilton has become, in mob parlance, an open city, meaning any gangster can take as big a bite out of it as he is capable of swallowing. Mobsters have wasted little time in exercising this newfound freedom.

"The purse strings have been opened up," said one mob-linked career criminal of Hamilton's underworld. "There is now more money to go around. John kept things pretty tight."

In the years since Johnny's death—and, perhaps more importantly, since the Musitanos were imprisoned—an understanding has slowly emerged of why this murderous turmoil was visited on gangland. Several credible sources on both sides of the law have pieced together a picture of why some members of the Musitano organization might have had animosity towards Johnny.

Pat Musitano, it seems, had a dramatically different vision of his family's place in the underworld than did his father, Dominic, who earned and maintained respect by understanding his delicate relationship with the Papalias. Dominic was content to take care of business without antagonizing Johnny. A seasoned police investigator who has worked undercover probing the Hamilton mob used this metaphor: Once the most powerful people eat their dinner, the others get the leftovers. "That way, nobody gets upset. But if I take your steak, then you have a problem," he said. Pat seems to have wanted steak. He had dreams of seeing the Musitanos move up in the pecking order, and he chafed at the subservient role his father accepted.

Always a dutiful son, so long as Dominic was alive, Pat's vision remained only a dream. After his father's sudden death in 1995, however, Pat's designs for the family set off a subtle power struggle the likes of which Hamilton had not seen in many years. For starters, Pat was allegedly more open than his father had been to working with Toronto gangsters, a former Musitano associate said. "Dominic didn't allow certain people from Toronto to interact with his family. He didn't trust a lot of people from Toronto. When Dominic was removed from the situation, they just came out of the woodwork. Pat developed relationships with these people and the next thing you know, they're around."

Johnny did not take the rumblings seriously at first, but a year or two after Dominic was buried, he found it harder to ignore the challenges. Feeling he was being pushed and tested, Johnny eventually did what he had done a thousand times before: he made a sweeping pronouncement—Pat and his young crew were to be banished.

"He died with his father," is how Johnny's decree on Pat went out to the underworld, according to one insider. Though Johnny's command lacked some of the authority of the past, word still circulated that The Enforcer wanted no one of consequence to do business with the youngsters. Of course, many discreetly ignored the decree—as hoods tend to do with any order that interferes with making a buck—but it is said to have put the Musitanos in a bit of a bind. Though Pat had dreamed of becoming so much more than his father, he suddenly faced the unnerving prospect of slipping considerably backwards.

Getting out from under such a black mark would require considerable effort if he tried to claw back respect inch by hard-fought inch.

Alternatively, a single daringly bold strike might counter it almost immediately.

TORONTO, ONTARIO

Anyone taking Hamilton away from Johnny would be in an enviable position within the underworld. The city—and much of the province of Ontario—could then be offered up to the Rizzuto organization in Montreal, a clan police now consider to be the biggest in Canadian crime.

Sure enough, it was not long after Johnny's death that the long shadow of Montreal's powerful Rizzuto operation started to creep across much of Southern Ontario. Vito Rizzuto himself, allegedly the boss of the Montreal clan, started making regular trips to Toronto. On October 23, 1997—exactly three months after Barillaro was killed—Rizzuto and his man in Ontario, Gaetano Panepinto, had a long, late-night meeting in a Woodbridge restaurant with Pat Musitano, who was accompanied by his cousin and confidant, Guiseppe (Joey) Avignone, according to a report by Montreal police recently filed in a Quebec court. By the time the Musitanos were arrested, Rizzuto was already making the rounds of certain restaurants and cafés of Southern Ontario at least every two weeks.

Rizzuto is described in court documents prepared by Revenue Canada in a dispute over unpaid taxes as the "Godfather of the Italian Mafia in Montreal" and in a secret RCMP report as the head of "one of the most influential and powerful Traditional Organized Crime groups in North America." Being perceived as a crime boss and being convicted of criminal activity clearly do not equate. Despite his notoriety, Rizzuto has not been convicted of any criminal offence since 1972, although he has twice faced serious drug charges and has repeatedly been named in police investigations and court proceedings.

Rizzuto's presence in Ontario could hardly be missed by the underworld élite or curious police. Standing six feet tall and unfailingly dressed in an elegant suit, he is always accompanied by at least two male companions constantly watching his back. When he attended the funeral of murdered Toronto *mafioso* Gaetano Panepinto in October

2000, he was never far from five men who arrived with him by minivan—a contrast to his routine in Montreal, where he typically travels alone.

The last time Montreal so lustily eyed Ontario was when Réal Simard was looking for action on behalf of Frank Cotroni in the 1980s. He dutifully paid his respect to the Papalias. There is no evidence of such niceties this time, however.

For many in the underworld who bore no particular love or loyalty to Johnny, the arrival of the Rizzuto organization in Ontario was greeted with a cautious sigh of relief. It was like an established but moribund company suddenly gaining a hip new CEO—one with solid international connections and a remarkable record of achievement: there were high hopes for a new golden age of prosperity and promotion; that, and a lot of jealousy.

The change re-invigorated police as well as crooks.

In April 2001, police proudly announced that they had dismantled an elaborate illegal gambling ring that had used high-tech devices, Internet links and storefront businesses in Ontario and Quebec to take in $200 million in bets on sports games and races. The sprawling network of bookmakers and debt collectors allegedly operated in Montreal, Ottawa, Hamilton and Toronto, accepting wagers—as high as $100,000 on a single football game from one man—at video rental stores and gas stations. The thoroughly modern bookies carried hand-held wireless computers. Among those arrested were relatives of long-time Rizzuto family associates and the proprietors of establishments in Toronto that Rizzuto frequented. As it turns out, that was merely the tip of the iceberg.

In the years since Johnny's death, detectives with the York Regional Police based north of Toronto, had noticed a lot more swagger in the stride of Gaetano Panepinto, a hulking Mafia enforcer who was muscling his way to prominence in a variety of criminal enterprises. Looking like a swarthy Arnold Schwarzenegger, Panepinto also operated a bizarre business: the Toronto branch of Casket Royale, a firm that offered discount coffins from storefront shops. His caskets ran from $295 for decorated pressboard to a $4,900 bronze luxury model; he offered a denim-covered model with cowboy decorations and children's coffins for free. Police were pretty certain Panepinto's power stemmed from his position as Montreal's new man in Ontario.

On October 3, 2000, just one month after police launched their investigation, Panepinto was shot repeatedly from a van that had pulled up beside his Cadillac. That spun the police probe in a new direction and also offered a code name for their operation: Project RIP, for "rest in peace," a line reserved for tombstones. A year later, wiretaps were running on several members of Panepinto's old crew. It did not take detectives long to realize there was a new man in charge: Juan Ramon Fernandez, better known by his alias, Joe Bravo.

That the Spaniard was even in this country was a puzzle. Months earlier, he had been deported under armed escort with orders not to return, his third such order from immigration authorities. Born on Boxing Day, 1956, Fernandez came to Canada at the age of five but never applied for citizenship. By his early 20s, he had made a name for himself in Montreal through break and enters, assaults and fraud, but he came to true notoriety in 1982 when he was convicted of manslaughter after beating a 17-year-old exotic dancer who later died. Upon his release from prison, he ignored a deportation order and was soon working again in Montreal, selling luxury Jaguars and running a nightclub and a juice bar. Drug convictions followed for Fernandez in the 1990s, and when he was last released from prison in 1999 he was once more sent packing. By May 2001, however, he was again unlawfully in Canada, this time in Ontario. Officers familiar with his background were amazed to hear he was back in Canada and living large. Somewhere along the way, he attracted the attention of Vito Rizzuto. As the police continued to watch Fernandez, they learned of meetings between Rizzuto and officials with OMG Media, a company with municipal contracts in Toronto, Montreal and Ottawa to place recycling bins on street corners, court heard. Fernandez himself claimed he had financial involvement with OMG; entered into the court record were transcripts of a secretly recorded conversation between Rizzuto, Fernandez and Frank Campoli, whom Rosemary Warren, a federal prosecutor, described in court as a director of the company. Campoli had indeed been listed on corporate records for OMG, but by this time his name as a director no longer appeared on the company's public filings. No charges against Campoli or OMG were ever laid. As police tried to keep track of it all, their investigation was, for a second time, rudely interrupted by violence.

In May 2002, Fernandez passed a dirty sock to a man he took to be an underworld assassin, the sides of the footwear bulging to accommodate a powerful pistol and a handful of bullets hidden inside. Fernandez told the man to use the gun to kill a despised rival, Gus Alevizos, which would be no small feat: the intended target earned his nickname "Big Gus" the hard way—he stood six-foot-six and weighed 500 pounds. What Fernandez did not know was that the man he gave the loaded sock to was an informant working with the Montreal police. Officers felt they had to intervene to prevent a murder. Police closed down Highway 407, north of Toronto, while a heavily armed police tactical squad surrounded an SUV in which Fernandez was hiding. In late June 2004, Fernandez pleaded guilty to counselling to commit murder, large-scale fraud, conspiracy to import narcotics and immigration violations. He was sentenced to 12 years in prison.

Fernandez's activities were striking evidence of a large-scale incursion into Ontario by the Rizzuto crime group following Johnny's demise.

In a further sign that Ontario has fallen tightly into Montreal's orbit, a Rizzuto representative has even been bold enough to ensconce himself in Hamilton. The man, who relocated from north of Toronto to live in Dundas, a pleasant suburban community recently amalgamated into the city of Hamilton, has been meeting quietly for months with business and underworld contacts, with seeming impunity.

But just when Canada's underworld seemed to be settling into a new world order, everything was again thrown into flux. This time, it was police, not rival gangsters, that caused the turmoil.

MONTREAL, QUEBEC

It began with a sharp knock on the front door of Rizzuto's 4,507-square-foot Montreal mansion, with its imposing cut-stone facade and Tudor-style leaded windows. It was 6:15 a.m. on January 21,

2004, and Rizzuto, wearing a bathrobe over his pajamas, followed his wife to the door. Waiting outside were two detectives with the Montreal police. The officers explained to Rizzuto, in English and French, that he was being charged in connection with three murders, based on indictments in the United States. Rizzuto was cooperative; his wife remained composed.

An officer followed him to his bedroom, where Rizzuto dressed. Uncharacteristically, he decided against wearing a tie, and instead picked out a camel-coloured turtleneck, dress pants and a sports jacket. Within 15 minutes, he was inside an unmarked police car with the detectives, as four uniformed officers in their cruisers hovered nearby. Rizzuto was soon in a police holding cell, awaiting what is certain to be lengthy legal wrangling over his extradition. Rizzuto was the only Canadian arrested that day in a sweeping probe that saw U.S. police arrest 27 people in New York for 15 murders and murder conspiracies, all linked to the New York–based Bonanno organization, authorities said.

Rizzuto's dignified departure from his home stands in stark contrast to his portrayal in documents written by U.S. prosecutors and given to Canadian authorities to support his arrest and extradition. According to court documents, on May 5, 1981, Rizzuto had a pistol in his hand and a ski mask covering his face as he hid in a closet in a Brooklyn building awaiting a signal from a Montreal colleague to come out shooting, U.S. authorities claim. The documents further allege that a high-ranking Bonanno member has agreed to testify against his underworld colleagues and has detailed the plot for police.

The rift between factions of the Bonanno family had moved from quiet disdain to open hostility by the spring of 1981. It was an internal affair that did not involve Johnny or his Buffalo masters, but the Bonanno-led families in Montreal could not avoid being drawn into the rivalry. Three New York captains, each heading a crew of foot soldiers and associates, were conspiring to depose family boss Phil Rastelli. A pre-emptive strike was planned to quell the insurrection, and the three rebellious captains were lured to a meeting in Brooklyn, U.S. authorities allege. The plan called for loyal Bonanno soldiers to be brought from Canada to do the hit, according to the police informant's claims. The plot went like clockwork, police said. Gerlando Sciascia, a Montrealer known in the United States as "George from Canada," lured the rival captains to the designated room and then ran his fingers through his silvery hair, the signal for the attack to begin. The three captains, Alphonse "Sonny Red" Indelicato, Philip "Phil Lucky" Giaccone and Dominick "Big Trin" Trinchera, were all killed. (The murders became a rich part of Mafia lore after the scene was recreated by Hollywood in the hit movie *Donnie Brasco*, starring Al Pacino and Johnny Depp.)

Rizzuto's lawyer says his client is innocent of the charges. While the courts work to adjudicate the government's claims, Canada's underworld is again in disarray. One criminal figure described life in Ontario's mob as living in a bizarre "holding pattern," where Johnny and Barillaro lie dead, the Musitanos linger in prison and Rizzuto remains sidelined while under arrest.

"It's like being in stupendous animation," he said, without a hint as to whether his line was misspoken or a purposeful play on words. The rank-and-file gangsters, rounders, associates, hangers-on and wannabes do not yet know how the final hand will play out. The fallout will not be known, several underworld characters say, until it is all sorted out on the street rather than in the courts.

KINGSTON, ONTARIO

Back at The Joyce, Ang Musitano's meeting with the parole officials ended just as Pat's did; both were denied additional freedom.

With that, he was excused, had a last chat with his lawyer, and was escorted back along the corridor towards a green metal gate. The barrier opened as Ang and the guard walked towards it in lockstep; Ang plodded through it once again, his hands stuffed back into his jacket pockets, and he was greeted by some of his fellow inmates who milled about on the other side. Ang nodded back—just as he had nodded to the parole board members minutes earlier—and disappeared back into the prison population. With a low buzz and a dull clang, the gate slid slowly shut.

Until next time.

ACKNOWLEDGEMENTS

When now-retired reporter Peter Moon introduced me to a very sensitive and confidential source for this book, the man asked a very specific question. This always-suspicious career criminal wanted to know—before he opened up to me—how Peter and I knew each other. The question was not idle chit-chat. To ease his mind, he was looking, I think, to hear that Peter and I went way back through years, if not decades, of close friendship. The fact was, Peter and I had only recently met, over coffee and a sandwich, to discuss Johnny Papalia. But before I blew this important interview with an improper response, Peter wisely jumped in.

"Adrian and I belong to the same mafia," he said.

The source and I both looked at him quizzically; Peter quickly explained. Our mafia, he said, is called journalism and it bears striking similarities to the Mafia this source was very familiar with, apart, of course, from the criminality. We had "cells" or "families" in every city in the country, he said. We could phone up a "made member" at a newspaper in another city and expect some assistance. We had a common code of behaviour and honour, and even our own brand of *omertà*, the Mafia's code of silence. That's how Peter knew me; that's how he could trust me, he said. The source was satisfied.

Yes, there is a powerful mafia, of sorts, out there which I called upon to piece together the story of Johnny Pops, and I was graciously answered by a host of people with uncanny knowledge and a willingness to help.

Very special appreciation is heaped upon the following: Antonio Nicaso and Lee Lamothe, two knowledgeable organized crime authors who are among the most gracious men I know; Peter Moon, who recently retired from the *Globe and Mail* after a remarkable career; pioneering organized crime author and journalist James Dubro; Mathew McCarthy, photographer at the *Kitchener-Waterloo Record*; Jim Holt, formerly of the *Hamilton Spectator* now based in Los Angeles; *Spectator* reporters Dan Nolan, Bill Dunphy, Paul Legall, Barbara Brown, Rick Hughes, and Carmelina Prete; Peter Edwards and David Beer at *The Toronto Star*; Eric Mayne at the *Windsor Star*; Gerry Nott, a former *Spectator* crime reporter who is currently editor-in-chief at CanWest News Service; Michel Auger at *Journal de Montréal*; Andre Cedilot at *La Presse*; Philip Mathias, Graeme Hamilton and Elizabeth Schaal at the *National Post*; Jerry Gladman at *The Toronto Sun*; Peter Bregg at *Maclean's*; Elizabeth Kelly at *Hamilton Magazine*; Stevie Cameron at *Elm Street Magazine*; Peter Gentile and his colleagues at MDF Productions; and Ron Lalone of Karma Film Production, Inc.

Thanks to my editors at the *National Post*, past and present, Martin Newland, Alison Uncles, John Geiger, Mark Stevenson, Steve Meurice and John Racovali, who allowed me some latitude in keeping tabs on the mob; and to my former editors at the *Spectator*, especially Kirk LaPointe, Dana Robbins, and Roger Gillespie, for investing a tremendous amount both in me and my early mob research.

It is unfortunate that some of the most helpful and cooperative people involved with this project should probably not be named.

To those members of the underworld who, for whatever reason, agreed to speak with me about one of their own, I say thank you. Some day I hope to understand the significance of all of the names, places, dates and events you so confidently spoke of.

Also reluctant to be named are many current and retired members of various Canadian and American law enforcement agencies. From chiefs to constables, your insight and information was essential.

Some officers I might be able to get away with expressing special gratitude to for assistance over the years include: Staff Inspector (ret.)

Ron Sandelli of the Metro Toronto Police, Corporal Reg King of the Royal Canadian Mounted Police, Constable (ret.) Jack McCombs and Constable (ret.) Ian Knox of the Ontario Provincial Police, Chief (ret.) Ken Robertson of the Hamilton Police, and RCMP Chief Superintendent Ben Soave, head of the Greater Toronto Area Combined Forces Special Enforcement Unit.

To each of the dozens of private citizens who were comfortable talking to me about what were sometimes very uncomfortable topics, especially when the chats took place in crowded cafés in central Hamilton and along Toronto's Danforth, I give thanks.

Appreciation also to Tammie Danciu at the *Spec*'s library, Kate Jennison at the *Post*, the staff at Hamilton Public Library's Special Collections department, and certain staff members with Revenue Canada, Industry Canada, the City of Hamilton, and municipal and university libraries across the continent; Pat Milikin at the National Archives of Canada; Richard Gelbke at the United States National Archives and Records Administration in New York City; Dr. Terry Miosi, who read drafts of the manuscript and offered valuable input; Vicki White and Bert Bruser for legal advice and insight; Dr. Derek Hunt for interpretation of and information about medical issues; Richard Vanderlubbe, of TripCentral.ca in Hamilton, for his fine travel arrangements; Dr. Catherine Salmon for transcription assistance; Paul Palango for various bits of assistance; and to Sue Swiggum and Marj Kohli of www.theshipslist.com for help tracking down old immigrant records and passenger manifests.

Thanks also to all at HarperCollins—especially my original editor, Don Loney, and the editor of the revised edition, Jim Gifford—for their interest in, and dedication to, this project. Also thanks to David, Vivienne, Ann, Terry, Norm, and Gail.

Above all, special praise and appreciation is heaped upon Paula, who gave up more than she should ever have had to for this project.

NOTES

CHAPTER 1

Information on Ken Murdock's murderous acts, here and in chapters 24 and 25, come from a series of interviews with this author from his prison cell, blended with information from the *Agreed Statement of Facts*, entered into the court record on November 24, 1998, a second *Agreed Statement* entered on February 4, 2000, and the *Transcript of Proceeding*, Vol. 1, 2 and 3, dated June 16–18, June 21–23, 1999, of *Her Majesty the Queen vs. Angelo Musitano and Pasquale Musitano*. The quotes from Domenic Pugliese and Father Gerard Bergie are from *The Toronto Star*, June 6, 1997.

CHAPTER 2

Information on Antonio Papalia and the wartime internment comes largely from the National Archives of Canada in Ottawa, particularly from the RG 117 and RG 24 volumes. Information on Rocco Perri comes from archival searches, contemporary newspaper accounts, *King of the Mob*, by James Dubro and Robin F. Rowland and *Rocco Perri* by Antonio Nicaso. Some of the material on the Papalia family's life is from Peter Moon's exceptional feature on Johnny, "The Enforcer: Is powerful Hamilton mobster Johnny Pops muscling his way into Toronto's underworld?" published in the *Globe and Mail* on November 28, 1986. This is the sole interview of substance Johnny ever granted a journalist, and I thank Peter for revealing to me previously unpublished segments of their 2½-hour chat, for opening up his files to me, and for introducing me to key sources. The Black Hand bombings were well-covered at the time by the *Hamilton Spectator*, *Hamilton Herald*, and *Hamilton Times*. The National Archives also highlight some specific cases of Black Hand activity in their RG 13 files. An understanding of the history of the Mafia here and elsewhere was aided by

Global Mafia by Antonio Nicaso and Lee Lamothe, and *Blood and Power* by Stephen Fox. The code of the *Picciotteria* is taken from *Deadly Silence*, by Peter Edwards and Nicaso, as are some of the details on the Musolinos. More on the Musolino legend, including the folk song, comes from Nicaso's *Alle Origini Della 'Ndrangheta: La Picciotteria*.

CHAPTER 3

Most of the information on Johnny's early health problems comes from his medical records, obtained by this author.

CHAPTER 4

The information on Johnny's early criminal life comes from a variety of interviews with former friends, neighbours, and associates of the Papalias. *Their Town: The Mafia, the Media and the Party Machine* by Bill Freeman and Marsha Hewitt was also helpful on some points. The quotes from Johnny himself come from the Moon interview, and the description of the Lansdowne Athletic Club comes from Dick Beddoes's *Globe* column, March 30, 1967.

CHAPTER 5

Some of the details on Montreal, the Cotronis, and Carmine Galante come from police reports, *Blood Brothers* by Peter Edwards, *The Canadian Connection* by Jean-Pierre Charbonneau, and "The Mafia in Canada," by Alan Phillips in *Maclean's*, August 24, 1963. "He is pure steel" quote is from *Last Days of the Sicilians*, by Ralph Blumenthal.

CHAPTER 6

The description of the stock broker extortion comes from "Organized crime's grip on Ontario," the second article in Phillips's *Maclean's* series, September 21, 1963. Quotes from Johnny are from the Moon interview. James J. Parker's quotes are from a Jim Kernaghan column in the *London Free Press*, October 10, 1998.

CHAPTER 7

Danny Gasbarrini's quotes are from the *Hamilton Spectator*, October 13, 1963.

CHAPTER 8

Quotes from Joe Valachi, here and elsewhere, are from Peter Maas's book, *The Valachi Papers*.

CHAPTER 9

The La Cosa Nostra initiation ceremony and analysis by Joseph Pistone are from *The Ceremony: The Mafia Initiation Tapes*. The 'Ndrangheta initiation ceremony ("Project Oaf") comes from a transcript of a police wiretap. Thanks to Lee Lamothe for opening up his files for this and other important documents. The quote from Giacomo Luppino comes from the wiretaps in his home, known as the "Orbit Tapes." Thanks to Gerry Nott for opening up his files.

CHAPTER 10

Quotes from Johnny are from the Moon interview, some of which are previously unreported. Quotes from Bluestein and the Town Tavern staff are culled from transcripts of the court proceedings, and a few are from contemporary media interviews, which are usually noted in the text.

CHAPTERS 11–15

Information on the French Connection comes largely from an extensive, week-long search by this author of court transcripts and other legal documents, police records, and affidavits filed by Johnny and his brother Frank at the United States National Archives and Records Administration office in New York City. Some of the information on heroin production and distribution comes from *The Heroin Trail*, *Canadian Connection*, and Phillips's *Maclean's* series. The Palermo meeting is described in Claire Sterling's *The Mafia*. Some of the information on Alberto Agueci, including his autopsy report and death certificate, comes from this author's access requests to the U.S. government. *Deadly Silence* provided additional details. Information on Lucky Luciano comes largely from contemporary newspaper accounts and *The Last Testament of Lucky Luciano* by Martin A. Gosch and Richard Hammer.

CHAPTER 16

Quotes from Frank come from court transcripts and the *Hamilton Spectator*. The quote from Tony Papalia is from the *Hamilton Spectator*, April 6, 1988. Information on Frank's germ phobia and Rocco's daily schedule, all quotes from Shirley Ryce, the Gold Key Club membership list, and how Ryce met the mob come from *Mob Mistress* by Dubro. Information on the police investigation is taken from my interviews with police officers, court records, and notes taken in court by Nott. Some of the information on the Papalia family abroad comes from Nicaso's research, contemporary newspaper accounts, *Mafia Business* by Pino Arlacchi, and *La 'Ndrangheta* by Luigi Malafarina.

CHAPTER 17

Art Tartaglia's sales pitch comes from Phillips's series. The quotes from Johnny are from the Moon interview. "You step on our grass . . ." quote comes from Barbara Brown's court coverage in the *Hamilton Spectator*, February 23, 1993. The Allind Distributors scenario was well-documented in the stories and files of Nott.

CHAPTER 18

Johnny's border crossing quotes come from the *Hamilton Spectator*, January 26, 1968. Quotes from Johnny's nosy neighbours come from Moon's story in *Canadian Panorama*, October 25, 1968. Danny Gasbarrini's denial comes from a Don Delaplante story in the *Globe*, July 6, 1970.

CHAPTER 19

The story is pieced together from interviews, newspaper coverage, court transcripts, and *Blood Brothers*. The jail house memories of Rosie Rowbotham were told to this author during their on-air discussion of Johnny on CBC Radio's *This Morning*, broadcast on September 29, 1999. Rosie is currently working on his memoirs.

CHAPTER 20

Ryce's quote on Jan Hayes, information on Hayes's wigs and eyelashes, and her habit of discreetly leaving the room are from *Mob Mistress*. Information on Johnny's visit with Réal Simard and Frank Majeau comes from the author's interviews as well as Simard's *The Nephew*, and Stevie Cameron's *On the Take*. The quotes from Johnny on Racco are previously unreported segments from the Moon interview, the quotes from Johnny on Greeks and Toronto are also from Moon.

CHAPTER 21

Jim Hunt's story was told in the *Toronto Sun*, June 3, 1997, and Jackie Washington's in the *Hamilton Spectator*, November 13, 1999.

CHAPTER 22

Johnny's quotes are, again, reported and unreported segments from the Moon interview. The nurse's quotes are from a letter to the editor in the *Toronto Star*, December 5, 1999.

CHAPTER 23

This chapter started out as a feature by this author in the *Hamilton Spectator*, as part of the Gangland: The New Face of the Mafia series. See "The Mob busters," June 3, 1998. Thanks to Sally Pauloski for remembering things she would rather forget.

CHAPTER 25

Tom Ireson's quotes are from the *Hamilton Spectator*'s coverage of the Musitanos' arrests. The November 25, 1998 edition of the paper is an essential document in this unfolding drama. Johnny's quotes come from unreported segments of the Moon interview. Portions of the Musitano family history originally appeared in this author's Gangland series, "The Sons Also Rise," *Hamilton Spectator*, June 1, 1998. The "champagne . . . on ice" quote is from the *Spec*, August 13, 1996. Birrel's quote is from CBC's *Disclosure*, and some Project Expiate details are from Bill Dunphy.

CHAPTER 26

Johnny's quotes are from the Moon interview.

EPILOGUE

Information on the underworld's more recent state of affairs comes from dozens of interviews with qualified sources and from this author's personal observations, such as at Pat's and Angelo Musitano's aborted parole hearings, for which observer status was granted, and interviews from prison with Ken Murdock. Information on Vito Rizzuto also comes from numerous police reports and court filings. Some portions of the chapter evolved from stories by this author in the *National Post*, including: "The man they call the Canadian Godfather," February 26, 2001; "Loaded sock brings down a gangster," June 30, 2004; "Dead mobster's crew arrested," September 19, 2002; "Mob enforcer killed in 'professional, organized hit,'" October 5, 2000; and "Arrest called 'biggest blow' to Canada's mob," January 21, 2004.

BIBLIOGRAPHY

Contemporary news accounts were extremely helpful, particularly stories from Canadian Press, *Globe and Mail*, *Hamilton Spectator*, *Hamilton This Month*, *London Free Press*, *Maclean's*, *National Post*, *New York Mirror*, *New York Times*, *New York Daily News*, *Ottawa Citizen*, *Time*, *Toronto Star*, *Toronto Sun*, *Toronto Telegram*, and *Windsor Star*.

Arlacchi, Pino. 1988. *Mafia Business: The Mafia Ethics and the Spirit of Capitalism* (translated by Martin Ryle). London: Oxford University Press.

Arlacchi, Pino. 1992. *Men of Dishonour: Inside the Sicilian Mafia*. New York: William Morrow and Company.

Beare, Margaret E. 1996. *Criminal Conspiracies: Organized Crime in Canada*. Toronto: Nelson Canada.

Berton, Pierre. 1971. "Middle-Class Rackets in the Big City," in *Social Deviance in Canada*, ed. W.E. Mann. Toronto: Social Science Publishers.

Blumenthal, Ralph. 1989. *Last Days of the Sicilians: The FBI's War Against the Mafia*. New York: Pocket Books.

Cameron, Stevie. 1994. *On The Take: Crime, Corruption and Greed in the Mulroney Years*. Toronto: Macfarlane Walter & Ross.

Charbonneau, Jean-Pierre. 1976. *The Canadian Connection: An Exposé on the Mafia in Canada and its International Ramifications* (translated by James Stewart). Montréal: Optimum Publishing.

de Champlain, Pierre. 1986. *Le Crime Organisé à Montréal (1940–1980)*. Montréal: Éditions Asticou.

Dubro, James. 1985. *Mob Rule: Inside the Canadian Mafia*. Toronto: Macmillan Canada.

Dubro, James and Robin F. Rowland. 1987. *King of the Mob: Rocco Perri and the Women Who Ran His Rackets*. Markham: Penguin Books Canada.

Dubro, James. 1988. *Mob Mistress: How a Canadian Housewife Became a Mafia Playgirl*. Toronto: Macmillan Canada.

Edwards, Peter. 1990. *Blood Brothers: How Canada's Most Powerful Mafia Family Runs its Business*. Toronto: Key Porter Books Limited.

Edwards, Peter and Antonio Nicaso. 1993. *Deadly Silence: Canadian Mafia Murders*. Toronto: Macmillan Canada.

Follain, John. 1995. *A Dishonoured Society: The Sicilian Mafia's Threat to Europe*. London: Warner Books.

Fox, Stephen. 1989. *Blood and Power: Organized Crime in Twentieth-Century America*. New York: William Morrow and Company.

Freeman, Bill, and Marsha Hewitt. 1979. "The Hamilton Mob and the Politics of Organized Crime," in *Their Town: The Mafia, the Media and the Party Machine*. Toronto: James Lorimer & Company.

Ginsborg, Paul. 1990. *A History of Contemporary Italy: Politics and Society 1943–1988*. New York: Penguin.

Gosch, Martin A. and Richard Hammer. 1974. *The Last Testament of Lucky Luciano*. Boston: Little, Brown and Company.

Harney, Robert F. 1978. *Italians in Canada*. Toronto: The Multicultural History Society of Ontario.

Harney, Robert F. 1981. "Toronto's Little Italy 1885–1945," in *Little Italies in North America*, ed. Robert F. Harney and Vincenza Scarpaci. Toronto: The Multicultural History Society of Ontario.

Kirby, Cecil and Thomas C. Renner. 1986. *Mafia Assassin: The Inside Story of a Canadian Biker, Hitman and Police Informer*. Toronto: Methuen.

Maas, Peter. 1968. *The Valachi Papers*. New York: G.P. Putnam's Sons.

Malafarina, Luigi. 1986. *La 'Ndrangheta*. Reggio Calabria: Gangemi.

Monaco, Richard and Lionel Bascom. 1991. *Rubouts: Mob Murders in America*. New York: Avon Books.

Moore, Robin. 1970. *The French Connection: The World's Most Crucial Narcotics Investigation*. Toronto: Bantam Books.

Moore, William Howard. 1974. *The Kefauver Committee and the Politics of Crime: 1950–1952*. Columbia: University of Missouri Press.

Morton, James. 1998. *Gangland International: An Informal History of the Mafia and other Mobs in the Twentieth Century*. London: Little, Brown and Company (UK).

Murphy, Mark G. 1998. *Police Undercover: The True Story of the Biker, the Mafia and the Mountie*. Toronto: Avalon House.

Newsday, staff and editors. 1973. *The Heroin Trail*. New York: Holt, Rinehart and Winston.

Nicaso, Antonio and Lee Lamothe. 1995. *Global Mafia: The New World Order of Organized Crime*. Toronto: Macmillan Canada.

Nicaso, Antonio and Diego Minuti. 1994. *'Ndranghete: Le Filiali Della Mafia Calabrese*. Vibo Valentia: Monteleone.

Nicaso, Antonio. 1990. *Alle Origini Della 'Ndrangheta: La Picciotteria*. Soveria Mannelli: Rubbettino Editore.

Pistone, Joseph D., ed. 1992. *The Ceremony: The Mafia Initiation Tapes*. New York: Dell Publishing.

Short, Martin. 1997. *Crime Inc.: The Story of Organized Crime (Updated)*. London: Arrow Books Limited.

Simard, Réal and Michel Vastel. 1988. *The Nephew: The Making of a Mafia Hitman*. Scarborough: Prentice-Hall Canada.

Sterling, Claire. 1990. *The Mafia: The Long Reach of the International Sicilian Mafia*. London: Hamish Hamilton Limited.

Stille, Alexander. 1995. *Excellent Cadavers: The Mafia and the Death of the First Italian Republic*. New York: Vintage Books.

Wismer, Catherine. 1980. *Sweethearts: The Builders, the Mob and the Men*. Toronto: James Lorimer & Company.

1940. "Speeches of the Minister of Justice, 11 and 13 June, 1940, House of Commons (Canada)," *Debates*, vol. 1.

1951. *Investigation of Organized Crime in Interstate Commerce: Hearings Before the Special Committee* (a.k.a. The Kefauver Committee). Washington, D.C.: United States Senate, 81 Congress, Second Session–82 Congress, First Session, May 26, 1950–August 7, 1951.

1961. *Gambling and Organized Crime: Hearings Before the Permanent Subcommittee*

on Investigations of the Committee on Government Operations. Washington, D.C.:
United States Senate, 87 Congress, First Session, August 22–September 8,
1961.

1961. *Report of the Hon. Mr. Justice Wilfred D. Roach as a Commissioner
Appointed Under the Public Inquiries Act by Letters Patent Dated December 11,
1961* (a.k.a. The Roach Report). Toronto: Queen's Printer and Publisher.

1964. *Organized Crime and Illicit Traffic in Narcotics: Hearings Before the Perma-
nent Subcommittee on Investigations of the Committee on Government
Operations.* Washington, D.C.: United States Senate, 88 Congress, First
Session, September 25, 1963–August 5, 1964.

1968. *The Federal Effort Against Organized Crime: Hearings Before a Subcommittee
of the Committee on Government Operations.* Washington, D.C.: United States
House of Representatives, 90 Congress, First Session, April 5, 1967–
February 8, 1968.

1968. *Impact of Crime on Small Business: Hearings Before the Select Committee on
Small Business.* Washington, D.C.: United States Senate, 90 Congress, First
Session, April 24, 1967–May 16, 1968.

1970. *Inquiry Re. Alleged Improper Relationships Between Personnel of the Ontario
Provincial Police Force and Persons of Known Criminal Activity Under the* Public
Inquiries Act *by Letters Patent Dated 28th July, 1970* (a.k.a. The Duke
Inquiry). Toronto: Queen's Printer and Publisher.

1974. *Report of the Royal Commission on Certain Sectors of the Building Industry*
(a.k.a. The Waisberg Commission). Toronto: Queen's Printer and Publisher.

INDEX